SOCIAL POLICY FOR

NURSES

CARING PROFESSIONS

Louise Ackers and
Pamela Abbott

OPEN UNIVERSITY PRESS

Buckingham • Philadelphia

Open University Press
Celtic Court
22 Ballmoor
Buckingham
MK18 1XW

email: enquiries@openup.co.uk
world wide web: http://www.openup.co.uk

and
325 Chestnut Street
Philadelphia, PA 19106, USA

First Published 1996
Reprinted 1998

A catalogue record of this book is available from the British Library

ISBN 0 335 19359 5 (pb) 0 335 19360 9 (hb)

Library of Congress Cataloging-in-Publication Data

Ackers, Louise, 1960–
    Social policy for nurses and the caring professions / Louise
Ackers and Pamela Abbott.
        p. cm. — (Social science for nurses and the caring
professions)
    Includes bibliographical references and index.
    ISBN 0–335–19360–9. — ISBN 0–335–19359–5 (pbk.)
    1. Medical social work—Great Britain. 2. Great Britain—Social
policy. I. Abbott, Pamela. II. Title. III. Series.
HV687.5.G7A25   1996
362.1'0425—dc20   95–49768
                                                                CIP

Typeset by Graphicraft Limited, Hong Kong
Printed in Great Britain by Redwood Books, Trowbridge

This book is dedicated to our children,
Matthew, James and Gavin
and
Alasdair, Francesca and Nicole

CONTENTS

SERIES EDITOR'S PREFACE

It is now widely recognized that the social sciences are central to nurse education. Nursing as a profession needs to ground itself in an understanding of social structures and relations, state policies and their constraints on the behaviour and experience of individuals and groups. The series of which this is one volume aims to provide nurses and others in the caring professions with lively and accessible introductions to the issues and debates within the social science disciplines.

This book is about social policy as a discipline and social policy as the development and operation of welfare policies and practices. The discipline of social policy (or social administration, as it has been called until recently) has developed alongside the welfare state, and its subject area has principally been the statutory welfare services – that is, those provided or funded by central and/or local government. The caring professions are centrally concerned with welfare – providing care and helping individuals and groups to meet their needs. They are part of the 'welfare system', however, and often in an ambiguous situation; they act on behalf of the state and tend to have a control function over individuals in terms of their structural position, at the same time as the conscious motivation of individual workers may be to help, support and 'work on behalf of' their clients/patients. This ambiguity has been thoroughly explored in the case of social workers and to some extent with regard to health visitors and psychiatric nurses (see, for example, Abbott and Wallace 1990), but it is equally true of all who work within the welfare system, in whatever capacity.

Social policy as a discipline has as its purpose the analysis and understanding of the role of the state in welfare, and it is therefore a necessary area of study for those who work within the welfare state (including workers in the area of health and nursing care). In order to understand current debates, we need to know something of the history of the system and its potential diversity – how it came to take the shape it does in this country, and how other countries have adopted different patterns of welfare and health provision. The debates that go on, often 'above the heads' of workers 'at the front' who are delivering health and welfare care but which determine what they are free to do and what resources are allocated to them with which to do it, are political debates in more than a 'party political' sense. Social policy is about the moral responsibility of the state to provide for the welfare of its citizens; it is concerned not just with what governments do provide, but with what they should provide and how they should provide it. At a more ideological level, it is concerned with the tension between the rights and duties of individuals on the one hand and the collective responsibility of citizens for each other, and on the other, how these opposed models of moral action and the nature of social relations are 'played out' in welfare provision.

These apparently abstract and political issues are as important concerns for nurses, social workers, local government administrators, etc., as the concrete services they provide for individuals and families; current decisions and current debates will crucially determine what it is possible to do in a caring role in ten or twenty years' time. People become nurses or social workers, for example, because they want to help other people. However, their ability to do this is crucially determined by social policies. The ways in which services are actually organized and provided are determined not by the immediate providers of the services but by government policies. Changes in policy impinge on the service providers as well as on the recipients of services.

Each section of the welfare state needs, therefore, to understand the history and philosophy of its own service in order to locate current practice in its context and understand current trends. In addition, each needs to understand the roles of other caring professions, for more immediate and practical reasons. Nurses, for example, are concerned for the health of patients and make recommendations to patients (and others) about what should be done to promote health and aid recovery from current problems. Health is not something separate from the rest of the social context, but is inextricably bound up with income, housing, education and every other facet of the welfare state. There can be no lasting good health without income adequate to provide the required diet and clothing, or without adequate housing and the means to heat it. A similar point could be made about any branch of welfare provision. At a more general and 'political' level, we are all well aware of the wide discrepancy between the living standards and the standards of health of the rich and the poor. There can be no diminution of these inequalities unless the full range of needs is taken into account. Health is improved and health inequalities diminished not just, or even primarily, by attention to health – housing, income and all the other aspects of welfare are just as likely to be in need of attention and to be capable of making a contribution to the health of the populace.

The study of social policy is therefore fundamentally the study of people's lives and their needs. It focuses in particular on those who are deprived or vulnerable, but it also deals with life-stages through which we all must pass – childhood, parenthood and old age – and with the experience of large groups of the population who are at some disadvantage – women, for example, or Black people. Its concern is with people's needs, how they are met or not met, who should meet them and how what is needed can best be supplied. Beyond this, it looks at how such needs are met by and for that proportion of the population who are not deprived or vulnerable or disadvantaged, and what effect changes in provision and policy would have on us all. In other words, social policy is the unacknowledged, taken-for-grated basis or foundation upon which the work of the caring professions is supported.

Pamela Abbott

WHAT IS SOCIAL POLICY?

Introduction

This chapter outlines the scope of **social policy** as an area of study and introduces the reader to major themes and issues within the discipline of social policy concerning the role of the **state** in the provision of welfare, the key actors in the provision of social welfare, the complex interactions between these providers and the influence of **ideology** on social policy. All these issues will be explored in more depth throughout the text.

The discipline of social policy

The discipline of social policy is relatively new, at least in comparison with other social sciences. The first department of social policy opened at the London School of Economics in 1950 headed by Richard Titmuss. This department and those which followed it were concerned primarily with the training of welfare professionals during a period of expansion in the **welfare state**. This led to a focus, within the discipline, on the statutory sector – on what the welfare state itself provided. Close links between the then Labour government and Fabian socialists such as Titmuss led to a demand for information to guide the future expansion of the post-war welfare state. The scope of the discipline in these early years was therefore strongly influenced by the institutional structures of the welfare state. Housing policy was primarily concerned with the development of public housing and health policy with the setting up of the National Health Service (NHS). Optimism about the prospects of the post-war welfare state's ability to solve the social problems of the day and bring about greater social justice thus led to a very narrow disciplinary focus.

It was around this time that T.H. Marshall developed his work on welfare and social citizenship. Marshall argued that, prior to the welfare state, a person's access to social resources (such as food, education and health), their personal welfare, depended primarily on their income from paid employment. Those with higher income (and/or wealth) could thus command greater social resources and those with low or no incomes went without (or were dependent on the parish for Poor Law support). The development of a system of social entitlement which derived from citizenship (or membership of a given society) irrespective of ability to pay was, according to Marshall, the litmus test of a civilized society. The welfare state then, with its universal health service, pensions and state education was to modify existing patterns of inequality, based on social class, and ensure that certain key social goods were available to all. The relationship between income from paid work and individual welfare was thus mediated by the introduction of collective social policies provided by the state. Academic concern thus focused on the role of the state as the primary provider of welfare.

The changing nature of social policy

The discipline has since broadened considerably in response to a number of pressures. First, there has been increasing recognition of the role of other actors which contribute in important ways to individual welfare; it is not only the state which provides welfare and not all welfare professionals are employed by the state. Second, the role of the state in relation to social policy has changed considerably. Housing departments are now responsible for the privatization of municipal housing (via council house sales) and they have worked in partnership with the voluntary sector (housing associations and cooperatives) in the provision of new housing. Health policy similarly has become less concerned with the institutional operation of the NHS (although this remains an important area of policy) and has become involved in measures to facilitate the growth of private health care.

The discipline of social policy is thus no longer concerned solely with what the state itself provides in terms of welfare, but more broadly with the whole structure of social entitlement and social responsibility in society which forms the basis of citizenship. Early concerns regarding the narrow focus of the discipline led Richard Titmuss to write an essay on the 'Social Division of Welfare' in 1955 (reprinted in Abel-Smith and Titmuss 1987). Titmuss drew attention to the contribution of two areas of welfare provision (in addition to that provided directly by the state) hitherto neglected in academic study, **fiscal welfare** (that provided for individuals via taxation policy), such as mortgage tax relief, and **occu-pational welfare** (welfare resources provided via employers to their employees), including various forms of occupational perks such as low-interest mortgages, creches, company cars, tied housing, etc. Titmuss argued that it was necessary to consider the contribution of all three sectors in order to understand the redistributive impact of welfare. While some aspects of state provision may indeed modify the relationship between income and access to welfare (such as universal free health care, for example), the contribution of the other sectors may in practice compound existing inequalities as welfare entitlement increases with status. Occupational welfare, for example, typically benefits those in white-collar jobs and is often regressive; that is, the more you earn the greater the value of the 'perk'. It was for this reason that Titmuss referred to occupational welfare as the 'concealed multiplier of occupational success'. Referring specifically to the development of occupational pension schemes, Titmuss noted that the cost to the Exchequer (in 1955) of such schemes was 'substantially in excess of the cost of national insurance pensions . . . contrary to the intentions of the 1920 Royal Commission, which considered tax relief for such schemes appropriate for poorer taxpayers, the benefits have increasingly favoured the wealthier' (Abel-Smith and Titmuss 1987: 50). Similarly, mortgage tax relief, at least until recent changes in policy, has provided a greater financial incentive to higher taxpayers and to those purchasing more expensive properties. The impact of modern welfare systems on social inequality is thus quite complex and requires an understanding not only of direct provision of welfare goods by the state, but also of the role of the state in other areas as a financier and regulator of policy.

Since the 1950s, it has become increasingly recognized within the discipline that even this categorization is inadequate if we are to understand fully the redistributive implications of social policy. In addition to these areas of provision, we might add a further three: the contribution of the **voluntary sector** (through agencies such as Age Concern, the National Society for the Prevention of Cruelty to Children or the Red Cross), the role of the **commercial sector** (through the purchase of welfare directly from commercial agencies) and, finally, the enormous contribution of **informal care** provided by families, neighbours and friends. Despite their importance historically in meeting welfare needs, these systems have been largely ignored or treated as marginal, as the focus of attention has been on the state provision of welfare services rather than on the influence of public policy more generally. It is important to remember that we are not talking simply about three parallel systems of resource distribution operating independently of the state, but of a complex relationship between the state and these sectors which has profound implications for citizenship and the distributional implications of social policy. We are not simply concerned, then, with what the state itself provides, but how it uses the power and resources vested in it to control and determine the whole basis of social provision through the regulation and financing of private and voluntary support. Clearly the broader aspects of public policy are important here (such as economic policy and taxation), but so too are areas of non-decision making or **policy vacuums**. In many cases, the lack of provision is just as significant as policy intervention. Nowhere is this more evident than the way in which state welfare providers have ignored and thereby failed to acknowledge the important and essential role of informal welfare – especially that which is provided by wives and mothers.

The mixed economy of welfare

It is important to recognize that the model of the government as welfare monopolist or the main provider of welfare is not and *has never been* a correct one. Not only does it ignore or marginalize the role of the private, commercial and voluntary sectors, but it also 'naturalizes' informal provision. Feminists in particular have pointed to the major contribution made by women to the provision of informal, unpaid welfare.

Recognition of the complex and changing nature of the state in contemporary welfare systems has been reflected in the introduction of the concept of **welfare pluralism** or the '**mixed economy of welfare**' in place of the term 'welfare state'. This concept emphasizes the need to consider the contribution of a plurality of providers to individual welfare. Figure 1.1 illustrates the broader impact of public policy on individual

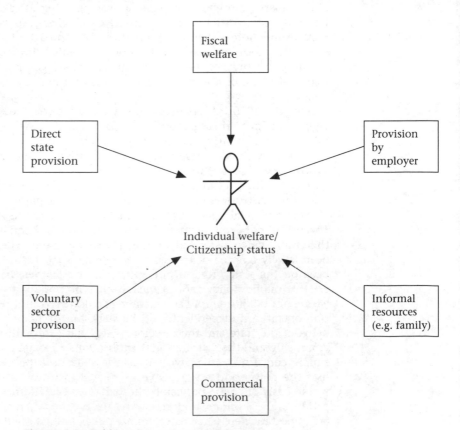

Figure 1.1 Public policy and individual welfare.

access to welfare, and Box 1.1 illustrates how the mixed economy works in practice in the context of health care.

> **Box 1.1   Provision of health care by the six welfare systems**
>
> The service provided by the NHS is **statutory welfare**, as is, for example, the provision of sports and recreational facilities/services – they are provided directly by central or local government. Examples of fiscal welfare (welfare promoted through the taxation system) include tax incentives for older people to subscribe to commercial health schemes. Voluntary provision includes the contribution of organizations such as the MacMillan Foundation, which provides nurses for cancer patients, or the hospice movement for the care of people who are terminally ill. (Charities such as these also benefit from certain forms of tax relief; that is, they benefit from fiscal policy as well.) **Occupational schemes** include the provision of private health insurance, health education classes and sports facilities by employers for their employees. Some employers, for example, provide their own ante-natal classes for pregnant employees. The **informal sector** is responsible for many areas of health care, including the care of people at home (by family and friends), the provision of transport to hospital and educating children about health care. Commercial health care includes the buying in of private nursing care at home as well as purchasing in- or out-patient hospital treatment, or paying for homeopathy, physiotherapy or acupuncture as a supplement to, or a substitute for, NHS provision.

We can see from the above examples how a person's health status – or their access to health resources – is dependent on a range of providers, all of whom are influenced to a greater or lesser extent by public policy. Moreover, our health status depends not only on what is construed as 'health' policy specifically (as in the example above), but also on many other aspects of social policy. There is a range of policies that have important implications for personal health status, including policy on the environment, on housing, employment and education. Indeed, the main cause of childhood mortality is accidental death, often as a result of proximity to road traffic, lack of adequate play areas and poor environmental planning. Employment status, for example, also has an important impact on personal health (see Chapter 3).

Health is not something separate from the rest of the social context: it is inextricably bound up with income, housing, education and every other facet of public policy. There can be no lasting good health without income adequate to provide the required diet and clothing, or without adequate housing and the means to heat it. Health is improved and health inequalities diminished not just, or even primarily, by attention to health – housing, income and all the other aspects of welfare are just as likely to be in need of attention and to be capable of making a contribution to the health of the populace. A similar point could be made about any branch of welfare provision.

Thus while it is important for health professionals to understand the history and philosophy of their own service in order to locate current practice in its context and understand current trends, they also need to understand the contribution of other aspects of policy and the role of other caring professions. Provision for children with special educational needs provides a useful example of the need for welfare professionals to be aware of their respective roles and services in order to plan effectively to meet the complex physical, psychological and educational needs of this group of children.

So far, we have seen how the scope of study of social policy extends to all aspects of the mixed economy of welfare of which the 'welfare state' is only one component. We have emphasized the fact that welfare pluralism is nothing new. In Britain after the Second World War, there was already a mixed economy of welfare with the state as the main provider. The state provided welfare (e.g. hospitals), subsidized private provision (e.g. through income tax relief on mortgage interest to homeowners) and supplied surveillance and regulation (e.g. the regulations of the private rental sector in housing). The government also made a commitment to maintain full employment. However, employers, the voluntary sector, the commercial sector and informal provision were all expected to continue to make a contribution to meeting people's welfare needs. Indeed, Beveridge, who is often seen as the architect of the welfare state in Britain, preferred the term 'welfare society', a society in which people's welfare needs were met by a partnership between statutory and voluntary services. The specific *balance of responsibilities* within this welfare mix has, however, been subject to change.

Perspectives on welfare: The influence of ideology

We saw earlier how Marshall regarded the development of the modern welfare state as a benchmark of a civilized society substantially altering the basis of social entitlement from one simply of ability to pay (reflecting labour market status and personal wealth) to one based on some notion of citizenship. Neither Marshall nor Beveridge expected to eliminate social inequality in this process, but they did want to reduce the effect of such disparities on access to basic social goods. Thus the introduction of comprehensive, free health care would result in a broad equality of health status and a universal education system would produce a broad equality of life chances or equality of opportunity if not of outcome. Under such conditions, the persistence of other aspects of inequality in society would be both tolerable and legitimate – on the grounds that those with greater income and wealth had achieved it via greater effort or ability.

Marshall's vision of the welfare state, then, was one of a redistributive system promoting social justice and consensus. We have seen that, when we take into account other aspects of state intervention (and non-intervention), this redistribution may not in practice have occurred. However, the very notion of a welfare state as redistributive, fulfilling broader moral objectives, is not universally accepted. It is important to be aware of the extent to which policy making and implementation are part of a wider political process, which is affected by both political expediency (often, electoral considerations) and ideology (a set of more or less coherent ideas about the way in which social welfare should be organized). Ideas about the role and function of the state in social policy (and particularly about the nature of the welfare state itself) are conditioned by and reflect specific moral, political and ideological positions about the causes of social problems and the apportionment of responsibilities. Where **social problems**, such as unemployment, ill-health or poor housing, are interpreted as the fault of individuals (a reflection of personal failure), there may be some question about the responsibility of the state to rectify the problem. Indeed, it could be argued that state intervention in such circumstances may be counter-productive, providing incentives for people not to work or to provide adequately for their families or to apply themselves to their studies! On the other hand, if social problems are interpreted as a reflection of the failure of the state itself, perhaps of its economic policy resulting in inadequate wages and lack of employment prospects, then it could be argued that the state has a responsibility to those in need as a result (subjects we return to in Chapter 2).

Much of the debate in social policy is concerned with ideas about moral responsibility and the meaning of citizenship, about when and how the state should assume responsibility and when it should be left to individuals and their families. The shifting nature of this debate and the dominance of particular perspectives over time has resulted in a re-ordering of the balance of responsibilities between the sectors involved in the welfare mix.

'Residual' and 'institutional' welfare states

One of the first attempts to illustrate the impact of ideology on social policy was Richard Titmuss' classical distinction between 'residual' and 'institutional' welfare states. These 'models' of social policy reflect different theoretical perspectives on the causes of social inequality and the appropriate response of the state. The *residual welfare state model* is based on individualistic explanations of social problems and places responsibility firmly in the hands of individuals (and their families). The state only assumes responsibility when the **family** or the market fails; it thus limits its commitment to those marginal and 'deserving' groups who lack sufficient resources either to purchase welfare support from the commercial sector or draw on family support. Supporters of this type of system argue that collective provision stifles initiative because it demands high levels of taxation and encourages dependency – that is, reliance on welfare benefits and services. Individual responsibility, initiative and self-help are not rewarded by collectivist welfare systems; indeed, they are positively undermined. The welfare state, according to this model, should exist to perform a residual safety-net function to prevent people falling into abject poverty (which may itself result in social problems such as crime, disease or political unrest) but in such a way as to avoid undermining the work ethic. State benefits under such a scheme are '**targeted**' at the poorest sections of society, providing a low level of benefit (in order not to **deter** them from taking low paid work). Services are provided on a **selective**, as opposed to **universal**, basis requiring extensive means testing of claimants (which Titmuss found to be **stigmatizing** and inefficient). This form of welfare system plays a structure-maintenance role, reinforcing the relationship between work performance (via paid work) and individual well-being.

The *institutional/redistributive model*, on the other hand, was the one favoured by Titmuss and Marshall. It provided a platform of universal services for the whole population, reflecting an institutionalized commitment to collectively financed and provided welfare. The objectives of this model were not restricted to preventing people falling below a certain basic modicum of welfare, but sought instead to promote social justice and to modify patterns of social inequality.

Welfare regimes

Titmuss' approach has been developed in recent years, in comparative social policy research, as the basis for classifying and categorizing contemporary welfare states. The work of Esping-Anderson (1990) has been influential in this regard and has sought to develop a typology of 'welfare regimes' according to the ways in which different societies allocate social goods. Esping-Anderson begins with Marshall's proposition that social citizenship constitutes the core idea of the welfare state and that the development of social citizenship rights will modify systems of social stratification (the distribution of resources between social groups such as class, gender or race). Esping-Anderson (1990: 21), however, argues that Marshall's approach 'must be fleshed out . . . the welfare state cannot be understood just in terms of the rights it grants. We must also take into account how state activities are interlocked with the market's and family's role in social provision'. He then goes on to examine how different forms of social policy in different countries have modified the relationship between paid work and welfare status. In practice, he identifies three 'regime-types', the first of which is dominated by social assistance provision (similar to Titmuss' residual model). Here social rights do not reflect work performance or citizenship but demonstrable need – providing generally meagre and means-tested (selective) benefits. In countries where this strong **Liberal** model dominates welfare provision, such as the United States, the welfare system actually reinforces existing inequalities through work-enforcing, stigmatizing benefits reserved for those unable to compete in the market. A second dominant model he refers to as '**Conservative**' and gives the example of Germany. This system is typified by compulsory contributory benefits with fairly generous entitlements. Here the state has assumed responsibility over individual welfare by requiring employers and employees to provide social insurance cover. The impact of this type of system on the distribution of social resources is to reward occupational achievement via the welfare state. It does therefore contain an element of redistribution – in favour of those who have paid higher contributions – but it ties social entitlement to work performance (disadvantaging those groups unable to contribute via labour market activity, such as married women). The final model identified by Esping-Anderson is the 'social democratic' model, typified by countries such as Sweden which have developed generous systems of universal benefits available to all citizens irrespective of prior earnings, contributions or performance and of a sufficiently high quality enabling 'citizens [to] freely, and without potential loss of job, income, or general welfare, opt out of work when they consider it necessary' (Esping-Anderson 1990: 23). This includes adequate provision for sickness, unemployment and, maternity, parental and educational leave, with guaranteed benefits equal to normal earnings. Only social democratic systems meet Marshall's notions of social citizenship by providing a broad equality of status for all citizens.

As with any system of classification, a level of generalization is required to illustrate key points and it would be unrealistic to expect any given country to fit exactly within Esping-Anderson's typology. Britain provides a good example of a welfare system which contains elements of all three models (including a core of universal services alongside occupational and means-tested benefits), although British social policy is clearly moving in the direction of the Liberal model. The Conservative government ordered a fundamental review of all its spending in 1994. The Chief Secretary to the Treasury, Michael Portillo, who is Chair of the Review, has indicated that, 'Throughout the public sector it is right to question whether existing spending patterns and levels are appropriate to give serious thought to the fundamental question of the government's proper role' (Portillo 1993). The government's view is that Britain can no longer afford the kind of welfare state – universal and solidaristic – that was founded in the 1940s. They argue that welfare services need to be targeted at those most in need. This increasingly means moving from universal benefits to selective benefits and a safety-net provision for those unable to provide for themselves and their families.

We need to be clear that the debate between selectivity and universalism is not just about efficiency – it is a debate about the type of society we want. As Wicks (1995: 283) has pointed out:

> ... 'selective' implies a particular society: a fundamentally unequal society, but a society of alleged equal opportunity, with the poor on the outside, excluded from mainstream society, different from ordinary citizens. Means testing is about doing good to these poor, but according to strict, defined rules ... Universalism, by contrast, is not about poverty first – and last – but about citizenship. It is about the range of risks all citizens face during their lives, about the good society intervening to produce greater equity. It recognises that if, as a general principle, we construct social policies for all citizens, then all citizens have an interest. They are utilised by all on a regular basis and can be defended by all. They are forces for unity and solidarity. Means testing, by contrast, is a force for division, resentment and poor policy ... Today dressed up as 'targeting', the means test rears its ugly head again.

The welfare state and individual freedom

While the institutional model claims moral support for collective social provision on the grounds that this promotes social justice and **equality**, supporters of the residual model would contend that this type of welfare system requires unacceptable levels of state intervention in the personal lives of citizens. The maintenance of this type of welfare system requires high levels of taxation and this perceived incursion into personal freedom has been criticized on the grounds that people are entitled to the fruits of their labour to spend as they wish. Although the existence of, for example, universal health care increases the quality of life of those without adequate means to purchase private care, the burden of taxation may restrict the ability of others who, if they were taxed less, could have exercised their right to purchase from the commercial sector – either by buying private health insurance or by paying for it directly. Compulsory taxation has reduced their disposable income; they have been forced to contribute towards the cost of the state-provided services, whether – given a choice – they would use them or not, and indeed whether they do use them or not. It also means that such people may be unable to buy in alternative types of service not available on the NHS, because of their 'reduced' income.

Feminist and black criticisms of state welfare

Concerns about the impact of interventionist, universal welfare systems have also been raised in other quarters, by feminist and Black academics and by the disabled persons movement. While the type of welfare system envisaged by Marshall would doubtless improve the quality of life of many people, the unquestioned benevolence of welfare and the association of welfare with the 'good society' failed to deal with important questions about institutional power and social control. Clearly, such large bureaucratic welfare organizations wield enormous power and may become the mechanism for controlling the lives of citizens as much as helping them. Education policy, for example, may be as much about reinforcing traditional class boundaries – by selecting and sorting and inculcating norms into the prospective workforce – as it is about the promotion of **equal** opportunity and merit. The caring professions themselves are centrally concerned with welfare, providing care and helping individuals and groups to meet their needs. They are part of the 'welfare *system*', however, and often in an ambiguous situation; they act on behalf of the state and tend to have a control function over individuals in terms of their structural position, at the same time as the conscious motivation of individual workers may be to help, support and 'work on behalf of' their clients/ patients. This ambiguity has been thoroughly explored in the case of social workers and to some extent with regard to health visitors and psychiatric nurses (see, for example, Abbott and Wallace 1990b), but it is equally true of all who work within the welfare system, in whatever capacity. The Labour Party's Commission on Social Justice, for example, has emphasized the enabling role of the welfare state and the opportunities it provides for 'life-long living, work, good health, a safe environment and financial independence', which will 'be the basis of social cohesion and economic security' – that is, the 'active society' (Commission on Social Justice 1993) – in contrast to the New Right view of welfare dependency.

The role of the state as an instrument of social control responsible for reinforcing existing patterns of social inequality, has been highlighted in the work of feminist social policy academics (Dale and Foster 1986; Williams 1989; Abbott and Wallace 1990a). Gillian Pascall (1986: 6) notes: 'While Marshall asserts the rights of citizenship, nowhere does he analyse the problematic relationship between citizenship and dependency in the family as he does between citizenship and social class'. In a similar vein, Lewis (1992: 161) argues that recent comparative work 'misses one of the central issues in the structuring of welfare regimes: the problem of valuing the unpaid work that is done primarily by women in providing welfare, mainly within the family, and in securing those providers social entitlements'. On the basis of this analysis she develops an alternative framework that stresses the broad commonality of women's experience and the dominance of the male breadwinner family model which cuts across established typologies of welfare regimes. Although the strength of this model varies depending upon the extent and nature of social entitlement, Lewis (1992: 162) emphasizes its persistence and universal impact:

> Modern welfare regimes have all subscribed to some degree to the idea of a male breadwinner model – the strength or weakness of [that] model serves as an indicator of the way in which women have been treated in social security systems; of the level of social service provision particularly in regard to childcare; and of the nature of married women's position in the labour market.

Issues of welfare provision are thus bound up with ideologically motivated notions about gender relations which restrict women's involvement in paid work (and their financial autonomy), effectively creating a vast army of unpaid workers upon whom the welfare state depends. As a result, many married women have no independent social entitlement but instead gain access to social resources (such as income support and pensions) via their male breadwinning partners. The impact on women's autonomy has been well documented (Lister 1990b; Lewis 1992; Ackers 1994).

The following section looks in a little more detail at the evolution of British social policy and the changing balance of social responsibility.

The development of the welfare mix in Britain

In Britain, the welfare state is seen as having moved from a residual (safety-net) position to a more collectivist one, although in the last fifteen years there has been some movement back towards a more residual position. The history of the post-war British welfare state is generally presented as the progressive development of social policies designed to stamp out want, poverty, ignorance, ill health, etc. – the move towards the gradual and progressive assumption by the state of responsibility for the welfare of all citizens. A civilized society is seen as one that cares for and provides for all its members, especially the weak and vulnerable. Indeed, Titmuss (1968) has argued that the collective provision of welfare encourages collective **altruism** – that is, a concern for the welfare of others. He uses blood donation as an example, pointing out that in Britain people are prepared to donate their blood without charge, thus ensuring a supply of good quality. In Britain, the NHS is often presented as the pinnacle of the idea of state welfare – a free health service, provided equally to all, based on need and not the ability to pay.

Until the 1970s, there was a general consensus in Britain that the state should be the main provider of welfare services. The major concern then was about providing *more* services, about funding the growth of state welfare services. The concern now is whether the state *should be* the main provider or even the main funder of welfare services, and the extent to which the welfare state actually does meet people's welfare needs.

It became clear from the 1970s onwards that all sides in Britain were dissatisfied with aspects of the old system of welfare. The **New Right** denounced the profligacy of public services and the traditional Left questioned their **paternalistic** and **bureaucratic** character. Furthermore, it had become evident that welfare policies did not meet the needs of the British Black and southern Asian populations and were often racist. Feminists have pointed out not only the **patriarchal** assumptions that informed much social policy, but also the ways in which state policies assumed the **nuclear family** with dependent wife as natural and inevitable. Debates centred on the causes of the social problems to which welfare was directed and the proper role of the state in its provision.

One response has been to argue for 'welfare provision which is universal in that it meets all people's needs, but also diverse and not uniform, reflects people's own changing definitions of difference and not simply the structural differentiation of the society at large' (Williams 1989: 209). However, the response of Conservative governments, which have been in power since 1979, has been to argue for a reduction in the provision of state welfare, the more effective targeting of benefits and services, and the reorganization and reduction of public services. In doing so, they have reinforced the idea of the primary responsibility of individuals and their families – especially in caring for children and dependent relatives, whose care is seen primarily as a matter of private concern rather than a collective responsibility:

> Our view is that it is for the parents who go out to work to decide how best to care for their children. If they want or need help in this task they should make the appropriate arrangements and meet the costs.
>
> (*Hansard*, 17 July 1988, Col. 150)

This contrasts sharply with a number of European countries, for example Sweden and France, where there is considerable state provision of care for children younger than school age (Abbott and Ackers, in press).

The Conservatives have also stressed the central role of the voluntary sector:

We must do more to help people to help themselves and families to look after their own. We must also encourage the voluntary movement and self-help groups working in partnership with statutory services.

(The Times, 1 September 1979, p. 292)

... in this way [via increased tax relief for charitable giving] the scope of individual responsibility is increased, the family is strengthened and voluntary bodies flourish; state power is checked.

(Conservative Party 1987: 11)

The role of the commercial and voluntary sectors has been emphasized, especially in terms of competitive tendering for the provision of meals and laundry services in the NHS and in providing community care, as well as in the privatization of public utilities and other previously state-owned services. The government has also tried to introduce market forces (competition) in health, the personal social services and education by the creation of what can be seen as quasi-markets or **managed markets** – and in the case of health and personal social services, they have encouraged purchasers (health authorities, GP fundholders and local authority social services departments) to buy services from the commercial and voluntary sectors as well as from NHS Trusts and local authority social services.

There has not, however, been a fast rate of growth across the board in the proportion of the population purchasing services in preference to using those provided by the state. Despite all the changes in the welfare mix that have taken place in the last 15–20 years, Hills (1993: 350) has concluded that 'the welfare state ... is very robust ... Welfare policy successfully weathered an economic hurricane in the mid 1970s and an ideological blizzard in the 1980s'. There has nevertheless been a substantial growth in home ownership, with a significant number of former tenants purchasing their council houses. In addition, restrictions on local councils building housing for rent has resulted in housing associations becoming more prominent and in the growth of shared-ownership schemes. Changes in legislation on pensions has meant an increase in employees contributing to private pension schemes (see Chapter 5). Furthermore, there has been concern that the level of spending on welfare services, especially personal social services, education and health, is not providing an adequate level of service, while the number of homeless has increased and inequalities have also increased (see, for example, Abbott and Wallace 1992).

While the Conservatives have not 'rolled back' the welfare state, and indeed the percentage of gross domestic product spent on state welfare has remained remarkably constant, there have been significant changes in the way in which the welfare state itself is organized and administered. The reshaping of the welfare state included the introduction of appropriate (i.e. private sector) managerial strategies and techniques to enable performance to be measured and rewarded. Managerialism, it is argued, will result in economy, efficiency and effectiveness. The strategies introduced include **performance indicators**, managed markets, compulsory competitive tendering and a public sector pay policy, including performance-

related pay (see, for example, Clarke *et al.* 1994). Taylor-Gooby and Lawson
(1993) have suggested that 'the pressures of continuing economic difficulty, the demand for more flexible services and the widespread dissatis-
faction . . . suggest that the process of restructuring will continue into the
next millenium, whichever party is in power'.

Social policy and social goods

This chapter has so far looked at the scope of social policy as a discipline.
It has emphasized the need to consider the whole breadth of welfare
provision within a mixed-economy approach and the complex and changing nature of the state. A central aspect of this involves consideration of
the welfare state in the provision and regulation of welfare. The concept
of the welfare state itself has been shown to be highly sensitive not only
to economic expedients but also to ideological, moral and politically motivated pressures. The final point to be made here concerns the concept
of a social resource itself. We have noted the concern of social policy with
systems of social distribution, or how social goods are distributed in society and needs are met. But we have not yet defined which 'goods' or
resources are 'social' as opposed to economic, political or simply luxury.

Traditionally, concern has focused on resources such as health care,
domiciliary care, social work, education, income support, housing, employment and education. Michael Cahill (1994), however, has suggested
five additional 'social goods' that should be included within the study of
social policy:

1 *Communicating*: telephone, fax, letters, e-mail.
2 *Viewing*: radio, television.
3 *Travelling*: rail, road and air transport.
4 *Shopping*: location and planning of shopping centres.
5 *Playing*: provision of leisure facilities, swimming pools, youth clubs, etc.

Cahill goes on to point out that studying these areas is important not
only for understanding old and new inequalities, but also because policies
are interdependent. We cannot, he suggests, understand or evaluate policies in isolation:

> . . . we can only provide good social policies if we are sensitive to the
> context in which government policy programmes operate . . . Adopting
> this perspective does mean that we must see social policy as part of
> a wider public policy. Health care is a good example, where govern-
> ments now acknowledge that many other public policies have a health
> dimension. But the process should work the other way as well: trans-
> port policies are dependent on housing and retailing policies, retail-
> ing policies have health dimensions, and so on. One could produce
> a long list of these policy inter-dependencies.
>
> (Cahill 1994: 2)

We might add to this list the issue of environmental policy, which is increasingly seen to fall within the parameters of social policy and which has important implications for health status (George and Wilding 1994).

Conclusions

The remainder of the book explores many of the issues raised here in more depth, mainly adopting a 'case-study' approach. Chapter 2 examines the evolution of the British welfare state, using health as a major example, as it is only through an understanding of how the welfare state evolved that we can come to understand where it is today. Chapter 3, again using health as an example, examines the extent to which welfare services have met one of the major objectives of the founders of the welfare state, a reduction in the inequalities between social classes. Chapter 4 then examines the extent to which another major objective, the reduction of poverty, has been achieved. Using the example of income maintenance and welfare benefits, Chapter 5 looks at the ways in which state welfare is provided. In Chapter 6, we consider both the ways in which private sector management practices and market forces have been introduced into public sector services and the privatization of welfare primarily provided by the state sector, using the health services and pensions as examples. Chapter 7 uses housing as a case study to examine the role of the voluntary sector in the welfare mix. In Chapter 8, we focus on the role of informal welfare – the provision of care by family, friends and relatives. Chapter 9, using the example of community care, considers the ways in which the different sectors contribute to the provision of welfare. Each chapter considers how the boundaries between these sectors have been progressively blurred in recent years as welfare state retrenchment has resulted in more complex liaisons and increased state intervention. The final chapter draws out themes arising in the previous chapters to examine the changing role of the state in social policy. It asks whether the evolution of this new balance of responsibility within the mixed economy of welfare has met with the criticisms of the post-war welfare state and considers the implications of these new forms of partnership for social equality and citizenship.

Summary

- The study of social policy has evolved from a narrow concern with the development and evaluation of state welfare to a broader concern with the whole basis of social entitlement and social responsibility.

- The concept of welfare pluralism is used to describe welfare systems in which social needs are met through a wide range of sources including the voluntary, commercial, informal and state sectors.

- These sectors do not operate independently of each other but rather interact in a complex manner with other welfare providers and with other aspects of public policy (on the economy and environment, for example).

- Whilst a mixed economy of provision characterizes the whole history of social policy in Britain, political ideology has an important impact on the balance between the main providers of welfare.

- The influence of ideology is illustrated through the concept of welfare 'models' (the residual and institutional models) – and subsequently welfare regimes.

Further reading

Abbott, P.A. and Wallace, C. (1992) *The Family and the New Right*. London: Pluto.
Titmuss, R. (1968) *Commitment to Welfare*. London: Allen and Unwin.

THE DEVELOPMENT OF A WELFARE STATE

Introduction

In this chapter, we consider the development of state welfare provision in Britain. We pay particular attention to the development of medical care provision but also briefly consider other state provision. The chapter will examine the debates concerning the extent to which the state should intervene in family life and civil society and the ways in which it does so; although much of the focus is on health, we use this as the basis for exploring debates about the provision of welfare which apply more broadly.

During the course of the nineteenth and twentieth centuries, the state gradually became involved in the supervision and direct organization of

welfare – of formal welfare services – most notably health, income maintenance, housing, education, employment and personal social services.
Nevertheless, the commercial sector, employers, the voluntary sector and
most notably the informal sector have continued to play an important
role in the provision of welfare. Indeed, the informal sector – the welfare
we provide for ourselves and others – has always been and continues to
be the main provider of welfare. The development of state-provided welfare has resulted in increased **surveillance** and regulation of the population and in increased power for welfare professionals, including doctors,
teachers and social workers (Abbott and Wallace 1990c).

It is only in the twentieth century that the British state has come to
play a major role in organizing welfare services and meeting the welfare
needs of the population. Indeed, all western societies have developed welfare states in the twentieth century, although the extent of state provision
and the range of services provided varies considerably. Such provision
ranges from that in Scandinavia and Britain, which provides comprehensive welfare services for all citizens, primarily funded out of general taxation,
to that in countries like the United States where universal provision is
limited and the role of the state is seen as providing a **safety net** for
those who are unable to make provision for themselves out of their own
resources (see, for example, Ginsberg 1992).

There is considerable variation as to the extent to which it is thought
desirable for government to make provision for citizens and the extent to
which it is thought to be individuals' responsibility to meet their own
needs, with the state intervening only when individuals are unable to
provide for themselves and their families. The role that the state plays in
the provision of welfare and the ways in which this role changes and
develops is to a considerable extent the outcome of these competing
ideas – between the state playing a major and a residual role. Those who
take the former position tend to argue that most needs are the result of
factors outside the individual's control, such as old age, unemployment,
sickness and low wages, and therefore that costs should be socialized (i.e.
paid for collectively). Those who take the latter view tend to argue that
most needs are the result of individual inadequacies and failings and that
state provision tends to create welfare **dependency**. In this latter view,
unemployment, for example, is often seen as the unwillingness of the
unemployed to take available jobs, and poverty in old age as the the result
of not saving money when in employment. In contemporary Britain, the
former view is more generally espoused by the Labour Party and the latter
by the Conservative Party.

State welfare and state intervention

Laissez-faire

In the early part of the nineteenth century, the dominant view was that
the state should *not* provide for the welfare of the population and indeed
that it should deter the able-bodied from becoming unemployed. This

view was underpinned by the idea of **laissez faire** (which literally means 'leave alone'), that the state should not interfere in the private sphere of the family, nor in the economy. This meant that individuals should be responsible for providing for all their own and their family's needs and that market forces should determine the price of goods and services, including the price of labour. For example, if income support is provided for the unemployed, the level at which it is provided influences the price of labour and the labour market. People will be unwilling, it is suggested, to take employment that pays a lower wage than that provided by state support, and if state support provides an adequate standard of living, then people may not be prepared to take available jobs, preferring to live on state benefit or wait until more attractive employment becomes available. The Victorians also believed that most poverty was the result of personal inadequacy, an unwillingness to work, spending money inappropriately and failing to save for sickness and old age. It was thought that if the state provided for the unemployed, not only would there be no incentive for them to take employment, but others could be encouraged not to continue in employment. The Victorians argued that the respectable poor would be contaminated by the **residuum** – the non-respectable poor.

During the course of the nineteenth century, the state did come increasingly to intervene in the private sphere of the family and in the economy and to take on more responsibility for providing for the welfare needs of the population. *Laissez faire* remained the dominant influence, however, and it is not until the early twentieth century, following the publication of surveys challenging the view that poverty was mainly caused by individual failure, that the state began to provide for individual welfare. Reforms in the nineteenth century were targeted at whole populations (e.g. **sanitary reform**), or at protecting what were seen as vulnerable groups (e.g. factory legislation) or at developing a resource (e.g. the Education Acts). Charitable endeavour developed alongside the increasing state intervention in the private sphere of the family and in the market.

Schooling, for instance, was provided by voluntary organizations, albeit with some government support after 1832, until the late nineteenth century. It was not until the Foster Education Act of 1870 that local School Boards were set up with the powers to provide schools, and not until 1880 that schooling was made compulsory from the ages of five to ten. Charitable organizations made considerable efforts to help the poor, weak and vulnerable, and notable individuals spearheaded campaigns for reform in a number of areas. The 'visiting movement' of Victorian times – charities whose primary purpose was the visitation of the poor – were mostly concerned with inculcating habits of thrift, cleanliness and middle-class morality in working-class families. **Mutual aid organizations**, **Friendly Societies** that enabled working-class men to provide for unemployment, sickness and old age collectively, also developed and grew in the nineteenth century (Green 1993).

The challenge to individualistic explanation

By the beginning of the twentieth century, however, ideas about the causes of poverty and the 'social problem group' (the undeserving poor) were beginning to change, influenced on the one hand by research suggesting that a significant proportion of the poor were not responsible for their plight. Poverty, it was suggested, was not generally the result of personal inadequacies but of low wages, the scarcity of employment, old age or sickness; it also became recognized that most working-class people did not earn sufficient when in employment to make adequate provision for periods of unemployment or sickness or for their old age. The other influence was the concern that the health and fitness of the British population was in decline and that this threatened Britain's position as a leading industrial nation. This concern was fuelled by the condition of working-class men who volunteered to fight in the Boer War: three out of five were rejected as unfit, due, it was said, to chronic sickness, the result of degenerate and shiftless lifestyles such as early marriage and the ignorance of mothers (Abbott 1982).

In the ensuing debates, the view developed that health, hygiene and the fitness of the population were keys to progress. However, although the interdepartmental committee set up to investigate the lives of the poor which reported in 1904, made fifty-three recommendations mainly concerning the importance of physical conditions, housing, poverty, diet, etc., the ones that were taken up and developed focused on the role of motherhood as the key to a healthy population. The emphasis on the mother and women more generally as having a 'duty of care' has continued to the present day, so that women are now seen as natural carers and those who 'fail' to fulfil this duty are seen as inadequate, in an almost biological as well as a social sense (Abbott and Sapsford 1990). This ideology also underpins the assumption that informal care is to be preferred to formal care and is the 'natural' duty of women.

While the emphasis on the prevention of ill health changed from the collectivist one of the nineteenth century – sanitary reforms aimed at the whole population – to an individualistic one in the twentieth century, there was also an increasing recognition that state intervention was necessary to alleviate ill health and poverty. Nevertheless, the tension between ideologies that stress a need for collective measures to overcome social problems such as poverty, ill health, inadequate diet and the like on the one hand and those that stress individual responsibility and personal inadequacy on the other continued to underpin the changing provision made by the British state. The welfare state legislation of the 1940s was concerned to provide for the welfare needs of the population and included the NHS, the **social security** system, the education system and the personal social services. However, the extent to which these measures were intended to result in a more equal society, or have resulted in one, or merely to provide a safety net, has been a matter of considerable debate (see Chapters 3 and 4).

The public provision of medicine

The public provision of welfare, including public health provision, can be traced through the nineteenth century, back to the voluntary hospitals of the eighteenth century and earlier such as Westminster, St Thomas' and

St Bartholemew's, and the Elizabethan Poor Law of 1603. But it is the period from the 1830s to just before the First World War which saw an increasing trend of state intervention in matters of health, sanitation and welfare generally, areas which had once been regarded as *private* (see Box 2.1).

Box 2.1 Key developments in nineteenth-century Britain

1833   Factory Act – limited the number of hours children could work
1834   The New Poor Law
1844   Health of Towns Movement founded
1847   The 10 Hour Act – limited the working day of women and children
1848   Public Health Act
1853   Infant vaccination against smallpox made compulsory
1857   Foundation of the Ladies' National Association for the Reform of Sanitary Conditions
1860   Adulteration of food made illegal
       First district nurse began work in Liverpool
       Nightingale Nursing School started at St Thomas' Hospital, London
1861   Foundation of Manchester Ladies' Sanitary Reform Society
1864   Poor Law Board argues that Poor Law Unions could pay for basic medicines
1866   Sanitary Act
1867   Poor Law Unions allowed to build infirmaries away from workhouses and to open separate fever hospitals
1868   Artisans' Dwelling Act
1869   Formation of **Charity Organizations Society**
1870   Foster's Education Act – Local School Boards permitted to provide elementary schools
1875   Public Health Act
       Food and Drugs Act
       Artisans' and Labourers' Building Improvement Act
1878   Formation of the Salvation Army
1879   Artisans and Labourers Building Improvement Act
1880   Education Act – compulsory schooling for children aged 5–10 years
1890   Poor sick no longer had to go to the Relieving Officer before they could be treated at the public infirmary
1890   Housing Act
1891   State education made free
1891   Publication of Charles Booth's *The Life and Labour of the People of London*, Volume 1

Poverty and health

In the early nineteenth century, the conditions brought about by industrialization became a cause for considerable concern. The Poor Law Amendment

Act 1834 can be seen as an outcome of this, a measure to 'persuade' the poor to work rather than to seek relief – that is, blaming the poverty of the poor on themselves. The Act was intended to deter the able-bodied from seeking relief. They were to be offered only 'indoor' relief, in the workhouse, and the conditions of the workhouse were to be less desirable than those of the poorest outside. The aim was to reduce public expenditure and to encourage the able-bodied to take any available work. By distinguishing between the able-bodied and those deemed unable to work, the Act created *paupers*, an underclass of those assumed to be lazy, indigent and unwilling to work.

What we find in this period is a new way of defining what came to be known as 'the social question', a new technique for characterizing and regulating the population. The conditions in which the poor lived were seen as a potential source of contagious disease and also of social and moral corruption. To counteract this, reformers suggested a programme of social hygiene reforms, improving welfare and at the same time obtaining detailed information about the lives of the poor. This programme was aimed not only at disease but at the chain of conditions which were seen as linking susceptibility to contagion with criminality, moral depravity and political sedition. The family was seen as the prime target for intervention. Jacques Donzelot (1980) refers to this strategy of surveillance as 'the policing of the family'; that is, the use of political power to investigate the details of the population's everyday lives and to secure its wellbeing and happiness, its fitness for work, its morality and discipline, the quality of its health, and so on.

The early Victorians thought that poverty was inextricably linked with health, and this led to a concern with the health of the poor. Edwin Chadwick, the architect of the 1834 Poor Law, began by 1838 to recognize that much poverty was caused by sickness and that much sickness could be prevented. It was evident that cholera, typhus, tuberculosis and other diseases spread among the population in the poor areas of crowded towns. The growth in the urban population in early nineteenth-century Britain resulted in **endemic** and **epidemic** contagious diseases. Cholera first broke out in Britain in 1831–32 and reoccurred in 1848–49, 1854 and 1867, and although it started in the poor districts of towns it quickly spread to middle-class areas. Typhus and typhoid fever were mainly diseases of the poor, and there were epidemic outbreaks in 1826–27, 1831–32, 1837 and 1846–47, coinciding with periods of economic recession and high unemployment. Both of these diseases were endemic; that is, there were high incidence rates even in the periods between epidemics. Tuberculosis was also mainly a disease of the poor.

Sanitary conditions and health

The Inquiry into the Sanitary Conditions of the Poor headed by Chadwick, which reported in 1842, demonstrated a close relationship between insanitary living conditions, overcrowding, lack of sewers, etc., and the death rate. One of the responses to the report was the formation of the Health of Towns Association in 1844, which carried out a propaganda campaign for the implementation of sanitary legislation. The (male) membership comprised leading citizens, including doctors and lawyers. Local sanitary associations were also founded in a number of cities.

In Victorian England, the course of reform was set by the clashes and debates between factory owners and **philanthropically** inclined reformers whose wealth came from land: between those who saw a need for the state to regulate the conditions under which diseases like cholera flourished and the shopkeepers and other middle-class groups who would pay for proposed reforms through local rates; between those who feared political centralization and those who saw it as necessary if greater evils were to the avoided. Most public health reforms of the early period challenged the principle of *laissez faire* directly, though in a limited way. The Factory Acts limited the hours that could be worked by labourers, particularly women and children, and laid down basic minimum conditions. The Royal Commission on the Health of Towns (1842) led to the Public Health Act of 1848, which set up a general Board of Health. Municipalities were permitted to set up their own boards of health to consolidate and extend public health networks and to appoint staff, including a medical officer of health. They were, in addition, given powers to deal with sewage and drainage, street-sweeping and cleaning. They had powers to register slaughter-houses and common lodging houses, to regulate offensive trades and dangerous chemical wastes, and to clean and purify 'unwholesome homes'. All new houses built after the Act was passed were required to have a w.c., a cesspit and drains. The legislation was enabling rather than mandatory for precisely the reason that the costs fell on local ratepayers: local authorities were *empowered* to carry out these works but were never *required* to do so. However, the General Board of Health could enforce action if it received a petition signed by one-tenth of the ratepayers in an area or if the death rate exceeded 23 in every thousand.

What is usually referred to as 'the sanitary movement' continued throughout the Victorian period and into Edwardian England. Its aims rested on a discourse which changed and evolved, but certain elements remained constant throughout the period:

1 First, the reformers made a connection between dirt and disease, which has been part of our taken-for-granted common sense for many years, but which was vehemently denied by many in early and mid-Victorian Britain. A germ theory of disease was not fully accepted until the 1860s.
2 The second element of the discourse was the recognition that public health was indivisible – that the illness of one class was a problem for all classes. The ideological implications of this recognition were important because it meant that the state could and should intervene in private lives and in independent local government. *Laissez faire* could not be allowed to run as far as imperilling ratepayers' lives. As Lord Macaulay reluctantly put it in 1846,

> I am as firmly attached as any gentleman in this House to the principle of free trade properly stated, and I should state the principle in these terms: that it is not desirable that the state should interfere in the contracts of persons of ripe age and sound mind, touching matters purely commercial, but you would fall into error

if you apply the principle of non-interference . . . where the public
health or the public morality is concerned.

There was considerable opposition to the reforms, not only from ratepayers and municipal authorities but also from the medical profession,
who were concerned that treatment for epidemics was being prescribed by
sanitary engineers as opposed to medical professionals, However, in 1866
the Sanitary Act made the provisions of the 1848 Act mandatory, though
without central control, and the 1875 Public Health Act consolidated all
the sanitary legislation and required all municipalities to appoint a medical officer of health. Municipalities were prepared to accept the legislation
because there was no central control, and by the time of the 1866 Act
the medical profession, whose status had been enhanced by the Medical
Qualifications Act 1858, came to recognize the value of preventive medicine (and, indeed, turned it into a medical specialism).

The concern about public health also resulted in reforms to improve
housing and clear slums. The Artisans' and Labourers' Building Improvement Acts of 1875 and 1879 gave local authorities the power to purchase
land in slum areas and redevelop it. The Housing Act 1890 gave them the
power to clear whole areas, repair and improve houses and build new
ones of better quality. The 'public good' aspect of health – the view that
the state should intervene on behalf of society to ensure the availability
of services for which the commercial market would not pay – led to public
provision of clean water, sewage, cemeteries, factory inspection, compulsory vaccination against smallpox, controls on house-building and regulation of overcrowding. All these reforms raised public expenditure and
were resisted for this reason by the minority who paid local rates, despite
the arguments of people like Chadwick, who had calculated that getting
rid of avoidable disease would actually save money, principally by les-
sening demands on the Poor Law, which was paid for and spent locally.
The public good cannot be seen simply as providing services to the poor
which they could not afford to buy. Public health and sanitation measures
also meant regulation and control of the poor. Controls on overcrowding, for example, raised rents and were resisted by the poor. We are now
so used to seeing the great Victorian reforms as bringing in desirable
improvements that it is easy to lose sight of the fact that many of
them were regarded at the time as profligate with the public purse, an
invasion of privacy and an erosion of the rights of families and individuals to keep their living and health arrangements private.

The Victorian reforms greatly expanded the power of the state – that is,
both central and local government – to intervene in the personal and
private matters of health and health-related issues. The intervention was
not neutral in ideological terms but embodied values and social con-
structions which continued into later schemes for the public provision of
health care: into the Liberal government's reforms of the National Insurance Act (1911) and into the National Health Service Act (1946).

Public health and personal health

Richard Titmuss (1968) has identified two features of publicly funded
health care: it is collectivist and it is preventive. It cannot be supplied

on an individual basis: clean water supplies and efficient sewage disposal (which between them eradicated epidemic diseases such as cholera) cannot be supplied to some people and not others without the attendant risk that those who do not receive them will infect those who do. Everyone, according to collectivists, has an interest in seeing that minimum standards of water purity and sewage disposal are enjoyed by all and, if necessary, imposing (through the state) the requirement that all conform to the regulations in this area. Public goods like clean water cannot be provided on a pay-as-you-consume basis because of the danger that some will not pay for them. That is why there is strong pressure to finance such public services from taxation; everyone pays for them, to varying extents, and everyone enjoys the benefits. This argument for limited state intervention was accepted in Britain by the 1870s, when Disraeli's government passed a number of Acts regulating public health and sanitation which extended or strengthened the reforms of the early Victorian period.

Individual health

Personal health is individual health, the complaints which now take us to our general practitioner (GP) or result in us being admitted to hospital. Clearly, the public and personal merge into one another because diseases caught due to a lack of public facilities (e.g. clean water) will lead to personal illness, but the distinction can be maintained in diseases which appear to be accidental, of unknown origin or appear to arise due to personal neglect. The patterning of individual health problems is not random, as we shall see in Chapter 3, but follows divisions of social class, gender, ethnicity and region. This patterning makes it increasingly difficult to maintain a clear distinction between personal and public health, but we are concerned at the moment with how the Victorians and Edwardians saw the connection and how the 'health debate' evolved then.

The connection between poverty and disease was graphically illustrated by a number of research reports in the early and mid-Victorian periods. The consequences of poverty in the rapidly expanding cities of industrializing Britain were seen as overcrowding, damp and insanitary housing, a poor diet and defective public provision of services such as water and sewage disposal. These in turn led to chronic ill health and shortened **life expectancy**, and in particular to a high infant **mortality** rate. The Victorian public health and planning reforms were aimed at some of these consequences but in themselves did nothing to deal directly with poverty as such – simply with some of its consequences which had public health implications.

However, arguments that the personal health of the poor also required attention were advanced as early as 1844 by the Royal Commission on the Health of Towns, which itself was fundamentally arguing for solutions to collective problems rather than individual ones. Personal health treatment for the poor was a patchwork of **Poor Law infirmaries**, voluntary hospitals (which were of higher status and increasingly became more interested in acute and 'interesting' diseases than in chronic conditions) and charitable efforts by doctors and medical missionaries. In short, the poor received preventive health measures, but curative care was extremely uncertain and readily available only to those of the skilled working class and tradesmen who voluntarily insured with Provident and Friendly Societies and with the craft trades unions. The middle and lower middle classes could buy personal health care according to their means; the amount of health care received depended on the ability to pay for it or, in the case of better-paid working-class men, membership of a voluntary insurance scheme run by a Friendly Society. For the poor there were means-tested voluntary (charity) hospitals (which until the twentieth century normally took *only* patients unable to pay for medical care, these generally being nominated by one of the financial supporters of the hospital); these were not spread evenly throughout the country, took only acute as opposed to chronic cases and even then were selective in the cases they took on. Apart from these, the poor in casual and unskilled jobs and the unemployed were thrown entirely on to the Poor Law provision, and there was a strong tendency to identify Poor Law infirmaries with workhouses.

Personal health measures came much later than public health ones and resulted from the confluence of several different strands in the debate between the '*laissez-faire* lobby' and the interventionists. The main debate concerned the causes of poverty and, by extension, of ill health. Edwin Chadwick, although a noted sanitary reformer and therefore interventionist in the matter of public health measures, was also Secretary to the Poor Law Commissioners and a strong supporter of the new Poor Law, whose principle of **lesser eligibility** was aimed directly at forcing the poor into employment and tightening up the laxity of the 1834 Poor Law which, in the opinion of the new Act's supporters, pandered to the very moral defects which led to poverty and unemployment. The same moral defects of the poor which were responsible for their poverty also showed themselves in poor hygiene, poor parenting, drunkenness and poor **household** management, all defects which might have public health implications, given the slum housing into which the poor were crowded. (Housing remained in short supply throughout the nineteenth century in all the expanding cities, and as the population increased so overcrowding became more rife.)

The growth of social work in late nineteenth-century Britain

The social work of the late Victorian period was aimed at the remoralization of the poor. Two particularly notable organizations involved in this provision were the Charity Organisations Society and the Ladies' Sanitary Reform Association. These two associations can be seen as the outcome both of a growing feminism in Victorian times (see Banks 1981) and of class-conscious philanthropy associated with the evangelical revival. Philanthropic good works were an outlet for upper middle-class Victorian women who were denied a role in production, were no longer satisfied with themselves as wives and mothers but continued to share Victorian middle-class attitudes to women. Philanthropy can be distinguished from charity: while the latter means the outright support of the poor by individuals or state agencies, the former in nineteenth-century Britain was a private intervention in the problem of poverty, a strategy for intervention under the Liberal state. It deflected the problem of poverty and **pauperism** from the field of political right to the field of personal conduct and industry. Philanthropy was provided in two ways: (1) assistance and aid and (2) the diffusion of medical and hygienic norms. It was based on an ideology of self-help and self-reliance.

The Charity Organisations Society

The Charity Organisations Society (COS) was the originator of the idea of 'case-work', whereby a case-worker made direct interventions into individual families to 'remould' them, in exchange for charitable payments. Thrift, temperance and habits of industry were what the poor needed. It grew out of the view that some of the poor – the 'deserving' poor – could be helped to become respectable, self-supporting members of society if given the right blend of assistance and advice. It was also influenced by the evangelical Christian argument the charity *per se* demoralized the poor. They argued that the deserving poor (the sick, the elderly and widows) should be trained in thrift and self-help. The COS, founded in London in 1869, was concerned to ensure that a clear distinction was drawn between the deserving and the undeserving poor. It was underpinned by moral values that were used to determine which individuals were 'in real need' and which were 'playing the system'. The dominant *laissez-faire* ideology that underpinned its moral values saw two causes of poverty: some were poor through natural disasters (such as widowhood) and some through their own 'moral failing' (unwillingness to work, or spending money on drink and gambling). The deserving poor were those whose poverty was no fault of their own and who displayed a willingness to help themselves – those who exhibited the moral values of thrift, sobriety and self-discipline were to be assisted. An officer of the COS assessed and classified different kinds of applicants. A 'case-work' approach to individual applicants developed, whereby they were exhorted and encouraged to conform to 'virtuous' middle-class models of what the family life of the poor should be like. Only those assessed as deserving were given assistance, and they were followed up to see how the money was spent; the officers kept 'case notes' for all those who were assisted.

Ladies' Sanitary Reform Societies

This spirit of personal moral challenge in social work ruled in health matters also, particularly where hygiene and the removal of squalor and filth were concerned. It was the mothers who were the first target for change. The Ladies' National Association for the Reform of Sanitary Conditions was a philanthropic organization established to educate the poor with specific reference to hygiene and cleanliness. The association was founded in London and Brighton in 1857, based on the view that the mother is the key person in health education and that the instruction of mothers, especially working-class mothers, in hygiene was essential. The main aim of the association was the preservation of child life – to reduce mortality rates among children under five – and the main target was mothers. Many of the lady members already visited the poor on behalf of the parish, the Bible Society, etc., and they started to take 'sanitary tracts' with them as well as religious ones. In London, Mrs Raynor, a founding member of the Ladies' National Association, felt that *lady* visitors might not be able to influence poorer women, and she began to use working-class women to visit the poor as female sanitary missionaries. This idea spread to other parts of the country as local branches of the association were established. However, the Manchester Ladies' Sanitary Reform Society (founded in 1861), which employed working-class women to visit mothers at home and instruct them in the need for cleanliness and good diet, is often thought to be the first organized hygiene movement. Its example spread widely in Britain in the late nineteenth century, and most cities came to possess charitable societies with the same purpose.

These organizations, like other similar Victorian ones, were founded, run and charitably supported by middle-class Victorians out of a sense of a duty to help the deserving poor. They can also, however, be seen as the precursors of social work and health visiting – both services that have been developed and provided by the state in twentieth-century Britain. The latter has become a mandatory and universal service; the majority of health authorities require their health visitors to have regular contact with all families with children under the age of five. Social work has remained a selective service, targeted now not so much at those in financial need as those who are deemed to be unable to cope with their daily lives. A key concept here was the idea of dysfunctional families – families unable to cope and thus neglecting or abusing their children (see, for example, Clarke 1988; Abbott and Wallace 1990c).

The twentieth century

The collective challenge

Towards the end of the nineteenth century, the view that poverty was the result of individual failure came increasingly to be challenged. Particularly influential in the debates surrounding the causes of poverty were the results of surveys carried out by Charles Booth in London and Seebohm Rowntree in York. In his first study, Booth divided the population into eight classes (see Box 2.2).

Booth found that 30.7 per cent of the population fell into classes A–D and were in 'poverty'. Classes E and F, in which 51.5 per cent of the population being surveyed fell, were in 'comfort'. In York in 1899, Rowntree found that over 50 per cent of those living in poverty were poor because of a large family. He also found that the chances of being in poverty varied over the **life-course** – those most likely to be living in poverty were young single people, families with dependent children and people over sixty years. Those least likely to be in poverty were married couples

> **Box 2.2   Classes of the poor in Booth's London survey**
>
> A   The lowest class – occasional labourers, loafers and
>   semi-casuals
> B   The very poor – casual labourers, hand-to-mouth existence,
>   chronic want
> C, D   The poor, including those whose earnings were small because
>   of irregularity of employment and those whose work, though
>   regular, was low paid
> E, F   The regularly employed and fairly paid working class of all
>   grades
> G, H   Lower and upper middle class and all above

with no dependent children, with both partners in employment. Booth and Rowntree argued that not all – or even a majority – of the poor were responsible for their plight. The main causes were a lack of regular employment, low wages, sickness and old age.

By late in Victoria's reign the poor had come to be viewed as a health problem in a wider sense than the perceived public health threat of the earlier period. The private sickness of many of the poor was now seen as a problem demanding public intervention – at first charitable intervention, but increasingly provided by the state. The principle of non-interference was eroded further by the enormous outcry after the Boer War (1899–1901) when a high proportion of potential army recruits had had to be turned away as unfit for service (Abbott and Sapsford 1990). However, the debate continued between those who saw poverty and want as a result of individual failing and those who argued that it was a result of factors beyond the control of individuals.

National efficiency

The debate on '**national efficiency**', as it was called, was the immediate background to the Liberal government's health and welfare reforms in the Edwardian period, reforms now widely acknowledged as the beginnings of the British welfare state (see Box 2.3).

The state's interest in children as a resource followed on the revelations about the health of Boer War recruits, but it also intermeshed with a more general debate on national efficiency and **eugenics** – a fear that the decline in the racial stock meant Britain was losing out to its competitors both commercially/industrially (the USA and Germany) and militarily (particularly Germany). For the first time, the working class were seen as a national resource, and the health and physique of working-class children as requiring state intervention. Health measures were increasingly targeted at individuals rather than, as in the case of sanitary reform, at whole populations. The first responses were free school meals (1906), the medical inspection of schoolchildren (1907) and the Notification of Births

---

Box 2.3   Key developments in Edwardian Britain

1904   Report of Interdepartmental Committee on National Efficiency
1905   Royal Commission on the Poor Law established
1906   School Meals Act
1907   School Medicals Act
       Workmen's Compensation Act
       Notification of Births Act
1908   Old Age **Pensions** Act
       Labour Exchange Act
       Children Act
1909   Majority and Minority Reports of the Royal Commission on
       the Poor Law published
1911   National Insurance Act

Act 1907. (This last measure, whose provisions were made mandatory in
1915, was to enable health visitors to visit the homes of all newborn
babies and give advice on hygiene and child care.) More generally, there
was a commitment to improving 'the quality of mothering', for example
by the provision of mother and baby clinics and health visitors by local
authorities. 'Concentrate on the mother. What the mother is the children
are. Let us glorify, dignify and purify motherhood by every means in our
power', said John Burns, once a trades union agitator and later President
of the Local Government Board, at a conference in 1906 on infant mortality. (However, non-employed women and children were excluded from
the provisions of the 1911 National Insurance Act, arguably because they
were not economically productive – see below.)

These interventionist reforms continued to be opposed, however, by
those who argued that state welfare resulted in dependency. The Charity
Organisations Society, for example, said of school meals provision, that

> to feed the children is to debase the moral standard . . . by prudently
> inviting parents . . . to spend in idleness or drink the time and money
> which should have been given to making provision for their family.
>   (From an 1883 COS pamphlet, quoted in Owen 1965: 242)

This concern that parents and especially men should be encouraged to
take their responsibilities seriously, or at least not deterred from doing so,
underpinned the legislative reforms to a large extent. Health visiting, for
example, was introduced as a result of an inquiry in 1904 by an interdepartmental committee set up to investigate why the physical condition
of working-class recruits for the Boer War was so poor. It found that the
major factors were poverty and poor housing, although inadequate mothering was also seen as contributory. The committee made a large number
of recommendations designed to reduce poverty and improve the housing
conditions of the poor, but the main recommendation taken up was the

introduction of health visiting. Although medical inspection of school children was introduced, it remained the responsibility of parents to ensure that their children received medical care.

The Liberal reforms

Other welfare measures of this period included: the Workmen's Compensation Act 1907; the Children Act 1908, which was concerned with measures to combat cruelty to children; the Probation of Offenders Act 1908, which first introduced probation as an alternative to imprisonment; the Labour Exchange Act 1908; and the Old Age Pensioners Act 1908, which introduced a non-contributory **pension** of 5 shillings per week at age 70 for both men and women. (Those who had an income of less than £21 a year received a full pension, and those whose income went up to £31 10/– a proportion of it. Those who had been habitually drunk, served a prison sentence in the previous ten years, been on poor relief or habitually failed to support themselves were excluded on moral grounds.) The Widows, Orphans and Old Age Pensions Act 1925 introduced additional contributory schemes to cover the risks of bereavement and old age.

The Liberal government did not, however, reform the Poor Law. The Royal Commission on the Poor Law, which was set up in 1905, resulted in two reports, a report from the majority and one from the minority. The Charity Organisations Society was opposed to any state intervention and argued that every case of poverty needed to be investigated in order to distinguish between the deserving and the undeserving. The **Fabian Movement**, whose views were expressed in the Minority Report and who were represented on the commission by Beatrice Webb, argued that much poverty was not the fault of the poor and that the state should make provision. The Fabian view had been influenced by the surveys of Booth in London and Rowntree in York, which had demonstrated that a substantial proportion of poverty could be attributed to the unavailability of jobs, low pay (preventing saving), sickness and old age. A report written for the commission by Professor William Smart showed that poverty affected women more than men and children and the elderly more than the young. In a sample of paupers, 27 per cent were men, 29 per cent children and 43 per cent women. About 3/1000 people aged 15–20 years were in poverty, less than 7/1000 aged 25–34, 16/1000 of those aged 65–74, 276/1000 aged 75–84 and 353/1000 aged 85+. A report on 150,000 children on poor relief found that they were under-nourished, poorly dressed and bare-footed (see Jones, 1994). Despite evidence of the extent of poverty and the arguments and research on its causes, no major reform of the Poor Law was undertaken until the 1940s. The argument that state relief would demoralize the poor and that outdoor relief would greatly increase costs to ratepayers held sway.

The poor still relied on charitable medical care, although the number of hospitals offering free care to acute cases expanded slowly but steadily in Edwardian Britain, as local authorities took over many Poor Law infirmaries (following the abolition of the Poor Law wards in 1929) and built new ones. A considerable and diverse range of local authority municipal hospitals was founded, including infectious diseases hospitals, hospitals specializing in the treatment of tuberculosis, maternity hospitals, mental hospitals and general hospitals.

The most significant change in personal health care provision was due to the Liberals' National Insurance Act of 1911, partly copied from Bismarck's reforms in Germany. Lloyd George appealed both to the self-interests of employers in supporting reform and to the hygiene movement's fear of racial decline when he spoke in favour of the new Act. The Act was in two parts: Unemployment Insurance and Sickness Benefit. Contributions were made by employees, employers and the state.

The unemployment provision applied only to workers in fluctuating trades (e.g. building, shipbuilding) and no benefit was paid for wives or children. Benefits were paid at the new labour exchanges, where the genuineness of the claim was tested by ensuring there was no suitable work available. In 1920, the scheme was extended to virtually all manual workers earning less than £250 per year. However, as unemployment rose during the 1920s, benefits were cut and contributions increased (Jones 1991). At the same time, dependants' benefits were introduced and transitional benefit, at a lower rate, was introduced for workers who had exhausted their benefit right. In 1930, the term 'Poor Law' was replaced by 'public assistance', 'paupers' became 'rate-aided persons', and workhouses (now controlled by local authorities) became public assistance institutions. In 1934, an Act of Parliament established the Unemployment Assistance Board, which provided benefit for those whose entitlement to unemployment benefit had become exhausted. Benefits were paid at a lower rate than public assistance, with a considerably harder **means test** – the Household Means Test – which included calculations based on the income of the total household, including working children, aged parents and lodgers.

The health scheme was administered by local insurance committees, which included representatives of approved societies, local authorities and **GPs**, with a residual scheme organized through post offices for those refused by the voluntary sector. The sickness provisions applied to all **manual workers** (both men and women) aged 16–70 years who were earning less than £250 per year – about 2 million people – although this was later increased to £420, and non-manual workers earning less than £160 a year were included. The benefits, however, were restricted to GP care, drugs and medicines, and a modest entitlement to sickness and disablement benefits and a maternity grant. Hospital services were originally excluded, but they were gradually covered, and by 1939 about half the population were entitled to hospital care through one scheme or another.

The Act aroused opposition from employers, because of the contributions they had to pay, and from the British Medical Association (BMA), who believed that the remuneration for GPs under the scheme was inadequate. The government, however, removed the power of insurance committees over GPs' remuneration. The **middle classes** were excluded from the scheme, partly because the doctors feared losing their private patients and partly because the Liberals insisted that the scheme would be funded

entirely from contributions – the insurance principle. Only working people were in the health scheme; **non-employed** wives and children were
excluded, as were the **unemployed** and the self-employed. (It was feared
that if married women and children were included, this would deter men
from working to provide for their families.) Those who could not afford
the fees for private treatment had to turn to the local authority hospitals
(the old Poor Law infirmaries), which provided care mainly for the chronically sick, the elderly and the mentally ill, or rely on charitable medical
treatment, which was in general available only for acute illness. However,
by 1939, 43 per cent of the population were covered by National Health
Insurance and about 90 per cent of GPs participated in the scheme (Webster
1993).

The 1911 Act was the forerunner of the 1946 National Health Service
Act, which established universal health care funded from general taxation. The insurance principle was, however, retained for sickness benefit
and extended to unemployment, old age pensions and maternity benefits
in the 1946 Act.

Personal health care between the wars

The Liberal reforms and the slow extension of local authority hospitals
left a patchy and cumbersome system of personal health care in Britain
in the inter-war period. Access to health care in the pre-war health service
depended on geography and money. Access to high-quality health care
varied throughout the country. The poorest, who were entitled to free
care, and the wealthy who could afford to pay for it received medical care,
although even then the quality of the care they received varied considerably. Others depended either on insurance with Friendly Societies and
Provident Associations or hoped they would not need medical care.

The poor then, although provided for in the public and voluntary hospitals and under National Insurance, had an unhealthy and insecure existence and there were many gaps in the services designed to satisfy their
needs. The middle classes were the major source of finance and paid more
than their fair share of doctors' fees and hospital bills. The rich, voluntarily excluded themselves from some of the best hospital care, preferring
instead the small private hospital or nursing home with sometimes poor
facilities and inadequately trained staff.

Pressure for reform came from the Labour Movement and from middle-
class fears of medical costs. The organized medical profession, however,
resisted further reform, as it had resisted the 1911 scheme, on the grounds
that what was being advocated was a system of state-salaried doctors. The
BMA opposed the war-time proposals for a National Health Service; the
Labour government's Bill was accepted only after a lengthy opposition.
The eventual terms were much more favourable to the BMA's position
than the Labour Party had wanted – GPs were to remain independent
contractors rather than salaried employees, and hospital doctors were
permitted to combine private practice with employment in the NHS.

The National Health Service

The architect of the National Health Service, Aneurin Bevan, had to accept a scheme about which he had doubts concerning independent contractors (the GPs) and patients' freedom to choose the doctor they wanted, and also concerning the continuation of private practice. The need to extend health services to the dependants (primarily women and children) of the insured contributors (mainly men), however, and the need to provide hospital care and GP care in those parts of the country (predominantly the poorer parts) where provision had been very thin, overrode the Labour Movement's doubts. Legislation founded the health service that we have today, a centrally planned service with a commitment to health care based on need rather than on the ability to pay and a service available throughout the whole country and in poor areas as well as affluent ones, funded mainly out of general taxation.

The NHS, established in 1948, was under tripartite control (see Fig. 2.1). Local authorities were responsible for community and public health. Executive councils made up of part-time appointees nominated by the Ministry of Health, the local authorities and the independent contractors themselves were responsible for GP, dental, ophthalmic and pharmaceutical services. Hospital services, with the exception of the teaching

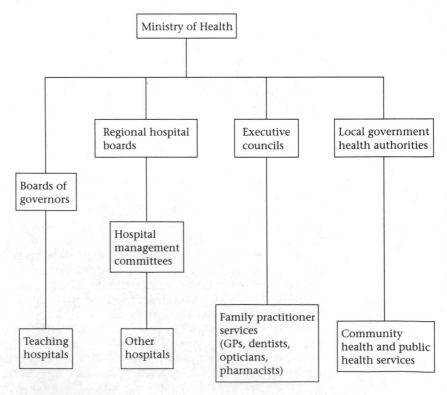

Figure 2.1 Structure of the NHS in England and Wales, 1948–74.

hospitals, were administered by Regional Hospital Boards (RHBs) responsible for the overall planning, coordination and supervision of services,
and Hospital Management Committees (HMCs) responsible for the day-
to-day running of local hospital services. Members of the RHBs were
appointed by the Minister of Health after consultation with local authorities and the medical profession. HMC members were appointed by the
RHB following consultation with local authorities, the medical profession
and voluntary associations. The teaching hospitals were administered by
boards of governors appointed by and accountable to the Minister of
Health.

The classic welfare state

The NHS was only one element of the reform that was undertaken in the
1940s and which resulted in a considerable extension of the state provision of welfare and was accompanied by a commitment to full employment. The aim was to eliminate Beveridge's 'five giants' – want, disease,
ignorance, squalor and idleness. The main measures included universal
free primary and secondary education, the NHS, compulsory insurance
benefit for all employees and the self-employed to cover for unemployment, old age and disability, as well as non-contributory benefits for
those not covered by insurance, local authority children's departments
staffed by qualified social workers, and increased provision of council
housing (see Box 2.4). However, the lynchpin of providing for the welfare of the population was the commitment to full employment – paid
employment for all adult men of working age who were fit to undertake
it. It was thought at the time that the government could ensure this by
economic policy and the provision of labour exchanges to ensure that
those seeking employment could be put in touch with employers with
suitable vacancies. As Lowe (1993: 99) indicates, 'the maintenance of
full employment was both a direct contribution to individual welfare and
an essential support for other welfare services, because it simultaneously
maximised revenue and minimised demand for them'.

Box 2.4 Main Legislation of the 1940s

1944   Butler Education Act
1945   Family Allowance Act
1946   National Insurance Act
       National Health Service Act
1947   Town and Country Planning Act
       New Towns Act
1948   Children Act
1949   Housing Act

The legislative period between 1946 and 1949 continued rather than redirected the legislation of the pre-war period, making the state provision of welfare more comprehensive and more rational, with a more coherent coordination of services. The commercial sector was not abolished; private schools, private health services and private insurances, for example, were not curtailed by the legislation. However, there was a national pooling of risk, with all those in paid employment making flat-rate contributions to the insurance schemes for unemployment, sickness, maternity, widowhood and old age and all receiving the same rate of benefit. Other state provision was funded out of general taxation, and given the **progressive taxation system** in Britain (tax increases with income, in percentage terms as well as absolutely) the better-off contributed relatively more than the less well-off to the provision of education and health services. There was also the safety net of means-tested income maintenance for those who fell outside the insurance network (see Chapter 5). The voluntary sector also continued to play a role, and informal care played a significant part in meeting **welfare needs** (see Chapters 7 and 8).

The legislation introduced in the 1940s founded what has been called 'the classic welfare state', one in which the state took the major responsibility for organizing and delivering welfare services and maintaining full employment. Welfare was paid for mainly out of taxation and from national insurance contributions, although the latter have never been sufficient to cover the costs of insured benefits. The welfare provision that was introduced was service-led and professionally dominated. It was assumed that experts knew the 'best' ways to organize and deliver services to meet the welfare needs of all citizens. There was a considerable degree of consensus about the desirability of the welfare state between the Conservative and Labour Parties, although there were dissenting voices in the Conservative Party.

Basically, the shape of the Welfare State remained as established in the 1940s, with the expansion of some services – especially personal social services in the 1970s (following the 1968 Seebohm Report) – the building of new hospitals, reforms to the organizational structure of the NHS and the introduction of new income maintenance benefits. There was a shift in emphasis from the late 1950s from residential to **community care** (see Chapter 9). An unanticipated development was that the number of people dependent on non-contributory benefits, which Beveridge had anticipated would decline, actually increased. What had been intended as an 'interim measure' now provides for the largest proportion of welfare expenditure (see Chapter 5).

It was not until the election of the Conservative government to power in 1979 that the classic welfare state was fundamentally challenged. The Conservatives have carried out a major programme of reform, critically reviewing all aspects of the welfare state. The programme of legislative reform has been concerned to move away from the state provision of welfare (though not necessarily from state funding for it), to target benefits and services at those most in need, to introduce commercial sector management techniques (the 'new managerialism') and to open up the provision of services to competition. The reforms have been underpinned by a will to challenge collective provision and to encourage the mixed economy of welfare, but with the state retaining a regulating role (Wilding 1992). Many of these changes are discussed in more detail in the following chapters, and in Chapter 10 we return to the question of ideology and the ways in which it shapes welfare policies.

Conclusions

In this chapter, we have considered how the ways in which welfare was provided, especially with respect to health services, changed during the nineteenth century and the first half of the twentieth century. We have focused in particular on the ways in which the state came to be a major provider of welfare services during that period, including the debates as to whether and why the state should be responsible for the collective funding and provison of welfare services. Those who have advocated the state provision of welfare have not always done so for purely humanitarian reasons, but on grounds of national efficiency. We have explored this in relation to health, but it is equally true, for example, that the arguments for introducing and expanding state education have included the need to inculcate habits of industry and diligence in children and young people, enabling Britain to compete with its industrial rivals and not 'wasting' the talent of young people. Arguments for the state provision of welfare have as often included reference to **social control** and meeting the needs of society as of humanitarian concern for the welfare of individuals.

The legislation passed in the 1940s laid down the framework for the state provision of welfare that continues to underpin welfare provision to the present day. Most subsequent changes have taken place within that framework, although the future pattern of the welfare state is now on the political agenda (Gladstone 1995b). Until 1979, when the first of Margaret Thatcher's administrations was elected, the main changes were to administrative structures and the extension of services; subsequently, the main changes have been in who actually provides welfare (but not who pays for it). As we shall see in subsequent chapters, the main provider and funder of welfare services in Britain continues to be the state, although the informal sector continues actually to provide most welfare care. The roles of the commercial and voluntary sectors have become more prominent, partly because of the emphasis by the Conservatives on the role they should and do play, and partly because the state is increasingly purchasing services from these sectors on behalf of clients. The actual increase in the purchase of services from the commercial sector by individuals and families, apart from private pension plans, has been modest to date. Similarly, the major growth in the voluntary sector has been in housing, with a growth in housing associations, as councils have been forced to sell housing to sitting tenants and restricted in the extent to which they can build new housing for rent.

It is important to recognize, however, that the Conservative government is committed to the development of alternatives to the state supply of social services and increasingly targeting those services supplied or purchased by the state at those most in need. To date there has been considerable resistance to the increased targeting of welfare based on insurance contributions (e.g. **retirement** pensions) and certain universal benefits (e.g. the NHS and Child Benefit). The government has most successfully increased targeting for means-tested benefits, but the implementation of the community care element of the National Health Service and Community Care Act 1990 from April 1993 has also resulted in increased targeting of domiciliary and day care (see Chapter 9).

The much more fundamental change has been in the disappearance of the commitment to full employment, abandoned in the 1970s. As we shall indicate in subsequent chapters, one of the consequences of this has been increasing inequalities in income between those in full-time permanent employment and those who are unemployed or who experience insecurity and low pay.

Summary

- This chapter has mapped the evolution of the welfare state in British social history from the industrial revolution to the present day. It has used the example of the development of medical care provision to illustrate broader trends and influences affecting social policy.

- This study shows the important contribution of the mixed economy of welfare provision since the nineteenth century, in particular the contribution of voluntary sector hospitals and the dominance of the informal sector throughout British history.

- Through an analysis of health care policy, this chapter evidences the influence of political ideology on social policy from a period of *laissez-faire* in the nineteenth century through a period of concern about poverty (in the early twentieth century) both in terms of 'contagion' and its impact on public morality. This lead to the development of social policies whose primary function was to control and reinforce certain patterns of social behaviour (such as the work ethic and 'normal' family relations).

- Post-war Britain witnessed the development of a political consensus during a period of social reconstruction resulting in more interventionist social policy founded on principles of social justice and citizenship. This period saw the birth of the 'modern' welfare state. Using the example of the development of the NHS this chapter shows how institutional welfare provision may both promote social equality and reduce individual freedom, through increasing the powers of welfare professionals and new forms of regulation and surveillance.

- The 1980s saw a return to *laissez-faire* principles under the policies of the New Right committed to monetarist economics and a 'return' to ideas about individual responsibility and the role of the welfare state in encouraging a dependency culture.

Further reading

Hill, M. (1993) *The Welfare State in Britain: A Political History Since 1945*. Cheltenham: Edward Elgar.

Jones, H. (1994) *Health and Society in Twentieth Century Britain*. Harlow: Longmans.

Jones, K. (1991) *The Making of Social Policy in Britain 1930–1990*. London: Athlone.

Lowe, R. (1993) *The Welfare State in Britain since 1945*. London: Macmillan.

Thane, P. (1982) *The Foundations of the Welfare State*. Harlow: Longmans.

THREE

HEALTH INEQUALITIES AND STATE HEALTH POLICIES

Introduction

We have indicated in Chapters 1 and 2 that there are debates about the extent to which the welfare state was introduced to bring about greater equality rather than just to provide a 'safety net'. We have suggested that the provision of certain services – especially education and health – was intended to ensure that everyone had access to these services and that, at the very least, there would be a considerable reduction in the inequalities that were based on **social class** and the ability to purchase the services (or not). The vast majority of the population use the National Health

Service (NHS) and send their children to state schools. Since the Second World War, a considerable amount of research has been carried out to determine the extent to which welfare state services are reducing inequalities and providing equality of opportunity.

In this chapter we consider, as a case study, the extent to which the provision of the NHS has brought about greater **equity** in health provision and discuss some of the ways in which welfare policies could be modified. We could have considered education and discuss the research which has been undertaken, which in general has indicated that class differentials (and indeed gender and ethnic ones) in educational achievement persist, and that they are not fully explained by differences in aptitude and ability (see, for example, Douglas 1964; Halsey *et al.* 1981). Focusing instead on the role of the NHS as the main provider of health care in Britain, this chapter aims to draw the reader's attention to the level of health inequalities which continue to exist. It also considers some of the different theories which have been proposed to account for such inequalities. The chapter will also encourage the reader to consider ways in which health is affected not just by NHS-provided health care, but also by other social policy areas such as housing, employment, the social security system and also the wider economic structure. A key issue raised in this chapter is the question of equity and the extent to which the NHS has provided more equitable access to health services in Britain since its introduction in 1948. Attention will be paid to the health policies that have followed from this or should follow, including *The Health of the Nation* (Department of Health 1992) strategy and criticisms of it.

The structure of the NHS

Most formal health care in Britain is provided by the NHS. The main provision is hospitals, primary care practices (doctors, dentists, pharmacists and opticians operating outside hospitals) and other community-based services (community nursing, health visiting and preventive medicine). The service is paid for mainly out of general taxation and, with the exception of dental and optical care and prescribed drugs, free at the point of delivery. Children and those on low incomes are exempt from charges for dental and optical care and for prescribed drugs; everyone else has to make a financial contribution. (The basic structure of the NHS is marginally different in Northern Ireland, Scotland and Wales; see Box 3.1.)

The original structure was tripartite, with hospitals, GPs, dentists and pharmacists and community services being administered separately (see Fig. 2.1). In 1974, community services were transferred from local authorities to health authorities, which were also responsible for hospital services. The Family Health Service Authorities (FHSAs) became responsible for GPs, dentists and pharmacy services. In addition, since the implementation of the National Health Service and Community Care Act 1990, hospital units have become NHS Trusts and an increasing number of GPs

---

Box 3.1 The NHS in Northern Ireland, Scotland and Wales

- The health service in each of these areas is the responsibility of a separate minister.
- In Northern Ireland there are four Health and Social Services Boards, divided into Districts.
- Scotland has 15 Health Boards, and Wales has 9 District Health Authorities.

(Derived from Webster 1993: 130)

---

are becoming fundholders. This Act was designed to bring about a split between providers and purchasers of health care, thus creating managed markets in the NHS (see Chapter 7). District Health Authorities (DHAs) are now responsible for purchasing hospital services on behalf of their populations and the NHS Trusts for providing these services. The GP fundholders are able to purchase hospital and other services on behalf of the patients on their list.

General practitioners, whether they are fundholders or not, are independent practitioners contracted to the FHSA. They are free to decide how they organize their practices and which patients they will take. They are paid a 'capitation fee', allowances for practice expenses and special payments for various tasks that they undertake. The majority of GPs now work in group practices, employ practice nurses and provide a wide range of services (Box 3.2 lists the services provided by one East Midlands general practice.) Opticians, dentists and pharmacists are paid on a fee-for-service basis, and these are the three services for which patients have been asked to make increased contributions to the cost of their treatment, especially since 1979.

Box 3.2 The range of services provided by one suburban GP practice

- Ante-natal care
- Post-natal care
- Baby clinic
- Childhood immunization
- Family planning
- Immunization for foreign travel
- Cervical smears
- Well person/coronary prevention clinic
- Hypertension clinic
- Asthma clinic
- Diabetic clinic
- Minor operations
- Health checks for new patients, the elderly and pre-school children
- Influenza injections
- Hormone replacement therapy/menopausal clinic

Since its inception, the goal of the NHS in Britain has been to make health care available to the population as a whole, via a general practice service. The vast majority of the population are registered with a GP, who can refer patients for specialist and hospital services. The original aim was to provide a comprehensive and universally coordinated service, state-funded and state-provided. (Indeed, since the introduction of the 'purchaser/provider split' under the 1990 legislation, hospitals are reluctant to treat patients who are *not* registered with a GP.) Subsequent reforms, including the 1990 Act, have not changed this fundamentally, with the possible exception of dentistry, where increasingly adults are being forced to become private patients, although it is possible that they will result in a reduction of state provision (as purchasers buy from the commercial and voluntary sectors as well as the state sector), but the state remains the main provider of health care. In Britain, about 84 per cent of health care spending is by the state, one of the highest proportions in the world. However, in total, Britain spends a relatively modest proportion of its **gross domestic product (GDP)** on health care, compared with other western countries (see, for example, Abbott and Giarchi, in press).

The NHS and equity

The founders of the NHS envisaged a first-class health service for all. The service was to be funded out of direct taxation in order that the better-off classes contributed more towards its costs, while the poor, it was assumed, would benefit most. A Ministry of Health publication in 1944 stated that the aims of the NHS were:

> to ensure that everybody in the country – irrespective of means, age, sex and occupation – shall have equal opportunity to benefit from the best and most up-to-date medical and allied services available. To provide, therefore, for all who want it, a comprehensive service covering every branch of medical and allied activity.
>
> (Ministry of Health 1944: 47)

A leaflet circulated to every household in Britain in 1948 explained the purpose of the new health service:

> It will provide you with all medical, dental and nursing care. Everyone – rich or poor, man or woman or child – can use it or any part of it. There are no charges, except for a few special items. There are no insurance qualifications. But it is not a 'charity'. You are all paying for it, mainly as taxpayers, and it will relieve your many worries in times of illness.
>
> (COI 1948)

The NHS was founded, then, on a principle of equity, and it was assumed that it would improve the health of the nation and more specifically of the poorer classes, who had previously had access to less comprehensive health care than the more advantaged classes who had been able to pay. It is certainly the case that the overall health of the population has improved since the NHS was introduced, although to what extent this is directly attributable to the service is more difficult to determine. Part of the general improvement in health is undoubtedly the result of improved living standards in Britain after the Second World War and elements of welfare provision other than the NHS itself. Indeed, Jones (1994: 53) has suggested that, 'Good Health Services do not produce a fit and healthy population overall; they produce an aging population with a higher proportion of handicapped and infirm'.

Despite increased spending on health care, there seems to be ever increasing demand for more spending, partly because of the increasing proportion of elderly people in the population, partly because of advances in medical science and particularly 'hi-tech' medicine, and partly because wage inflation (staffing costs) has been higher than the general growth in the economy. Also, there has been a need since the foundation of the NHS to replace old hospital buildings and provide hospital and other services where the existing provision proved inadequate.

The NHS has been evaluated in terms of the extent to which it has met its aims in relation to equity, although a number of other concerns have been expressed about health care and the way in which it is provided. These latter criticisms are concerned with the broader role of medicine and medical science and can broadly be referred to as 'the cultural critique of medicine'. They question on the one hand the extent to which medical science has improved health and is able to do so, and on the other hand the way in which medical science increasingly exerts control over people's lives (see, for example, Abbott and Sapsford 1988; Abbott and Wallace 1990a, 1996).

Social policy analysts have principally been concerned, however, with the question of equity. Whitehead (1994) has indicated that the NHS was built on at least eight components of equity or fairness, and it is possible to evaluate the extent to which it has operated in an equitable or fair manner. The evidence available indicates that some of the principles have been achieved, at least in part, whereas others have not:

1 *Universal entitlement.* In general, this principle has been achieved; everyone who is resident in Britain is entitled to the services provided by the NHS. However, there have been cases of, for example, families living in temporary bed and breakfast accommodation who have not been able to register with a GP, and homeless people find it difficult to register and gain access to health care. In recent years, it has become increasingly difficult, especially for adults, to find a dentist who is prepared to treat them on the NHS, though the FHSA has to provide people with details of a dentist who is prepared to take NHS patients.

2 *Pooling of financial risk.* The NHS has been and continues to be paid for out of general taxation. Taxes are generally progressive in Britain, meaning that the better off in general pay more in taxes than those who are less well off. However, since the election of the Conservatives to power in 1979, taxation in Britain has become less progressive – that is, as a result of the reforms, the less well off pay a higher proportion of their income in tax and the wealthiest a lower proportion (see Chapter 4; see also Abbott and Wallace 1992: ch.4).

3 *The health service*. There has been a move away from the original principle, which envisaged that health care would be free at the point of
delivery and that nobody would be deterred from using services because
of their cost. The principle of a free service was breached almost immediately the NHS was introduced, with the introduction of charges for
medicines and some appliances. Since then, charges for medicine, appliances, opticians and dental services have gradually increased, and
the rate of increase has accelerated under the Conservative government
since 1979. Charges are means-tested so that the least well off, and
children, are generally exempt. However, means tests act as a deterrent
to the poor seeking services, and many people who are not entitled to
a free service have difficulty in meeting charges. Also, the hidden costs
of health care are not taken into account, for example the cost of getting to the service in the first place and the loss of earnings resulting
from time taken off work. Manual workers are more likely to lose earnings if they take time off work. Poor people, the elderly and women are
more likely than middle-class people and men to have to use public
transport (where it exists), with the attendant costs in money and time
which its use entails.

4 *Equality of access*. That is, everyone should have access to a comprehensive range of services – primary, secondary and tertiary care.
Basically, the NHS nationalized the existing provision. This resulted in
considerable inequalities in spending on health care and the provision
of services in different regions. There has been some reduction in inter-
regional inequality in health service provision since the formation of
the Resource Allocation Working Party in 1976, a policy designed to
ensure a more equitable distribution of resources between health authorities (Mays and Bevan 1987). However, recent changes in resource
allocation due to the introduction in 1991 of the new RAWP formula
have reversed this trend, and more resources are being channelled back
towards the south-east of England and away from the north – mainly
because older people are highly weighted in the formula (Royston *et al.*
1992). There is also considerable evidence of 'distance decay and territorial injustice' (Giarchi 1990), especially with the greater centralization
of services; that is, the further someone lives from a service the less
likely they are to use it. This is particularly true for elderly or disabled
people (Whitehead 1987) and women with children (Graham 1984).
More resources in the NHS have been devoted to acute services than
those for the chronically ill, the latter being referred to as the 'Cinderella
services'. Despite repeated government assurances since the mid-1970s
that there should be a redistribution of resources to the chronic services
(for the elderly, mentally ill people, disabled people and people with
specific learning difficulties), little has changed, although there has been
some redistribution from hospital to community services since the early
1980s (see Webster 1993: 133, table 7). Wistow and Henwood (1991)
argue that 'the rights to universal and free health care for a large proportion of the population are being removed'. In particular they point
to the erosion of free NHS care for frail elderly people requiring non-
acute health care, including continuing care beds, during the 1980s.
Whitehead (1994) has argued that the introduction of the National

Health Service and Community Care Act 1990 will further erode the rights to universal and free health care of frail elderly people requiring continuing care beds, as they will now have their needs for care assessed by local authorities and will be means-tested if services are provided. Community care policies for the mentally ill have resulted in many people being in the community without adequate support or care. One report concluded that:

> Many psychiatrically very ill people are living like feral children in the centre of the city, scavenging for garbage and subsisting from charitable handouts. This sight is constantly before us – and yet we seem to be blind to the desperate plight of these vulnerable individuals.
>
> (Weller and Tobiensky 1989)

5 *Equality of care.* This is the principle that everyone should receive the same quality and level of service for the same need. In 1971, Tudor Hart argued that there is an 'inverse care law' in the NHS – those that have the greatest need for services have access to the poorest services. He suggested that this was because the more prosperous areas attract the greatest resources, including skilled health workers in primary and secondary care. [Whitehead (1987) argues that deprived areas continue to have a poorer provision of health services than more affluent ones, 20 years after Tudor Hart was writing.] Other research has suggested that middle-class people receive a better standard of care, are given more time by doctors and other health workers, and that doctors and other health workers are less likely to explain their health problems and treatment to working-class than to middle-class people (see, for example, Cartwright and Anderson 1983). Middle-class people also make more use of preventive services than working-class people, and are more knowledgeable about the services available and their right to them. LeGrand (1982) argued that the NHS systematically favours the better off, although he agrees that it is more equitable than the service it replaced, and it is arguably more equitable than what is available in many other countries (Ham *et al.* 1989).

6 *Selection on the basis of clinical need.* This is the principle that services should be provided on the basis of need and not ability to pay. It has generally been adhered to, although it is mediated by inequalities between regions (discussed above) and clinical judgement of the likelihood of benefit. There have, for instance, been cases of people denied treatment on the basis of age or lifestyle. It has also remained possible for people to pay privately for treatment in order to avoid a wait and/ or to have treatment that is not considered medically necessary. There has been some evidence that since the introduction of the National Health and Community Care Act 1990, GP fundholders have been able to get their patients treated more quickly than others (see Chapter 6).

7 *Non-exploitative ethos of science.* This is the view that medical care is based on value-free and objective knowledge. Concern has been expressed at the ways in which people from **ethnic minority** groups and women have been controlled by the medical professionals. At a more general level, it has been suggested that the power of the medical

professions has come from their successful claim to scientific status and the claimed efficacy of medical treatments (Foucault 1963; Armstrong 1984), which is not totally proven. Also, it has been argued that doctors have extended their status and power by medicalizing more and more areas of life (see, for example, Scull 1977; Witz 1992). This enables medical practitioners to maintain a high status and high economic rewards and a dominant position in the medical division of labour. Patients are seen as something to be worked on rather than people to be worked with (Savage 1986).

8 *Feel-good factor.* A feeling shared by all citizens that it is a good thing that all members of society have access to health care when they are ill. Despite all the criticisms and concerns that have been expressed about the NHS, there remains a feeling that it should remain; it continues to be a popular service in Britain.

The NHS, then, while it may not have achieved equity – whether this is defined as equal access for all, equal spending on all, services provided on the basis of need, equal treatment or equal outcome – remains a popular institution (1994 British Social Attitudes Survey). Furthermore, while the health of the population as a whole has generally improved since 1948 and the fear of having to pay for medical treatment has in the main disappeared, nevertheless the relative inequalities between the more advantaged and the more disadvantaged groups prior to 1948 have persisted, and some may even have increased since 1980, as we shall see in the next section.

Health inequalities in Britain

Poverty and health inequalities

Research in Britain and elsewhere in Europe has consistently demonstrated that disadvantaged groups have poorer health than more advantaged groups and a reduced access to health care (e.g. Townsend and Davidson 1982; Whitehead 1987; Benzeval *et al.* 1995a; Abbott and Giarchi, in press). Comparative research has indicated that in western societies life expectancy is highest in those countries with the most equitable income distribution (Wilkinson 1992) – that is, those with the least gap between the highest and lowest incomes.

The publication of the Black Report on Health Inequalities (Townsend and Davidson 1982) had a significant impact on both politicians and the medical and medical-sociology disciplines. The working group's main finding was the apparent failure of post-war social welfare and economic policy to reduce the differences in health experience between the most affluent and the most impoverished in British society. Except in the case of child health, the differential between occupational classes I and II (professional and managerial) and IV and V (semi- and unskilled manual) in terms of life expectancy had grown wider (Table 3.1). Mortality rates for the more affluent in society had fallen steadily, while the death rate for the poorest had fallen only marginally, thus widening the gap. Also, the

Table 3.1 Male mortality by occupational class, 1930–83 (standardized mortality ratios).

Occupational class[a]	1930–32	1949–53[b]	1959–63		1970–72		1979–80 + 1982–83	
			Unadjusted	Adjusted[c]	Unadjusted	Adjusted[c]	Unadjusted	Adjusted[d]
I Professional	90	86	76	75	77	75	66	70
II Managerial and administrative	94	92	81	—	81	—	76	—
IIIN Non-skilled, non-manual	97	101	100	—	104	—	94	—
IIIM Skilled manual							106	—
IV Partly skilled	102	104	103	—	114	—	116	—
V Unskilled	111	118	143	127	137	121	165	(124)

[a] **Registrar General's classification**.
[b] A standardized mortality ratio of 100 indicates that the subgroup has exactly the average mortality of the population as a whole. A ratio of 110 indicates 10 per cent more deaths than would be expected from the average, after allowing for differences in age and gender balance.
[c] Occupations in 1959–63 and 1970–72 have been reclassified according to the 1950 classification.
[d] Further allowance is made for occupational reclassification between 1970 and 1980.
Source: Townsend et al. (1988).

Table 3.2 Percentage changes in the extent of poverty in Britain, 1960–83.

Income in relation to supplementary benefit/national assistance standard	1960	1975	1979	1981	1983	1960	1975	1979	1981	1983
Below SB standard	1.3	1.8	2.1	2.6	2.7	2.3	3.5	4.0	4.9	5.0
Receiving SB	2.7	3.7	4.0	4.8	6.1	4.9	7.0	7.6	9.1	11.4
At or up to 40% above SB standard	3.5	7.0	5.5	7.2	7.6	6.4	13.2	10.4	13.5	14.1
Total	7.4	12.5	11.6	14.7	16.4	14.2	23.7	22.0	27.0	30.5

Source: For 1960, Abel-Smith and Townsend (1965); for other years, annual Family Expenditure Surveys.

number of people in poverty had risen, members of the lower social classes being more at risk of falling into poverty than those in the higher ones (Table 3.2).

The life expectancy of the least privileged in society is about 8 years less than that of the most affluent. The most disadvantaged are also likely to experience more illness and disability (see, for example, White et al. 1993). Since the 1980s, the gap in Britain between the rich and the poor has been widening, with the death rate in some of the most disadvantaged areas rising not only in relative terms when compared with more affluent areas, but actually rising in absolute terms among some age groups (Benzeval et al. 1995b).

Class, deprivation and health inequalities

Since the publication of the Black Report (Townsend and Davidson 1982), there has been extensive research by social scientists into **health**

inequalities, including a number of small-area studies. They have looked at a number of potential associations between social and material deprivation indicators and health indicators, moving away from occupational or social class as the sole indicator of differences in lifestyle. A number of factors have been found to be associated with different levels of mortality (death) and morbidity (ill health): occupational class, unemployment, car ownership, gender, ethnicity, age, marital status, area of residence, and so on (Townsend and Davidson 1982; MacIntyre 1986; Abbott (ed.) 1988; Marsh and Channing 1986; Moser *et al.* 1986; Townsend *et al.* 1986a; Wilkinson 1986; Whitehead 1987; Abbott and Sapsford 1994). Goldblatt (1990), for example, has shown using a longitudinal study that between 1976 and 1981 female and male owner-occupiers with access to a car had a standardized mortality ratio (SMR) of 78, compared with ratios of 138 and 129 for females and males, respectively, living in local authority

---

Box 3.3   Deprivation and ill health: Small-area studies

Study	*Findings*
Carstairs (1981): 37 municipal wards in Glasgow and 23 in Edinburgh	Clear evidence of higher mortality and morbidity rates in areas of greater deprivation (except for perinatal and infant deaths)
Fox *et al.* (1984): 36 clusters of wards	Pattern of low mortality in high-status clusters and high mortality in low-status clusters. Longitudinal study
Thunhurst (1985): 29 wards in Sheffield	Clear **correlation** between 'areas of poverty' and mortality. For men, life expectancy was more than 8 years longer in the more affluent wards
Townsend *et al.* (1985): 29 wards in Bristol	Poor health significantly correlated with **deprivation**
Townsend *et al.* (1987): 755 wards in London	Mortality rate of the most deprived wards nearly double that of the least deprived wards
Townsend *et al.* (1988): 678 wards in Northern Region	Correspondence between ill health and deprivation extremely close. The strongest association was with lack of car (proxy for low income)
Abbott (ed.) (1988): 85 wards in Plymouth Health District; Abbott and Sapsford (1994): 20 wards in Plymouth City	Significant correlation of deprivation indicators with health indicators; much more marked for urban than rural areas. The 1994 study is a replication in the Plymouth City area using more recent census data

accommodation with no access to a car. Small-area studies have consistently found an association between ill health and deprivation (Box 3.3), Townsend *et al.* (1988) arguing that deprivation measures are more highly **correlated** with health status than is social class (that is, with occupational categorizations such as the **Registrar General**'s – see Chapter 4).

Class is also problematic when used as a proxy indicator of household deprivation. The occupation of the head of household may not reflect the material circumstances of the household if there are other wage-earning members. Conversely, those households in which there is no economically active member are excluded from analysis; this means, for example, that households headed by **lone parents** who are not in employment are excluded from analyses of inequalities in child health, a group larger in numbers than either Class I or Class V. Studies that rely on social class, therefore, seriously underestimate inequalities in child health. Another problem emerges when social class is used in research into health inequalities among Britain's Afro-Caribbean and southern Asian populations. The occupational class of southern Asians in Britain, for example, often overestimates their socio-economic circumstances (Smaje 1995). For example, small shopkeepers are in the Registrar General's Class III, but their income may be much lower than the average for this class. A final difficulty with using social class is with respect to older people. While social class as measured by the occupation of the head of household prior to retirement is a good indicator of health inequalities for the younger elderly, it is less so for older people. This may be because the economic circumstances of old age have an increasing impact, or because the relative importance of material factors in explaining differences in health experience declines with age.

Unemployment and health inequalities

Looking at unemployment, Moser *el al.* (1986) found that even after socio-economic position is taken into account, there remains more ill health among the unemployed than would be expected, and this is not due to health selection. Morris *et al.* (1994) found significantly higher death rates among men whose unemployment was not obviously related to ill health, compared with men in employment (an odds ratio of 1:47). The stress associated with unemployment could be implicated in higher suicide rates among the unemployed, and mortality among women married to unemployed men is higher than among other married women. Wilkinson (1986) found that there was a statistically significant correlation between health status and changes of income, suggesting that small changes in the living standards of families in occupational Class V literally mean life or death to the babies born to them. Higher levels of mortality are associated with living in rented accommodation and with not having access to a car (see Table 3.3), both of these tending to be highly correlated with income. Homelessness is also associated with poor health (Stern *et al.* 1989), as is living in bed and breakfast accommodation (BMA 1987). Both the homeless and those in temporary accommodation have difficulty in gaining access to health care (Graham 1993a; Bines 1994).

Table 3.3 Mortality by housing tenure and access to a car in England and Wales, 1971–81.[a]

	Males	Females
Housing tenure		
Owner-occupier	84	83
Privately rented	109	106
Local authority	115	117
Access to a car		
Yes	85	83
No	121	135

[a] Standardized mortality ratios for deaths between the ages of 15 and 64 years.
Source: Goldblatt (1989).

Table 3.4 Mortality of men and married women.[a]

Social class	Men aged 20–64 years	Married women aged 20–59 years
I	3.75	1.45
II	4.25	1.81
IIIN	5.29	2.04
IIIM	5.97	2.29
IV	6.51	3.04
V	9.94	3.99
Armed Forces	9.60	1.12
Unoccupied	8.60	0.90

Note: Married women are classified by their husbands' occupations.
[a] Age-standardized annual death rates per 1000.
Source: OPCS (1986: tables GD19 and GD27).

Women and health inequalities

Differences in health between males and females are usually so obvious that they are taken for granted, and as such they are easily overlooked. Male mortality is higher than female mortality from before birth, although the difference has narrowed over the last 50 years (see Table 3.4). While more men die from heart disease, cancer is the major cause of death among women. Women live longer than men but have a higher self-reported rate of **morbidity** (ill health). When marital status is taken into account, married men have lower death and morbidity rates than men who have never been married or are widowed or divorced, but the reverse is true for women. Women have more physical illness and disability across the lifespan than men (Blaxter 1990), poorer psychosocial health, see GPs more often and are more frequently prescribed psychotropic drugs for anxiety or depression (Ashton 1991; Doyal 1995). We can sum up gender differences by suggesting that 'women get the quantity of life, men get the quality'.

Although, as we have already indicated, social class is not necessarily the best measure, and we should note that women do not always have equal access with men to household income (see Chapter 4), there are clear class differences in women's experience of health (see Table 3.4). Women who are married to men at the bottom of the class hierarchy report more physical symptoms and illness than women married to men in higher social classes (Blaxter 1990; OPCS 1991). Women married to men employed in semi- and unskilled manual work (Registrar General's Classes IV and V) are more likely to consult their GPs about health problems than women married to men in professional or managerial occupations (Classes I and II) (OPCS 1991). Black women are more likely to live in working-class households and be employed in lower-paid sectors of the economy and to experience racism as well as economic hardship, all of which have an adverse effect on their health.

Motherhood also has an adverse impact on women's health. Mothers are more likely than fathers to report recent ill health and less likely to rate their health as good (Popay and Jones 1990). Women who are married or cohabiting and owner/occupiers are less likely than tenants to have a long-standing illness and more likely to rate their health as having been good over the previous 12 months. Married/cohabiting women who are tenants and on benefit are more likely to report a long-standing illness and less likely to report their health as having been good in the previous year; lone-parent mothers' health status, controlling for housing tenure, is on the whole poorer than that of married/cohabiting women (Table 3.5).

One lone-parent mother explained her situation to Hilary Graham:

I've never had a health visitor since the baby's been born. I can't get registered with a doctor. I've lived here a year without one, and with a baby. He's been in hospital twice. He caught a virus from the hotel which was growing in his bowel. He lost over six pounds in a week. Then he had a blocked intestine so he was in hospital for nearly two weeks that time . . . I feel so old, I mean I don't class myself as being young. I'm 34, but I don't know – I feel so old now, so very, very old.

(Graham 1993a: 175)

Table 3.5 Mothers' health by housing tenure.

	Home owner	Tenant	
		Not on benefit	On benefit
Percentage reporting a long-standing illness			
Married/cohabiting women	22	28	34
Lone-parent mothers	25	32	39
Percentage reporting good health in previous year			
Married/cohabiting women	71	58	52
Lone-parent mothers	66	52	43

Source: Popay and Jones (1990: 517).

Sara Arber (1990) concludes from her analysis of the General Household Survey that women's own employment status and marital roles interact with their structural position to influence their health status. Married women in paid employment tend to be healthier than those who are not, and there is some evidence that paid employment 'protects' women from depression.

Age and health inequalities

Age is another variable which is frequently ignored as a factor in its own right. Age, like gender, carries with it a baggage of social meanings and expectations. There are difficulties in interpreting data of this kind, since we have very little information on which to differentiate between the physiological aspects of ageing and the social implications of 'passing age landmarks' – childhood, youth, years of fertility, middle age, old age. Mortality rates are high for the first 4 years of life and decrease thereafter; except for males, who have high mortality rates in the age range 15–24 years, accidents and violence being the predominant causes of death. There is also variation in self-reported illness with age. It is particularly high in the age groups 45–64 and 65–74 years, where the incidence of self-report by males is 41 and 58 per cent, respectively (1982 figures); the equivalent figures for females are 42 and 58 per cent. Health inequalities in old age relate to socio-economic circumstances prior to retirement (Goldblatt 1990; Arber and Ginn 1991), although the significance of social class declines with age. Cold and damp accommodation can also affect the health of the elderly, especially when the cost of heating means that they cannot afford, or are frightened that they cannot afford, to heat their accommodation adequately.

Ethnicity and health inequalities

The data available on ethnic groups are problematic. The Black Report found no significant differences in health status between white and non-white groups. Overall, there do not seem to be major differences, except in the area of mental health, but from the information which is available there would appear to be differences in cause of death. There is a high incidence of hypertension and stroke among immigrants from the Caribbean, but high rates of ischaemic heart disease, infections and diabetes among those from Asia. British southern Asian mothers also have a higher perinatal mortality rate than non-Asian mothers. The Black and Asian populations of Britain are disadvantaged in terms of housing, employment, education and other indicators of quality of social existence, when compared with the white population (Skellington and Morris 1992; Philpott 1994), and this has an impact on health. It is also necessary to consider the effect that race and racial discrimination have on health and access to health services (Oppenheim 1990; Benzeval et al. 1992); the pressures

Table 3.6 Regional mortality, 1982–83.[a]

Region	Men aged 20–64 years	Single women aged 20–59 years	Married women aged 20–59 years
Central Clydeside	7.86	1.78	3.23
Strathclyde	7.14	1.66	3.06
North	6.43	1.56	2.50
North-west	6.37	1.69	2.52
Remainder of Scotland	6.13	1.47	2.58
Wales	5.86	1.43	2.34
Yorkshire and Humberside	5.83	1.48	2.32
West Midlands	5.72	1.54	2.26
East Midlands	5.28	1.40	2.14
South-east	4.88	1.29	1.97
South-west	4.82	1.32	1.93
East Anglia	4.37	1.14	1.79

[a] Age-standardized annual death rates per 1000.
Source: Townsend *et al.* (1988).

of living in a racist society may have an adverse effect on health, especially mental health, and racial **discrimination** by service providers may deter people from seeking help, or at least delay them from doing so.

Regional variation in health status

Area of residence has long been associated with mortality and morbidity. In Britain there is a health gradient from north to south, death rates being highest in the north and west and lowest in the south and east (see Table 3.6). There is also an intra-regional gradient, with inner-city areas having higher mortality rates than rural areas (Fearn 1987); people from ethnic minority groups are often concentrated in these inner-city areas. As the Sheffield Health Study highlights, for example, there are also differences between wards in inner cities, the wards with the highest standardized mortality ratios (SMRs) being located in the most deprived areas, with the outlying suburbs (to the east of the city in the case of Sheffield) having the lowest SMRs for preventable deaths (see also Abbott 1988; Townsend *et al.* 1987; Abbott and Sapsford 1994).

Marsh and Channing's (1986) study of deprivation and health in one general practice found three times more mental illness, 60 per cent more hospital admissions and 75 per cent more casualty admissions in the 'deprived neighbourhood' sample than in a matched sample living in 'a more endowed community'. Abbott and Sapsford (1994) have demonstrated for Plymouth in the south-west of England that the association between health status and deprivation found using 1981 census data holds up using 1991 census data. Using the 1981 data, they found a correlation of 0.82 between health status and deprivation for the wards of the City of Plymouth; using 1991 data, the figure rose to 0.87. This suggests that for Plymouth, between 67 and 76 per cent of the variance in health status between wards is explained by **material deprivation**. An analysis of mortality data for the most deprived ward (St Peters) indicated that within the ward, the working class had poorer health than the middle class (Abbott 1988; for further discussion of small-area studies, see Whitehead 1987). The overall picture is depressingly repetitive – however one measures deprivation and health status, the gradient remains.

Explanations for health inequalities

One possible explanation for the persistence of health inequalities is that the NHS is not meeting its original objectives of providing free, high-quality health care for all, irrespective of ability to pay. Interested readers may wish also to refer to Chapters 4 and 6 of *The Health Divide* (Whitehead 1987) for a more detailed discussion. A number of explanations have been put forward for health inequalities, and these are discussed below.

Health services: Equal access for equal need?

The provision of a service which is theoretically 'free at the point of use' does not ensure that it is equally used in practice. For some people the cost of actually getting to the surgery or clinic may be prohibitive, and this may be affected by the availability of a hospital car service or subsidized public transport.

Whitehead (1987) summarizes the arguments raised by the studies reviewed in the report on the debate over whether the services offered by the NHS are equally accessible to all social groups:

> Some of the studies reviewed by the Black Working Group suggested that access to those who needed care was in some cases biased in favour of the non-manual socio-economic groups . . . Aspects of equality mentioned included: equal access to available care, equal treatment for equal cases and equal quality of care.
>
> (Whitehead 1987: 276)

In addition, the ideal of the NHS has been somewhat distorted as the service is no longer 'free'. The increasing cost of prescriptions and optical treatment and the dearth of NHS dental facilities in some areas, for example, may serve to reduce take-up of services among certain groups. There is also the issue of awareness of services, with some groups having more knowledge about available services and being more articulate in their demands.

The 'artefact' explanation

The **artefact explanation** of the apparent differences in health experienced by the lower and higher social classes argues that the method of measuring occupational class used by the Registrar General inflates the size and importance of health differences (Jones and Cameron 1984; Illsley 1986). In particular, it is argued that the changes in occupations assigned to each band of the classification over the years, together with a reduction in the proportion of employees in unskilled manual work and a corresponding increase in middle-class occupations, means that comparisons with early decades of the century are meaningless. However, recent studies that have tried to control for some of the measurement problems involved with occupational class (Goldblatt 1990; Marmot *et al.* 1991) continue to demonstrate the existence of a clear occupational class gradient, and research using indicators of inequality other than occupation has confirmed the pattern of health inequalities between the top and bottom of the social scale (see, for example, Rose and Marmot 1981; Marmot *et al.* 1991).

Theories of natural and social selection

Explanations in terms of health selection acknowledge the existence of health inequalities but attribute them to a process of 'natural selection' or 'the survival of the fittest'. In a way analogous to the theories of Darwin, it is suggested that those who are best fitted to survive are upwardly mobile socially, and those who are not are downwardly mobile. That is, people in poor health tend to move down the social class scale and become concentrated in the lower socio-economic groups, whereas those in good health experience upward mobility; in other words, it is health status that determines social class, not social class that determines health status. The gap between the higher and the lower classes is therefore inevitable, whatever overall improvements occur. For example, a healthy worker, it is argued, is able to perform his or her work more efficiently than an unhealthy worker and is, therefore, more likely to be promoted. It has also been found that taller women are likely to marry into a higher occupational group than short ones (height being a broad indicator of health before marriage; for a discussion of this position, see Knight 1984; Illsley 1986). Other research has indicated that serious illness in childhood affects social mobility, with boys who have experienced serious ill health being more likely than should be expected by chance to be in a lower social class at age 26 than their fathers were (Wadsworth 1986).

However, the effect of the downward social mobility of unhealthy people makes only a small difference in the overall figures. Indeed, other research has clearly indicated that health-related mobility between classes cannot explain the difference in health between them. Fogelman *et al.* (1987), for example, found that differences in health between socio-economic groups of young people who had remained static with respect to their parents were the same as the differences for those who had been upwardly or downwardly mobile between the generations. Whitehead (1987) concludes that there is some evidence for health selection but that it accounts for only a small proportion of the differences between social classes.

Cultural/behavioural explanations

Cultural/**behavioural explanations** stress differences in the ways in which different social groups 'choose' to live their lives – that is, the behaviour and 'voluntary' lifestyles they adopt:

> In this explanation inequalities in health evolve because lower social groups have adopted more dangerous and health-damaging behaviour than higher social groups, and may have less interest in protecting their health in the future.
>
> (Whitehead 1987: 289)

It has been suggested, for example, that lower social groups choose to smoke more, to drink more, to eat less healthy food and to exercise less than those in more advantaged social groups, all issues raised in *The Health of the Nation* report (Department of Health 1992). Edwina Currie, as a junior Health Minister, adopted such an explanation when she was shown research that indicated that 65 per cent of the variation in health in the Northern Health Region could be accounted for by material deprivation:

> I honestly don't think that [health] has anything to do with poverty. The problem very often for many people is just ignorance . . . and failing to realise that they do have some control over their own lives.
>
> (quoted in Townsend 1993: 383)

While this is undeniably true to some extent, it is insufficient to explain fully health inequalities.

Statistics have shown that even when we compare individuals from socio-economic Groups I and II whose smoking, eating, drinking and exercise habits are broadly similar to those of the working-class stereotype, health inequalities by class still persist. Pearson (1986: 16) has suggested, with respect to cultural explanations for ethnic differences in health, that:

> . . . the focus on cultural distinctiveness or cultural difference as an explanatory factor *per se* has led to some misleading and simplistic conclusions and definitions of 'problems'. Over-generalisations abound and the influences of social factors such as occupational class, unemployment and housing conditions are often denied in simplistic analyses which reduce such complex social phenomena to grossly over-generalised, stereotyped racial and ethnic categories.

The same can be said of less 'exotic' cultural explanations in terms of regional customs or working-class lifestyles.

Structural explanations

'Structural' explanations of the causes of health inequality stress the role of social circumstances that are outside the control of individuals. They maintain that the evidence indicates that the majority of health differentials between people defined on the basis of class, gender or ethnic group are avoidable and are intrinsically related to the wider life-chances of these groups.

Structuralist explanations thus emphasize the external environment and the conditions in which people live and work. (Research indicates that lay people are themselves aware of the effect that poor living conditions, low income, unsafe working conditions, pollution and so on have on their health; see, for example, Cornwell 1984; Ong 1993.) They also stress the importance of socio-economic pressures on low-income households to consume unhealthy products (such as cheap food) as important determinants of health status. One illustration of this argument is the increasing use of bed and breakfast accommodation to house homeless families (CSO 1992). Much of this type of accommodation lacks cooking and refrigeration facilities, so that many residents are dependent on 'take-away' food.

The Health Divide (Whitehead 1987) notes the interrelationship between behavioural and structuralist explanations, using as an example the incidence of childhood accidents. Here the behaviour of parents and children is clearly linked to structural issues such as the lack of safe play areas, fenced gardens and the problems of supervision in high-rise areas. Research on a Glasgow housing estate (Hunt et al. 1988) found that damp housing was a major cause of respiratory illness among children. It also showed that parental smoking was considerably less significant in relation to children's respiratory illnesses than poor housing.

In a study by Marmot et al. (1984), which looked at health inequalities within the civil service, it was found that mortality rates of low-grade civil servants were three times those of high-grade civil servants. Similarly, in a study of the British Army, Lynch and Oelman (1981) found that the mortality rates of lowest ranks was six times higher than that among the highest ranks. Marmot argued that evidence of this sort suggests that poverty itself is unable to explain the persistence of health inequalities, for while lower-grade employees or soldiers have less disposable income, they are not 'poor' as such. Marmot looked instead at explanations which highlight the importance of social and psychological stress as significant factors affecting health inequalities between different groups.

Other studies have focused on material deprivation and specifically on housing conditions, employment, poverty and an adverse environment. The explanation put forward by Marmot may be even more relevant when we acknowledge the relationship between these material factors and psychological and social stress. Furthermore, by looking at health inequalities from this perspective, we are able to appreciate the impact that all areas of social policy (including housing and employment, for example) have on health and the interdependence of and relationship between them.

Housing conditions were found by both The Black Report (Townsend and Davidson 1982) and Whitehead (1987) to be a major contributory factor determining health. It was found, for example, that people from areas of poor-quality housing were in poorer health, had more long-standing illness and showed more symptoms of depression than those living in 'good' housing areas. There are a number of reasons for this, including:

• Living in damp and mouldy housing is a major cause of respiratory/ bronchial problems (Hunt et al. 1988).

- Overcrowding can lead to stress within families, resulting in family breakdown and mental illness.
- A lack of decent amenities such as shops and play areas for children and the poor design of inter-connecting walkways between flats have been shown to contribute to ill health and accidents, especially among children (Young 1980).
- Young (1980) also points out the problems associated with poor refuse collection and infestation.

Employment status and unemployment have also been shown to be a cause of physical and mental ill health (see Whitehead 1987). Manual workers such as miners, builders and others whose jobs involve exposure to dust or toxic substances and possible accidents are clearly at more risk of ill health or even death than those in the professional classes. Some studies have also shown that the stress caused by unemployment is an important factor in mental health and may sometimes lead to suicide. Further proof of the impact of unemployment on health is to be found in studies which show that once the unemployed find their way back into work, their overall health improves markedly. A longitudinal study by Fox and Goldblatt (1982), for example, showed how mortality among the unemployed was raised by 20–30 per cent, with particular increases in suicide rates, cancers and heart disease. This study also showed how the effects of unemployment were similarly felt by the spouse and family of the unemployed person.

Income is another factor affecting health inequalities. It affects, among other things, the quality and quantity of food which people can afford. It is commonly found in studies of poorer families that when money is short, spending on food tends to be restricted (Graham 1984). Furthermore, given that the cheaper foods tend to be high in sugar and fat content, this leads to less healthy diets being adopted. Income also affects the type of housing a family can afford and the amount and type of heating available.

Health and healthy policies

Although The Black Report found that some improvements could be made within the NHS to ensure that health services are more equally distributed, it concluded that if we are to reduce health inequalities substantially in the UK, the main focus of government action should be to reduce inequalities in *other* areas of social life:

> While the health care service can play a significant part in reducing inequalities in health, measures to reduce differences in material standards of living at work, in the home and in everyday social and **community** life are of even greater importance.
>
> (Townsend and Davidson 1982: 304)

The Report maintained that, as a matter of the greatest importance, the government should make the abolition of child poverty its primary goal in order to improve the nation's health. Improvements in housing and working conditions were also recommended, as was a proper mechanism for coordinating health policy at a national and local level. Whitehead (1987) expressed concern that, some 8 years later, none of these recommendations had been implemented:

> In reality what has happened over the past eight years is a disturbing increase in the number of children growing up in poverty, and an increase in families becoming homeless. Policies deliberately designed to reduce child poverty have not been adopted, and the situation has been exacerbated by a sharp rise in the level of unemployment, which has affected families with young children in particular. A concerted effort to improve housing conditions has not been made and there is now growing concern over the shortage of houses and the poor state of repair of existing dwellings ... Mechanisms for coordinating policies on health in local and national government have not been set up ... although it is widely acknowledged that health promotion policies need to involve many agencies outside the health sector, such as housing, environmental control, transport, food and agriculture and – above all – the Treasury.
>
> (Whitehead 1987: 356)

The goal of the NHS is to provide health care to those in need of it. That is to say, having become ill, the NHS is there to cure us and look after us. However, the studies mentioned above have shown that in order to promote good health, it would be better to prevent us becoming ill in the first place. In order to develop this preventive role we need to consider other areas of government policy, such as housing, employment, social security payments and also education. As Webster (1993: 196) had argued:

> ... medicine alone is incapable of controlling disease and disability, a great part of which is attributable to poverty and exploitation. Low family income, unemployment and adverse working conditions have always been passports to malnutrition and disease associated with bad housing conditions and unhealthy occupations. Of course, entirely different diseases stem from affluence, but the burden is nothing like that carried by the poor. Indeed, the poor in all parts of the world are also 'afflicted' by impediments to health connected with affluent life-styles.

Healthy policies: The way forward

As we have seen above, the NHS is predominantly concerned with caring for the sick, and medicine is primarily concerned with curing the sick. However, Sigerist (1943: 24) suggested that 'the task of medicine is to promote health, to prevent disease, to treat the sick when prevention is broken down and to rehabilitate the people after they have been cured'.

Despite increased spending on health care in Britain after the Second World War – during the 1960s and early 1970s, for example, health care expenditure rose by 60 per cent – the improvement in health has not been dramatic. Between 1946 and 1970, for example, life expectancy in Britain for a newborn male rose by only 2.4 years, for males aged 25 by 0.8 years and for males aged 65 by 0.4 years. Blaxter (1990) reported that 29 per cent of her respondents reported themselves to be in less than good health. The General Household Survey (CSO 1992) reported that half the population do not indulge in any active sports, games or physical activity, and the Health Education Council (1992) has indicated that a third of the population fail to reach basic fitness levels. About 90 per cent of the adult population have at least one risk factor for heart disease and strokes (Department of Health/OPCS 1993). According to the General Household Survey for 1990 (OPCS 1994), a third of the population has a long-term illness and a fifth have a long-standing illness that limits their activities. Nearly a quarter of the population are sick at any one time, and a similar proportion of the adult population have at least one disability (OPCS 1988). Criticisms of the emphasis on health care have grown, and the focus has shifted to some extent towards prevention.

It has also become increasingly recognized that the major killer diseases of the late twentieth century – cardiovascular diseases, cancer, accidents and alcohol related conditions – are preventable. As we saw in Chapter 2, the same was true in the nineteenth century with the major killer diseases of the time – typhoid, smallpox and so on. A major concern of the nineteenth century was sanitary reform, with doctors prominent in the reform movement. It was recognized that reducing morbidity and mortality rates would be achieved best by environmental improvements necessitating state intervention:

> The completion of the Water Works would be a great blessing to the town – From the villas on the London Road, to the extremities of 'The Worth' and Belgran-Gate, fever and diarrhoea have spread their desolating blight. From these and other causes vast numbers of the poor are always in a low state of health. This is no doubt why they are perpetually seeking after the nostrums of quackery.
> (Rev Joseph, Dean of Leicester, quoted in Haynes 1991: 43–4)

Similarly, McKeown (1976) has argued that the main reasons for the decline in infant mortality rates in the twentieth century and the improvements in our health generally are to be found in the improved social, economic and environmental conditions in which we all now live. Although he recognizes that medical advances have been of some importance, he suggests that these have been of only marginal importance compared with improvements in our housing and working conditions, diets and general improvements in water supply and sanitation.

However, by the end of the nineteenth century, due to the influence of Social Darwinism, there was a shift in emphasis away from community interventions towards seeing individual behaviour as the major factor. Newman (1906: 257, 262), for example, suggested that:

> ... the problem of infant mortality is not one of sanitation alone or housing or indeed of **poverty** as such, but is mainly a question of motherhood ... death in infancy is probably more due to ignorance and negligence than to almost any other cause ... three measures are

needed to be carried out (a) instruction of mothers, (b) the appoint-
ment of lay health visitors, and (c) the education of girls in domestic
hygiene.

There has subsequently tended to be a bias towards blaming the victim,
to see poor health as the result of individual failings, whether by biological constitution or unhealthy lifestyles or by not using the services provided. There has been a focus on what individuals should do to promote
their own health. Women, as in the passage from Newman quoted above,
are especially seen as negligent not only on their own behalf but on
behalf of their husbands, children and other dependants for whom they
are seen to be responsible. People from ethnic minority groups are often
blamed because of their 'special diets', 'strange religions', 'funny habits' or
'inability to speak English'. There has consequently been a relative neglect, in public policy, of the social causes of ill health – unemployment,
poverty, environmental pollution and so on. Service providers have failed
to recognize that their services may not meet the needs of many potential
users, or indeed to recognize that the ways in which services are provided
are seen as patronizing and out of step with people's lived experiences.

Hilary Graham (1984), for example, has pointed to the difficulties of
mothers with young children getting to medical centres and hospitals.
Others have pointed to the impossibility of providing a 'healthy diet' on
low income and to the priority that mothers have to give to providing
food that will be eaten (see, for example, Blackburn 1991): poor mothers
cannot afford to experiment with food! Thus while research indicates that
knowledge about what amounts to a healthy diet is available even among
low-income groups (HEA 1989; Jones 1992), low-income groups cannot
afford a healthy diet (Blaxter 1990). At income support level it is necessary to spend 50 per cent of income on food to obtain the nutritional
standard recommended by the government's own advisory body (NACNE
1983). Furthermore, 'healthy' food (e.g. low-fat milk, brown bread and
low-fat spreads) are often not available in poorer districts (Ashton and
Seymour 1988; Jones 1992). Wilson (1989: 13) has maintained that in
poor households, 'it is more important to avoid waste than to try and
convert an over-stressed family to food it does not know. Health education has to be seen as an investment for better times. Its immediate effect
can only be increasing worry rather than leading to action.'

Jocelyn Cornwell (1984) has indicated that many working-class people
are well aware of the ways in which their work and the environment
in which they live 'cause' their ill health. Health education that targets
individuals and suggests that their chosen lifestyles are responsible for
their ill health will not, in such circumstances, have much impact. It is
notable, for example, that health education aimed at encouraging people
to stop cigarette smoking has been most successful among the middle-
classes and least successful at discouraging working-class women.

The Health of the Nation

The renewed interest in the environmental and lifestyle causes of ill health
has resulted in the development of what has been referred to as the 'New

Public Health', a recognition of its roots in the nineteenth-century Public Health Movement. The World Health Organization (WHO) has been especially active in promoting preventive action for health, with its declared target of 'Health for All by the Year 2000'. Especially influential in this development has been the LaLonde Report (1974), published by the Canadian Government, which argued that there are four elements to health: healthy biology, environment, lifestyle and health care organization. The 'New Public Health Movement' has taken a more structural approach to health promotion, recognizing the role that factors over which individuals have little control – income, housing, environment and public policies – play in ensuring health and in constraining the decisions individuals can make. This has meant accepting a need for state intervention, including legislation and fiscal policy.

However, the British Government has continued to emphasize individual responsibility and individual change, rather than acknowledging the need for more structural action. In 1976, a booklet issued by the government, *Prevention and Health: Everybody's Business* (DHSS 1976), emphasized the role of lifestyle and the responsibility of individuals for making their own lifestyle choices. More recently, *The Health of the Nation* (Department of Health 1992) re-emphasized the need for changing lifestyles and behaviours and for maximizing the efficiency of the NHS in improving health rather than working on other facets. There was, for example, no reference in the document to the WHO strategy which emphasizes the role that all government departments should play in developing health policies. Despite the emphasis on prevention in the White Paper, the government has been unable to accept the centrality of poverty and **social deprivation** as causes of ill health.

The 'Health of the Nation' strategy acknowledges that advances in medicine alone make only a small contribution to the nation's health, albeit a critical one, particularly in the area of preventive medicine and health promotion. The strategy defines an approach which envisages a balance between the government (including the NHS) and other organizations within wider society:

> ... although there is much that government and the NHS needs to do, the objectives and targets cannot be delivered by government and the NHS alone. They are truly for the nation – for all of us – to achieve. We must be clear about where responsibilities lie. We must get the balance right between what the government, and government alone, can do, what other organisations and agencies need to do, and finally, what individuals and families themselves must contribute if the strategy is to succeed.
>
> (Department of Health 1992: 3)

Thus despite increased spending on health promotion from £1.6 million in 1981 to £11.4 million in 1988, the emphasis continues to be on changing individual lives. Three main forms of health promotion have been developed: high-profile campaigns aimed at specific problems (e.g. drugs, AIDS), health screening, and GP health promotions such as childhood immunization. There is evidence that the benefits from these forms of health promotion are modest compared with their costs. Furthermore,

	Individualistic	Collectivist
Paternalist/ expert-directed/ prescriptive	Health persuasion techniques	Legislative action for health
	Corrective	Protects against environmental and economic risks
	Defective individual	
Participatory/ client-controlled	Personal counselling for health	Community development for health
	Empowering	Mobilizing embattled groups
	Concerned individual	

Figure 3.1 Strategies for health promotion.

little has been done to redress the balance between prevention and treatment. In the mid-1980s, for example, about £10 million per year was spent on programmes aimed at preventing coronary heart disease, compared with £500 million spent on treatment services. The continuing emphasis on lifestyle has meant ignoring the complex relationship that exists between lifestyle, environment and social constraints – and indeed the effects food policy, employment policy, fiscal policies and housing policy have on health and the ability of people to adopt healthy lifestyles. Blaxter (1990: 216) concludes that, 'if circumstances are good, "healthy" behaviour appears to have a strong influence on health. If they are bad, then behaviours make rather little difference'.

The New Public Health

There are alternative health promotion strategies, including those deriving from the WHO's 'Health for All by the Year 2000' campaign, that do take account of the structural constraints on people's lives. Beattie (1984, 1991) has suggested four strategies for health promotion (see Fig. 3.1). The strategies deriving from the WHO initiative tend to be collectivist rather than individualistic. The WHO European Region (1984) has suggested four basic prerequisites for health:

1 Peace and freedom from fear of war.
2 Equal opportunities for all.
3 The ability to satisfy basic needs, i.e. adequate food and income, a basic education, safe water and sanitation, decent housing, secure work and a satisfying role in life.
4 The will for change at an official level.

The WHO (1985) has also indicated that in health care the principle of equal justice 'means equal access to available care, equal treatment for equal cases and equal quality of care', and in health terms it means that 'ideally everyone should have the *same opportunity* to attain the highest level of health, and, more pragmatically, no-one should be unduly disadvantaged'.

The WHO initiative, especially as expressed in the **Healthy Cities Project** (see, for example, Ashton and Seymour 1988; Ashton 1991), has stressed health promotion and the prevention of disease by recognizing structural constraints. It has also stressed the need for cooperation between different government departments and the need for community participation – enjoining communities to take control of their own health as well as recognizing the need to provide adequate primary health care services to meet the needs of the community. While the British Government has not been an enthusiastic supporter of the initiative, a number of cities in Britain have become 'healthy cities' and adopted the WHO targets (see Box 3.4).

Box 3.4 Healthy cities

Healthy cities aim to provide all citizens with:

- a clean, safe environment;
- a way of life that is protective of the natural environment and material resources;
- community support;
- the opportunity for individuals to influence the decisions that affect their lives;
- provision to meet their basic needs (e.g. adequate food, water, health, shelter, safety and self-respect);
- adequate recreational and other facilities;
- work opportunities for all who need them;
- optimum levels of health care;
- provision for good physical and mental health and a low level of disease in the population.

Because the Healthy Cities Project is concerned to establish local strategies for improving health that go beyond educating individuals and address social issues such as poor housing, industrial pollution, traffic congestion and inadequate leisure facilities, which at the structural level mean interaction and cooperation between different agencies, there have been moves to facilitate such cooperation. Normally several of these elements occur at the same time and as part of the same project. For example, Liverpool, one of the poorest cities in Western Europe, has acknowledged the health inequalities which exist within its boundaries and has achieved a partnership between key city agencies, all committed to the Healthy Cities initiative. The objective is to achieve a measurable improvement in Liverpool's health by the year 2000, particularly in the city's poorer districts.

Liverpool has a City Health Plan comprising six target blocks: health, lifestyles, the environment, appropriate care, research, development. The biggest project is the Croxteth Health Action Area, based on two poor council estates. In the early 1980s, research indicated that poor housing was the biggest cause of ill health; subsequent improvements in housing have improved residents' health. The project also aims to involve residents actively in other aspects of improving their physical and social environment.

Range (1994) has suggested that the process of implementing 'Health for All' in Healthy City projects is probably as important in itself as the achievement of specific goals or targets. It is the recognition of the underlying causes of ill health and the constraints that preclude people adopting healthy lifestyles, in addition to the strategies that can make change possible, that is important. Jones (1994) has suggested that directors of public health – appointed by health authorities since 1990, following the recommendations of the Acheson Report (1988) – may influence the development of healthy policies. They are required to produce an annual report of the health of the population, and these, Jones suggests, will become the focus for local debate. Under the National Health Service and Community Care Act 1991, health authorities have become purchasers of care rather than providers. They now have the opportunity to purchase services that promote health, including the ability to loan safety equipment to mothers on low income or provide smoke detectors to members of vulnerable groups. While these are admittedly valuable services, they still have a paternalistic rather than an enabling focus, especially if provided by health visitors or other standard service providers.

Black critics of the welfare state have repeatedly drawn a sharp and clear distinction between paternalistic, victim-blaming strategies and enabling strategies that take full cognizance of structural inequalities. Thus 'the "ethnic sensitivity" approach tends to focus on the supposed "problems" of ethnic minority groups' (Parmar 1981: 291), while 'anti-racist perspectives focus on transforming the unequal social relations shaping interaction between black and white people into egalitarian ones' (Dominelli 1983: 3). The difference in these two approaches is clearly indicated by comparing the Asian Mother and Baby Campaign, funded by the DHSS and the Save the Children Fund between 1984 and 1987 (Mason 1990), with the Multi-Ethnic Women's Health Project started in 1980 at the Mothers' Hospital in Hackney (Parsons and Day 1992). The former was a health education project aimed at educating Asian women about the importance of the maternity services and providing them with interpreters. Its starting point was that Asian women did not understand the importance of maternity care and that they had insufficient command of English. Evaluation of the campaign suggests that it provided a valuable translation service for Asian women but was less successful in delivering health education (Mason 1990). The Multi-Ethnic Women's Health Project provided workers who acted not only as translators for Asian women using maternity services, but also as independent advocates (i.e. they were not employed by the NHS). Its starting point was that health workers did not speak Asian languages nor understand the health needs of Asian women. Evaluation suggests that it has been a successful and popular initiative (Parsons and Day 1992).

Conclusions

In this chapter, we have considered the basic principle of equity on which the NHS was founded and considered the extent to which this has been achieved. We have indicated that inequalities in access to health care and in health status have persisted, with more advantaged groups having better access to services and a better health status than materially disadvantaged groups. Further improvements in health, we have argued, are more likely to come from improvements in the general standard of living and from health promotion that recognises the structural constraints on individual choices than from health care *per se*.

Summary

- Those who see an important role for social policy in the promotion of social equality tend to favour the principle of universalism (in order to reduce the deterrent effect of stigma). Taking the example of the development of the NHS, this chapter evaluates the extent to which universal services provided on the basis of citizenship and medical need have, in practice, promoted greater social equality.

- Despite the institution of health services based on principles of universal entitlement, the pooling of financial risk and equality of access and quality of care, considerable evidence exists of the persistence of health inequalities in Britain – and in some cases increased levels of polarization both between social groups and regions.

- A variety of theories have developed to explain the persistence of health inequalities. Cultural/behavioural explanations have emphasized the role of individual responsibility; the NHS can only encourage healthy lifestyles and treat illnesses, it cannot force people to adopt them, i.e. to stop smoking or consume more healthy diets.

- Social reformists have attributed health inequalities to the institutional malfunctioning of the NHS itself and its failure to ensure equality of access, equality of care and territorial justice and to its focus on treatment as opposed to prevention.

- Other theories have suggested that inequalities in health status are a function of broader structural problems which cannot be remedied by changes in healthcare alone. Townsend's work demonstrated the impact of multiple deprivation on health status, in particular the impact of poor housing and unemployment. Employment status is also related to health status with a close association between certain occupations and industrial disease or stress. Furthermore, low income itself restricts a household's ability to adopt healthy lifestyles.

Further reading

Benzeval, M., Judge, K. and Whitehead, M. (eds) (1995) *Tackling Inequalities in Health*. London: King's Fund.

Blackburn, C. (1991) *Poverty and Health: Working With Families*. Buckingham: Open University Press.

Blaxter, M. (1990) *Health and Lifestyle*. London: Routledge.

Davies, J. and Kelly, M. (eds) (1992) *Healthy Cities: Research and Practice*. London: Routledge.

Department of Health (1992) *The Health of the Nation: A Strategy for Health in England*. Cm 1986. London: HMSO.

Smith, R. (1987) *Unemployment and Health: A Disaster and a Challenge*. Oxford: Oxford University Press.

Townsend, P., Whitehead, M. and Davidson, N. (eds) (1992) *Inequalities in Health: The Black Report and the Health Divide* (new edition). Harmondsworth: Penguin.

POVERTY, INEQUALITY AND SOCIAL POLICY

Introduction

We noted in Chapter 1 how attitudes about the role of the state in social policy reflect perspectives on the causes of social problems. When social problems are interpreted as a reflection of individual failure, for example, responsibility for those problems may be seen to rest with the individuals themselves. On the other hand, when social problems exist as a result of state action or the state's failure to act in certain circumstances (perhaps because of some inadequacy in its training programmes, or the lack of child care), then the state itself may be held responsible. We also saw how different explanations of the causes of social problems reflect ideologically motivated perspectives on the extent and nature of any state intervention. Those who see problems such as poverty as primarily the fault of individuals typically support the idea of a residual welfare state providing a safety net of selective welfare benefits, sufficient to avoid the social malaise associated with abject poverty, but not at such a level as to undermine the work ethic and personal freedom. On the other hand, those who see poverty in relative terms, as a reflection of broader inequalities in life chances between social groups, tend to support the notion of redistributive, universal welfare provision, which exists to promote social justice and consensus.

This chapter examines the nature and extent of poverty and social inequality. It begins by considering competing definitions of poverty and some of the problems of measurement before going on to examine the incidence of poverty and explanations for its persistence in contemporary British society. It is important to remember, as Hills (1993) has reminded us, that the original purpose of the welfare state was to prevent rather than to relieve poverty, by a system of social insurance.

Clearly, income inequality is only one aspect of social inequality, although it is arguably the most important consideration in terms of individual freedom, as equalization of income provides individuals with the widest range of choices within the mixed economy of welfare. We argued in Chapter 3 that deprivation and **material inequality** underpin health inequalities and that future improvements in health are more likely to come from improvements in the material circumstances of the worst-off people than from other measures. This raises a number of issues that we shall consider in this chapter: What is poverty? Which groups are poor? Is poverty a major problem in Britain? What social policies are there for countering poverty? And how successful are they?

One of the five 'giants' that Beveridge argued that the welfare state would (should) eliminate was want (poverty). There is considerable debate as to whether poverty persists as a social problem in Britain. The Conservative government, which has been in power since 1979, has consistently denied that poverty is a social problem in contemporary Britain; to the extent that some people still live in need, it is because they choose not to spend their income appropriately. Margaret Thatcher, for example, said in the House of Commons in 1983, that 'The fact remains that people who are living in need are fully and properly provided for' (quoted in Mack and Lansley 1985). In contrast, Peter Townsend (1993: 18) has argued that in Britain, 'Ill health, disability and premature death are . . . outcomes of inadequate resources underlying material and social deprivation. Poverty kills'. Indeed, Townsend, along with other commentators (e.g. Johnson 1990; Walker 1995), argues that not only have inequalities increased in the last 15 years, but the proportion of the population in poverty has also increased. Johnson (1990: 65) argues that this is a direct result of government policy:

The social security changes are . . . consistent with . . . promoting inequality. Benefits have been widened, there is greater reliance on means tests and more people find themselves in the **poverty trap**. The element of discretion is now much greater and rights have been eroded. The combined effect of unequal tax cuts, benefit reductions and punitive attitudes towards the poor has led to deeper divisions and wider disparities.

Townsend (1993: 17) goes further by indicating the ways in which poverty results in further deprivations:

> In the United Kingdom the polarisation of incomes has taken a variety of forms: people sleeping rough and beggars on the street; repossessions of homes; imprisonment of large numbers for debt; electricity disconnections; the reappearance of sweat shops and casual labour, including instances of illegal child labour; a rise in the number of accidents and deaths at work; the loss of employment rights and of different forms of work 'security'; the deterioration of public housing and inner city areas; a sharp increase in theft and crimes of violence; the growth of forms of multiple deprivation; the destruction of public administration and services and the deepening as well as the growth of mass poverty.

Indeed, inequalities widened more in the UK between 1980 and 1985 than in any other member state of the European Community (Eurostat 1990). The proportion of the population on or below-average incomes, at 60 per cent, has remained almost constant since 1961, but the proportions below 60 per cent of average incomes, below 50 per cent and below 40 per cent have increased since 1981 and at a faster rate since 1986 (CSO 1995: table 5.21). For example, in 1986, just over 20 per cent of people were on incomes below 60 per cent of the average; by 1992, this had increased to just over 30 per cent. Hills (1993) indicates that by the 1990s the gap between the highest and lowest paid was greater in Britain than at any time since 1886 (see Table 4.1; see also CSO 1995: table 5.19). From 1979 to 1989, the incomes of the richest tenth of the population rose by over 60 per cent, while the real incomes of the poorest tenth fell by 14 per cent (House of Commons 1993). Not only are the incomes of people at the top rising faster than those of people at the bottom, but tax reforms have differentially benefited the better-off. As a consequence of reforms in the 1980s, the top 10 per cent pay 32 per cent of their income in tax, while the bottom 10 per cent pay 43 per cent (Oppenheim 1990; see also Abbott and Wallace 1992; Davies *et al.* 1992). The increasing inequalities

Table 4.1 Real weekly income[a] of the lowest decile, as a percentage of the highest decile's income.

	1971	1981	1993
Single men, no children	42.7	41.3	34.2
Single women, no children	45.7	43.7	39.2
Single women, 2 children	44.6	54.5	44.5 (53.6)[b]
Married men, no children	44.6	43.23	35.3
Married men, 2 children	48.5	46.9	37.9 (40.0)[b]

[a] After income tax and national insurance, and including child benefit.
[b] Figures in brackets include family credit.
Source: CSO (1995: table 5.12).

have had a particular impact on children: in 1987, 10 per cent of children lived in households whose income (after housing costs) was less than half the average; by 1991, this had risen by 321 per cent (DSS 1992).

What is poverty? Issues of definition

The key issues in dispute here are (1) the definition of poverty and (2) the causes of poverty. Those who take the view that poverty is a minor problem in contemporary Britain argue that only those who are unable to provide for much more than the basic needs of food, clothing and shelter are poor (*subsistence* poverty). Those who argue that poverty persists as a significant social problem take a *relative* view – poverty is defined relative to the living standard of the population of the country under discussion – and they generally see poverty as the result of structural factors outside the control of the poor (**structural dependency**). In contrast, those who take the former view tend to see poverty as the outcome of individual failures: inappropriate behaviour patterns or the inappropriate spending of available income. The government policies of the last 15 years, they argue, have been designed to provide incentives – incentives to those at the bottom to work hard and take available jobs, and incentives to those at the top to be innovative and create jobs. This has been done on the one hand by reducing direct taxation, especially for high-income earners, and on the other by making employment more attractive than living on benefits. The latter has been achieved by reducing the real value of benefits, increasing the policing of the unemployed, introducing measures designed to help the unemployed back to work, and reform of social security to reduce the poverty trap.

However, critics of the government have indicated that not only have these policies not always had the desired outcome, but other government policies (e.g. economic and housing polices) have actually worked against the realization of these policies:

New barriers to seeking financial independence through work have been erected as a result of policy changes and developments in the labour market. Of central importance has been the 36 per cent fall in manufacturing jobs since 1979 and their only partial replacement by less skilled lower paid jobs in the service sector. The proportion of men in low-paid jobs increased by 15 per cent between 1984 and 1991. Ironically, attempts to lessen the effects of the unemployment and poverty traps by basing means tests on net rather than gross incomes and by introducing Family Credit more generously than its predecessor have made these traps wider if less deep. More people, well over four million, are caught in these traps. Also, those families affected have to earn more in order to break free of the penalising concentration of tax, national insurance and benefit withdrawal. The traps have been further exacerbated by the growth in owner occupation among lower-income families who are now affected by unemployment. Escalating social rents resulting from the policy of shifting housing subsidies away from bricks and mortar towards low-income tenants add further to the problem. (Walker 1995: 2)

As we have indicated above, there are debates as to what poverty is and how it can be defined. There is general agreement that those who do not have access to the resources to provide themselves and their families with basic needs such as shelter and food are living in poverty. Nor is there disagreement that inequalities exist in modern Britain. The debates are more concerned with what the basic needs are that must be met and what constitutes an adequate level. Nor is there much debate that needs and the ways that they can adequately be met are historically and cross-culturally variable. What would have been considered an adequate diet in Victorian England would not be thought adequate today. Indeed, changes in the law, for example regarding the parts of animals that can be sold for human consumption and food adulteration, would make it impossible to purchase the same foods as a working-class Victorian housewife could have done. Similarly, what is considered adequate housing in Britain, with planning and building regulations, is very different from what is considered adequate in some countries, where it is possible to construct a house out of freely available materials on land occupied as a squatter. Consequently, the debate is not simply between those who argue that there is only **subsistence poverty** and those who argue for the concept of **relative poverty**; it is a more complex debate, about what needs should be met and at what level. Those who argue that there is 'no such thing as poverty in contemporary Britain' are saying that everyone has access to sufficient resources to meet minimum needs at a basic level. Those who argue that there *is* a significant problem of poverty are arguing that some people do not have access to sufficient resources to meet socially agreed needs at a socially acceptable level. We can think of the debate as positions on two continua. One is a continuum of needs, with at one end a small number of essential needs and at the other a much broader range of socially agreed needs. The second continuum is one from provision at a minimum level (e.g. a diet that provides basic nutritional requirements) to one of provision at a socially acceptable level (e.g. the diet enjoyed by the majority of the population).

It is possible to identify four points along the continua to assist us in understanding the main definitions of poverty.

1 *Absolute poverty*. This is where individuals are unable to meet their basic needs at a minimum level. At the extreme are those who are starving and without shelter. Once we move away from this extreme, the question becomes what counts as an adequate diet and adequate shelter.

2 *Subsistence poverty*. This is where individuals are unable to provide for themselves and their families a minimum number of agreed basic requirements at a minimum level. For example, Rowntree, in carrying out a survey in York at the turn of the century, used a minimum standard that enabled him to determine the proportion of the population living at or below the absolute minimum level. He indicated that:

> A family living upon the scale allowed for in this estimate must never spend a penny on railway fares or omnibuses. They must never go into the countryside unless they walk. They must never purchase a halfpenny newspaper or spend a penny to buy a ticket

for a popular concert. They must write no letters to absent children, for they cannot afford to pay postage. They must never contribute anything to their church or chapel or give any help to a neighbour which costs them money. They cannot save, nor can they join a sick Club or Trade Union because they cannot pay the money subscription. The children must have no pocket money for dolls, marbles or sweets. The father must smoke no tobacco and must drink no beer. The mother must never buy any pretty clothes for herself or her children, the character of the family wardrobe as for the family diet being governed by the regulation 'nothing must be bought but that which is absolutely necessary for the maintenance of physical health, and what is bought must be of the plainest and most economical description'. Should a child fall ill, it must be attended by the parish doctor; should it die it must be buried by the parish. (Rowntree 1901: 334)

This fits the assistance benefit level paid in Great Britain and results in a standard of life markedly below that of the rest of the population, especially for those on benefit for long periods of time (Townsend 1979).

Box 4.1 Household budgets and consequent living standards

Low-cost budget (social coping)		Modest but adequate budget (social participation)	
Examples of items included	Examples of items excluded	Examples of items included	Examples of items excluded
Basic furniture, textiles and hardware	Antique, hand-made or precious household durables	Basic designs, mass-manufactured furniture, textiles and hardware	Antique, hand-made or precious household durables
First aid kit, medicine	Prescription, dental and sight care charges	Prescription charges, dental care, sight test	Spectacles, private health care
Fridge, washing machine, lawn mower, vacuum cleaner	Freezer, tumble-dryer, shower, electric blankets, microwave, food-mixer	Fridge-freezer, washing machine, microwave, food-mixer, sewing machine	Tumble-dryer, shower, electric blankets
Basic clothing (cheapest prices at C & A)	Second-hand, designer or high fashion clothing	Basic clothing, sensible designs	Second-hand, designer or high fashion clothing
TV, video hire, cassette player, basic camera	Hi-fi, children's TV compact discs, camcorder	TV, video hire, basic music system, basic camera	Children's TV, compact discs, camcorder

Public transport, children's bikes	Car, adult bikes, caravan, camping equipment	Second-hand 5-year-old car, second-hand adult bike, new children's bikes	A second car, caravan, camping equipment, mountain bikes
Clock, watches	Jewellery	Basic jewellery, watches	Precious jewellery
Haircuts	Cosmetics	Basic cosmetics, haircuts	Perfume, hair perm
	Alcohol/tobacco	Alcohol – 14 units for men, 10 for women (2/3 of HEA safe limit)	Tobacco
Day trip to Blackpool	Annual holiday	One-week annual holiday	Holiday abroad
Cinema twice a year; museums, etc., about twice a year	Concerts, panto, ballet or music lessons for children	Walking, swimming, cycling, football, cinema, panto every 2 years, youth clubs, scouts/guides	Fishing, water sports, horse-riding, creative or educational adult classes, ballet or music lessons for children

Source: Social Policy Research Findings, Joseph Rowntree Memorial Trust No. 31, November 1992.

3 ***Social coping***. This suggests that the poor are those who cannot enjoy the standard of living of the average working-class household (see Box 4.1). On this definition, a family would be living in poverty if they could not afford to buy the children birthday presents or new clothing. Piachaud (1979) has calculated that to achieve this standard of living, income must be substantially above benefit level. When he calculated the amount necessary, he found, for example, that it would be necessary to provide 50 per cent more than the assistance benefit paid for each child.

4 ***Social participation***. This defines the poor as those whose standard of living falls below the prevailing living standard (see Box 4.1). Townsend (1979: 3) sums it up by suggesting that people are living in poverty 'when they lack the resources to obtain the types of diet, participate in the activities and have the living conditions and amenities which are customary or at least widely encouraged or approved in the society in which they live'. The European Union has accepted this as a means of defining poverty and have defined as poor those who have a disposable income of less than half the average *per capita* income in their own country (Hantrais 1995).

Problems of measurement: The poverty line

Not only are there different definitions of poverty but also problems of how to measure it. There are basically three ways in which it can be measured:

1 *Professional*: for example, dietitians can provide details of an adequate diet that can then be costed. Those whose resources mean they cannot afford to purchase this diet and prepare and cook it are said to be in poverty.
2 *Conceptual*: for example, expenditure studies can determine how people live and this can be used to determine the minimum adequate income. Townsend (1979), for example, constructed a 60-item deprivation index which he used as a basis for determining the minimum income necessary to enjoy an average standard of living. This index was correlated with income, and he suggested that a threshold existed at incomes near 150 per cent of supplementary benefit levels.
3 *Public opinion*: for example, Mack and Lansley (1985) asked a random sample of people to indicate which of a list of 35 possible items they considered to be necessities. From this they constructed a list of essential items (Box 4.2). Using this list they were then able to work out how much money a family required in order to be able to afford them. They defined the poor as those who lacked three or more of the 14 items which the large majority agreed to be necessities.

Box 4.2 Items considered essential to standard of living by the public (in rank-order of importance)

1 Heating	14 Carpets
2 Indoor toilet	15 Celebrations on special
3 Damp-free home	occasions
4 Bath	16 Roast joint once a week
5 Bed for everyone	17 Washing machine
6 Public transport	18 New, not second-hand,
7 Warm waterproof coat	clothes
8 Three meals a day for	19 Hobby or leisure activity
children	20 Two hot meals a day
9 Self-contained	(adults)
accommodation	21 Meat/fish every other day
10 Two pairs of all-weather	22 Presents once a year
shoes	23 Holiday
11 Sufficient bedrooms for	24 Leisure equipment for
children	children
12 Refrigerator	25 Garden
13 Toys for children	26 Television

Source: Mack and Lansley (1985).

To summarize, we have suggested that in order to determine who is in poverty it is necessary to determine (1) how many of a person's requirements should be met, and (2) the quality of the provision. At one extreme, a minimum number of requirements would be met at a minimum quality, and at the other, a maximum number of requirements would be met at a maximum quality. It is not essential, for example, for adequate nutrition to include a roast dinner once a week, but it is considered normal in modern Britain. Purchasing new as opposed to second-hand clothes is not essential, but it is generally seen as desirable. In contemporary Britain, we generally define as poor those who cannot afford to purchase the goods and services to participate in normal activities. There is, nevertheless, debate as to what is the basic minimum.

In poverty research in Britain, the level of state benefit has generally been taken as a proxy for a 'poverty line'. State benefit, or more properly the **income support** level, has been seen as an official definition of what income is necessary for subsistence. This is nonetheless a relative measure, as the real value of benefits has increased over time (though not as fast as the real value of wages). In other words, as living standards have risen in general, so has the standard of living obtainable on benefit. However, the gap in living standard between those on benefits or benefit-level income and the rest of the population has widened, especially since 1979. This is because the level of benefits has been uprated since 1981 in line with prices, not wages; the latter have risen faster than the former since 1979. So as the general standard of living has increased, so have inequalities.

It is now accepted by most researchers that benefit levels are too stringent a measure of poverty. The Social Security Advisory Committee argued in 1983 (DHSS 1983) that assistance benefit level was 'too near the subsistence level to provide an adequate standard of living for the poorest people in our society'. In 1972, George and Wilding found that 72 per cent of lone fathers on assistance benefit found it inadequate, while Bradshaw *et al.* (1987) found that families on assistance benefit could not even afford an adequate diet or sufficient clothing. One respondent in Ritchie's (1990: 35) study said:

> I buy half a pound of stewing meat or something and give that to Sid and the kiddies and then I just have the gravy ... before, I used to buy soya things and substitutes to meat but I can't afford that now.

One of the lone mothers in Graham's (1992) study, a woman with two preschool children, commented:

> Food's the only place I find I can tighten up. The rest of it they take before you can get your hands on it really. So it's the food ... The only place I can get costs down is food ... You've got to balance nutrition with a large amount of food that will keep them not hungry. I'd like to give them fresh fruit, whereas the good food has to be limited. Terrible, isn't it, when you think about it?
>
> (Graham 1992: 219)

Recently, it has become common to measure poverty by reference to average male earnings – those in poverty being those with incomes below a certain percentage of mean income. The European Union, for example, defines poverty as earning an income less than 50 per cent of the average equivalent disposable income of the country under consideration. Many commentators have used 40 per cent of mean income as a measure. This is contentious, of course, because it means that poverty always exists, being measured in relative terms. However, at the present time in Britain, those on below average incomes not only have less command over resources but are also unable to enjoy the normal type of diet and participate in normal day-to-day activities.

What is evident is that, whatever definition and measure of poverty is used, there are still people living in poverty in contemporary Britain, and the absolute number and the percentage of the population living in poverty has increased. At the same time, inequalities have also increased, so that the differences in living standard between those at the top and bottom of society have actually widened. Poverty has increased in Britain not only because of the widening gap between benefit levels and average pay, but also because the proportion of the population on benefits has increased and the numbers of people in low-paid jobs has also risen. Walker (1995: 1) has indicated that:

> ...the precise amount by which poverty has increased depends on the measure used. If relative measures and a low threshold are used (40% of the contemporary average equivalent net household income) ...the poverty grew by a massive 333 per cent between 1979 and 1990/1. Assuming an 'absolute measure' is used, that is, holding the level of output constant at the 1979 threshold, poverty still increased by forty per cent.

Box 4.3   What is poverty?

- Poverty is not having sufficient money to buy the necessities of life and to participate in the life of the community.
- Poverty is constantly having to make choices about which necessities a person and the family shall go without.
- Poverty directly affects mobility, housing, leisure and social interaction, and it dramatically affects **life chances**. It is socially disabling.
- Poverty is closely linked to ill health.
- Poverty disproportionately affects working-class people throughout their lives, particularly when they are young or elderly, and especially if they are women or black or disabled.
- Poverty affects individuals and communities, but it is entirely preventable given the will on the part of government.

Source: Derbyshire Welfare Rights Service (1993: 1).

What is poverty?

Poverty is about more than income; it is about multiple deprivation (see Box 4.3). A respondent in Cohen's (1991) study described what it was like to be dependent on state benefit:

> We're not living on the **dole**. We're just existing barely... Going into the butcher's shop and asking 'Have you got some bones for the dog?' and then making a pot of soup... Living is when I could go

into a shop and say, 'I'd like a pair of shoes, fit them on my bairn and we'll take them'.

(Cohen 1991: 28)

However, not all those on low income are necessarily living in poverty. There are at least two reasons for this. One is that people's standard of living is determined by their immediately available resources, and people may have access to resources they do not have to purchase (e.g. housing, meals and/or food provided by their employer, transport and recreational facilities as part of their remuneration package). The second is that people may have savings and other 'stored' resources on which they are able to draw. Pensioners are an obvious example, who may have savings to supplement pension income as well as high-quality owner-occupied accommodation. They may also be assisted financially or in other ways by children. University students are another group who have low incomes but who are at the worst only temporarily in poverty, most having come from homes where they have not experienced poverty, and most on gaining degrees will gain employment with income well above the poverty level. The Church of England Working Party (1985) defined poverty as 'not only about shortage of money. It is about rights and relationships, about how people are treated and how they regard themselves, about powerlessness, exclusion and loss of dignity. Yet the lack of an adequate income is at the heart'. To be poor is to be multiply disadvantaged and to be excluded from participation in the normal day-to-day activities that are taken for granted.

Box 4.4 Factors closely associated with poverty

Physical factors
- Lack of adequate housing
- Insufficient food
- Unpleasant neighbourhood
- Unpleasant work environment
- Insufficient clothing

Health factors
- Short life span
- Frequent illness
- Chronic illness
- Permanent physical disability
- Permanent mental disability

Welfare values
- Personally unacceptable ratio of earned to total income
- Stigmatizing form of financial dependency
- Inability to perform socially valued role
- Lack of good-quality education
- Highly unfavourable self-concept
- Low aspirations/hopelessness about possibility of socio-economic mobility
- Severe family instability

Safety and security
- Unsafe housing
- Unsafe neighbourhood
- Lack of protection against major loss of assets
- Unsafe work environment
- Unsafe air or water
- Lack of protection against major decline in real income

Source: Adapted from Baratz and Grigsby (1971: 119–34).

Baratz and Grigsby (1971) have suggested a range of factors closely associated with poverty, grouped under four main headings (see Box 4.4). This list gives some indication of the range of factors that can be experienced by those living in poverty. There are some problems with the list, for example some of the factors are vague and some are debatable. It nevertheless highlights the ways in which poverty is associated with a range of material deprivations and social problems. The poor experience a range of deprivations – material, health, security, status and power/control. They are materially, physically, psychologically and socially deprived. Not all poor people necessarily experience everything on the list; for example, many of the poorest members of our society are unemployed. Some poor people have adequate housing because they live in council housing of a good standard, but many do not. Nor is the list comprehensive. It does not, for example, refer to inadequate transport, a major problem for many poor people, especially those living in rural areas (Giarchi 1990).

Finally, the poor are not simply those who lack basic goods and services, but those who are unable to meet their needs from their own resources. They cannot make the same choices as the majority of the population. The poor cannot afford to buy a television, pay for their children to go on school trips, buy Christmas and birthday presents. This inability often results in a lack of social participation – not having a television means an inability to join in conversations about popular TV programmes, and children may be kept at home on school trip days and not allowed to accept invitations to birthday parties because of the inability to buy a present. Furthermore, the poor often have to make undesirable or unpleasant choices; for example, whether to buy food or pay the rent, pay the electricity bill or buy shoes for the children. The income and other resources needed to provide basic necessities also vary. For example, transport costs are much higher in rural than urban areas; indeed, those living in rural areas may experience severe hardship if they do not have access to a car. However, changing patterns of shopping in modern Britain make food shopping difficult and expensive for women with families if they do not have access to a car, as more and more supermarkets move to out-of-town locations. The reduction in extra-curricular sporting activities in schools in recent years has meant that children are deprived of participation in sport and other activities if their parents cannot pay for them out of school. Furthermore, reductions in public transport mean that it is often necessary for parents to have a car if their children are to take part, for example, in swimming clubs, judo classes, ballet lessons, football training, the Girl Guides or even just a recreational swim. Elderly people also face social isolation because of their level of access to transport, which prevents them from participating.

Thus it is important to recognize that it is impossible to have a 'poverty line' below which people are poor, whereas above it they are not poor (Piachaud 1979). It is possible to define income levels that are sufficient to enable people to live in varying degrees of discomfort, and indeed to indicate a level of income that permits social participation (Townsend 1979, 1993). Cut-off points are always arbitrary, however, leaving some people only just above the line and not noticeably better off than those just below the line. It is probably more appropriate to consider people as more or less deprived when they have a standard of living below the societal norm, with the most deprived living in absolute poverty. All the poor are excluded from full membership of society, however; they lack the resources to obtain access to the conditions of life considered necessary not to be deprived.

Who are the poor? The incidence of poverty in Britain

It is estimated that in Britain in the 1990s one person in five lives either in poverty or in circumstances so constrained and restricted that they are living only just outside of poverty. This means that there are approximately twelve million people whose own or family income is insufficient to meet their needs (Oppenheim 1990). The main groups likely to be in poverty are people over retirement age, the unemployed, lone-parent families, the lowly paid and families with children (see Box 4.5).

> **Box 4.5   Households with below-average incomes – 1992 prices**
>
> An income below £104, net of tax but before living costs are subtracted – the lowest 20 per cent of incomes – could be from:
>
> - Basic income support for a couple and two children.
> - Wages for a 40-hour working week at £3.00 per hour (at the time this was the minimum hourly rate set by most wages councils).
> - A pensioner's income support together with a severe disability premium and attendance allowance.

Women are more likely than men to be living in poverty, and there is evidence to suggest (e.g. Graham 1984) that some women are living in poverty even when they are in a household with an average or above-average income. Afro-Caribbean and southern Asian British people are more likely to experience poverty than white Britons. The poorest fifth of the population includes 18 per cent of the white population but more than a third of the non-white population. The experience of poverty also tends to be cyclic, with people moving in and out of it across the life course, being most likely to experience it as children, as adults in a family with dependent children, and in old age. Those who experience poverty at these stages of their lives often have only barely adequate incomes at other times and are therefore unable to save or otherwise provide for these stages. For example, a working-class couple who may have an adequate income when they are first married but find themselves in poverty when they have children, experience a period of relative affluence when the children are older and both parents are able to hold down paid employment, but never earn sufficient to save or insure privately for old age. In 1991–93, for example, semi- and unskilled manual workers, together with personal service workers, were just over half as likely to be members of an employer **pension** scheme as professional and intermediate non-manual workers (CSO 1995: table 5.26). The risk of being in poverty, then, relates to stage in the life course, but also to gender, ethnicity and social class. The young, the elderly, women, Afro-Caribbean and southern Asian British, and working-class people, are more at risk of poverty than middle-class, white Britons, the middle-aged and men (Hills 1994). This remains the case by whatever means poverty is measured. Seventy per cent of households in the bottom 20 per cent have no earnings, being headed by pensioners, unemployed people, lone parents or long-term sick people. Fifty per cent of households with an unemployed head or spouse are in the poorest 10 per cent of households, as are lone-parent families and those with a long-term sick or disabled head of household (Hills 1994; see also CSO 1995: fig. 5.18).

Poverty and the elderly population

Those over retirement age are at major risk of poverty. In 1993, retired households comprised 26 per cent of all households, but comprised 39 per cent of households with incomes in the lowest 20 per cent of the income distribution and 47 per cent of households with incomes in the second lowest 20 per cent (CSO 1995: table 5.16).

The lives of most people change considerably on retiring from paid work. Generally speaking, people have less money and more time than previously. To some extent, retirement is a fairly modern convention, creating a fundamental change in people's lives at the appointed time. For many, retirement marks the passage between 'useful work' and 'old age', between earning a wage and depending on a pension. The specific impact of these changes varies between men and women (particularly if the woman has not been engaged in paid work), between individuals of different socio-economic backgrounds (some have financial investments and company pensions while others are reliant on a state pension alone), between able-bodied and disabled individuals, and between different cultures. The material and psychological impact of retirement is therefore quite complex and generalizations, as always, have their problems. However, for the majority of people (including those who have looked forward to it), the onset of retirement is often experienced as a time of relative loss. People may lose the status and income gained from paid employment and the sense of companionship of workmates and colleagues – and, perhaps more importantly, the sense of purpose in their lives. Many people lose their role as workers and have no other positive role with which to identify (for further discussion, see Phillipson 1982).

The Child Poverty Action Group (Oppenheim 1990: 75) noted that:

> The inequalities in working life between employment and unemployment, low-paid and high-paid work, between men and women, are compounded in old age. There are still two nations of the elderly: elderly people who are dependent on income support (the replacement for supplementary pension) and in council or private rented

housing without private or occupational pensions and with few or no savings; and elderly people who have the generous bonuses from a lifetime's secure and well paid employment.

The state pension scheme in Britain gives ones of the worst returns in Europe, with a ratio of 42.5 per cent of average earnings, compared with 66 per cent in France and 69 per cent in Germany. The married couple state pension in 1992–93 was worth only 26 per cent of 1992 average male earnings.

In addition, many pensioners entitled to means-tested benefits do not claim them. The take-up rate of supplementary pensions has been found to be between 67 and 78 per cent and for housing benefit between 88 and 95 per cent (DSS Analytical Services, quoted in CSO 1991), and indeed, old age poverty as measured by the assistance benefit level would disappear if older people applied for the benefits to which they were entitled. The failure to take up benefits is arguably due to the sheer complexity of the benefits system, lack of awareness of entitlement and the effect of stigma. Clearly, such low figures suggest that the existing benefits system is not effective in achieving its objective of preventing poverty in old age.

Many elderly people live in housing which is draughty, damp, inadequately insulated and fitted with inefficient heating systems. In such conditions, adequate heating is expensive, if not at times impossible to achieve. Confusion over **eligibility** for cold weather heating allowances, which are often paid retrospectively, compounds these problems. Elderly people and pressure groups such as Age Concern have argued forcefully for a solution to these problems, which result in the unnecessary deaths of many pensioners every year from hypothermia. One specific issue raised by pensioners is the injustice of the flat rate standing charges to low users of gas and electricity.

Poverty and disabled people

As with the elderly, a high proportion of disabled people are dependent on state benefits. Fifty-eight per cent of the income of disabled adults comes from state benefits; 55 per cent of severely disabled people are over 75 years of age and two-thirds are women. The only group of disabled people who do not receive the majority of their income from benefits are the married non-pensioner disabled. According to Martin and White (1988: 31), the mean income of disabled people is 72 per cent of that of the non-disabled. They also found that a higher proportion of households with a disabled member could not afford the basic items as defined by Mack and Lansley (1985). For example, 17 per cent of households with a disabled member could not afford to buy new clothes, compared with 6 per cent of households without a disabled member. Similarly, 15 per cent of households with a disabled member could not afford two pairs of all-weather shoes, compared with 9 per cent of households without a disabled member. Unmarried disabled people (mainly women) with children were the most deprived: 53 per cent could not afford new clothes and 50 per cent could not afford two pairs of all-weather shoes.

Disabled people are disadvantaged in the labour market and are more at risk of unemployment and low pay than other groups of workers. This means that they are likely to fare badly in occupational and private pension schemes (Groves 1991).

Disabled people are more likely than other groups to be dependent not only on state benefits – contributory, means-tested and universal – but also on state welfare services. Changes in the levels of service and the ways services are provided also affect disabled people and their ability to meet their own needs. The removal of the right to income support to pay for residential care or housework and its replacement with a system of care managers designing packages of care (see Chapter 9) has been severely criticized by disabled people, who

> generally pay a price for the services – for example, invasions of privacy by a veritable army of professionals and having to accept services the state thinks they should have or can afford, rather than those they know they need. There is often a further price to pay: being socialised into dependency – because services are provided for rather than with disabled people.
>
> (Oliver and Barnes 1991: 9)

Lone parents and poverty

In 1993, 19 per cent of all families were headed by a lone parent, in 90 per cent of cases by the mother. Nineteen per cent of households are headed by a lone mother, but 68 per cent of households with children dependent on income support are headed by a lone mother (CSO 1995). Forty-five per cent of the incomes of lone-parent families is from social security benefits, and 74 per cent of lone-parent families draw benefits, in some cases in combination with earnings. Lone-parent mothers are less likely to be in paid employment than married mothers with dependent children: 42 versus 54 per cent. Not all lone-parent families are living in poverty, but a majority are.

Low pay and poverty

Thirty-seven per cent of workers in Britain were on low pay in 1994 (TGWU 1994: 13). One in four of the poorest fifth of the population in 1990–91 had worked full-time in the previous year (CSO 1995). Low pay is a significant cause of poverty, although not all those on low pay live in poverty. Households with more than one income may not be living in poverty, although individual members may be earning poverty wages. Hilary Land (1991) has noted that the wages of employed wives keep a significant number of households out of poverty. Between 1973 and 1993, the proportion of households with a couple of working age with only one in employment declined from 45 to 29 per cent (Hills 1993). The impact of two-income households in reducing the incidence of poverty can be illustrated by comparing the proportion of employees on **low pay** with the proportion of households in poverty. Using the European Union threshold of 68 per cent of mean male gross earnings, 44 per cent of employees (31.7 per cent of males and 58.8 per cent of females) in Derbyshire were lowly paid in 1991, compared with 10.2 per cent of households (DOE 1991). However, it is important to recognize that those in low-paid employment are more at risk of unemployment than other groups and are less likely to be in employer pension schemes and therefore are at risk of poverty in old age.

Unemployment and poverty

Unemployment is a major cause of poverty in contemporary Britain. When it is short-term it is unlikely in itself to be an indication of poverty. The Beveridge system of benefits was not designed to deal with long-term unemployment, yet in July 1993, 40 per cent of registered unemployed men and 26 per cent of registered unemployed women had been unemployed for over a year (see Hills 1994). (This is probably an underestimate of long-term unemployment for women, as women are less likely to register as unemployed than men.) However, the long-term unemployed are likely to experience considerable poverty. Furthermore, the longer they are unemployed, the less likely they are to be re-employed. The way in which the benefits system works means that a household headed by an unemployed man is likely to have less income if the female partner has employment than if not. Some groups of the population and some areas of the country are more vulnerable to unemployment than others.

Sinfield (1981) considers the unequal burden of unemployment in Britain and notes the persistence of regional inequalities since the war, with Northern Ireland faring consistently worst, and the north, Wales, Scotland and the north-west suffering the highest rates in Britain. In the 1970s, the West Midlands was badly affected for the first time, and it has been suggested that the present increase in unemployment is beginning to affect the prosperity of the south-east, although it is as yet too early to assess the significance of these shifts.

Oliver (1990) and Lonsdale (1990) both discuss the importance of unemployment in the construction of dependency for disabled people, arguing that the processes of industrialization and development have effectively excluded many disabled people from work, resulting in economic dependency and social marginalization. Fennell et al. (1988), similarly, point to the impact of 'the universal social institution' of retirement on the lives of elderly men and women. It is not just retired folk who are affected disproportionately by unemployment but increasingly, in recent years, those over 50, who if made redundant have found it increasingly difficult to return to the labour market.

Hawkins (1987) and Sinfield (1981) consider the relationship of skill levels to the incidence of unemployment and demonstrate the over-representation of unskilled and semi-skilled manual workers among the unemployed (and particularly among the long-term unemployed) throughout the post-war period, suggesting a persistent lack of demand for unskilled labour. Philpott (1994), for example, notes that the unemployment rate is four times higher for unskilled than professional workers. One explanation for the differential impact on people with low levels of skill is that industry has invested less in them and that, because there is a ready supply of such labour, it is less risky to operate a 'hire and fire' policy depending on the state of the economy. Others have pointed to the decline in the manufacturing base of the British economy, resulting in a fall in the demand for unskilled labour, although there have been areas of growth in unskilled labour as a result of the expansion of non-manufacturing, service sector industries. The concept of structural unemployment is often used by economists to explain the mismatch that occurs, as the economy changes, between supply of jobs and the skills of available workers. It has been argued, for example, that the new jobs created since the major decline in manufacturing may be unsuitable for those rendered unemployed – often being lowly paid, part-time jobs in the service sector.

Women and poverty

Women predominate among those who are poor – as low-paid workers, as pensioners, as disabled people and as lone parents. In 1989, 60 per cent of income support recipients were women (Lewis and Piachaud 1992). Glendinning and Millar (1992: 60) has suggested that:

> Women bear the burden of managing poverty on a day-to-day basis. Whether they live alone or with a partner, on benefit or low earnings, it is usually women who are responsible for making ends meet and for managing the debts which result when they don't . . . As more women and men lose their jobs, and as benefits are cut or decline in value, women are increasingly caught in a daily struggle to feed and clothe their families . . . usually only at considerable personal sacrifice.

Glendinning and Millar (1992) note that when looking at women's poverty, we should not be concerned solely with the disparate levels of *income* which exist between men and women, but also with (1) their *access* to income and other resources, (2) the *time* spent generating income and resources, and (3) the *transfer* of these resources from some members of a household to others. Women's real gross weekly earnings are considerably lower than men's. For example, in 1994, men in the top decile earned on average just under £600 per week, compared with just over £400 for women. In the bottom decile, men earned just under £200 and women around £150 (CSO 1995: table 5.6). In April 1994, a third of women earned £190 a week or less, compared with 13 per cent of men. Only half the women but three-quarters of the men earned over £230 per week (CSO 1995: chart 5.7).

The Family Expenditure Survey provides useful information about single-person households broken down by gender. It shows that:

1 In 1988, women's incomes were only 86 per cent that of men's.
2 Women in retirement were far more reliant on social security benefits than men and were less likely to have annuities, pensions or investments.
3 The greater reliance on social security in retirement by women was the

outcome of lower earnings, intermittent work patterns and fewer rights to occupational pensions (see Oppenheim 1990).

In terms of low pay, the CPAG report (Oppenheim 1990) cites the findings of a study by Holly Sutherland at the London School of Economics, which found that:

1 In 1989, 6.4 million women were low-paid (i.e. 71 per cent of the total number of people on low wages). The Low Pay Unit defines low pay as less than two-thirds of median male earnings (at that time £4.16 per hour or £157 per week). Indeed, Esau and Berthoud (1991) have estimated that 4.6 million women had incomes of less than £25 per week in 1984 compared with 0.4 million men, or 20 per cent of all women compared with 2 per cent of all men.
2 There is a strong association between low pay and part-time working. In 1989, 4.3 million women worked part-time and 79 per cent of them were lowly paid (only 0.9 million men worked part-time).
3 Black women are likely to have even lower earnings and/or to do more shift work than white women.
4 In 1989, average hourly earnings for women were 68 per cent of men's (including overtime), or 76 per cent excluding overtime.

The benefits system was built on the assumption that married women would generally be dependent on their husbands for economic support. It is this ideological notion of dependency within the existing benefits system, despite the move to more formally equal treatment in the 1980s, which is the root cause of gender inequality. An important feature of the British benefits system is the division between benefits notionally funded from national insurance contributions and **means-tested benefits**. As long as sufficient contributions have been made, the former are paid on an individual basis regardless of income; means-tested benefits are based on a test of income and capital. Women are less likely than men to be eligible for contributory benefits, failing to have made sufficient contributions either because of interrupted employment or because they had been earning insufficient to have had to have made contributions. In 1988, over two million women fell into this category. The result is that they, and all those who are unable to work as a result of domestic responsibilities, have no right to claim national insurance funded benefits. Women are less likely than men, then, to to be able to claim state benefits in their own right (and, for the same reasons, employer/private ones) and more likely to be dependent on the social security system (and thus on means-tested benefits). In 1988, according to CPAG:

1 Over three times as many women as men over pension age were receiving income support.
2 Two-thirds of lone parents (mostly women) were reliant on 'income support.
3 Ninety-six per cent of lone parents on income support were women.

Furthermore, even when women live in a household with an adequate income, they may still live in poverty, as resources are not necessarily shared equitably (Graham 1984; Vogler 1989).

Race and poverty

Britain's Afro-Caribbean and southern Asian populations are more likely
to experience unemployment and low pay than other groups (Oppenheim
1990). Even after allowing for the differences in the age structure and
educational attainment of these groups compared with the white British
population, their unemployment level is twice that of whites (Philpott
1994). Arnott (1987) concluded that:

> Despite the lack of adequate statistics it is clear that many black
> people, and in particular black men and the 'never employed' black
> youth, are bearing a large part of the social impact of the govern-
> ment's policies, trapped by unemployment and low incomes in decay-
> ing minority areas where the very fabric of their surroundings is
> being eroded by neglect.
>
> (pp. 68–9)

There is also evidence of a considerable failure to take up means-tested
benefits among minority ethnic communities, especially southern Asian
households and households in which English is not spoken (Craig 1991;
NACAB 1991). However, Spicker (1993) points out that while the lifestyles
of different minority groups vary considerably, their housing conditions
are generally poorer than those of the white population. He concludes
that: '[the] available data does indicate that people in ethnic minorities
are relatively disadvantaged ... and are over-represented among the people who are poor' (p. 67).

Explaining the persistence of poverty and inequality

As Spicker (1993) points out, we do not have to understand the causes of
poverty (or, indeed, of any social problem) in order to respond to it.
Nevertheless, the understandings of poverty that people have shape their
responses. Those who see it as the outcome of individual failures suggest
different policies from those who see it as the outcome of structural factors. In 1972, Keith Joseph asked

> Why is it that, in spite of long periods of full employment and rel-
> ative prosperity ... deprivation and problems of maladjustment so
> conspicuously persist?

His answer was that

> We know only too certainly that among the children of this genera-
> tion there are some doomed to an uphill struggle against the disad-
> vantages of a deprived family background ... many will not be able
> to overcome their disadvantages and will become in their turn the
> parents of deprived children.

The National Consumer Council (NCC) report (quoted in Taylor-Gooby
and Dale 1981) on means-tested welfare presented a somewhat different
argument, stating that society can tackle poverty only by making changes

in the system of welfare benefits. Milliband (1969), a Marxist political scientist, presents a different analysis again:

> The bitter truth is that the abolition of poverty will have to wait until the abolition of the system which breeds it comes on the agenda; and this is a question which far transcends the issue of poverty itself.

These three examples illustrate three alternative ways of explaining the persistence of poverty in Britain, with important implications for policy. Murie and Forrest (1980) attempted a classification of different approaches to urban problems. They divided competing explanations into the following groups:

1 **Individualist**/*pathological explanations*: exemplified by the Conservative government's approach.
2 *Reformist explanations*: exemplified by the NCC report.
3 *Structuralist explanations*: exemplified by the Marxist approach.

A problem of people: Social pathology and cultural explanations

According to such views, poverty can be explained in terms of the characteristics of poor people themselves and the effects of their immediate social environment (i.e. poverty results from individual and subcultural factors). Individualistic views of poverty attribute poverty and deprivation to the faults of individuals, to their inadequacy and incompetence. Such inadequate individuals are deemed unable to compete effectively in 'normal' society and in some cases unable to rear their children to do so, resulting in the transmission of inequality. Those who take this view do recognize that some people are unable to provide for themselves adequately through no fault of their own, for example the mentally ill and those with physical disabilities. However, they are predominantly concerned with those who are assumed *not* to try – those who are said to be lazy.

The notion of a **'poverty cycle'** or subculture of poverty was promoted by Keith Joseph, who argued that poor families resulted from unstable marriages, poor accommodation and overcrowding, inadequate parenting and lack of occupational skill. Inner cities, according to this view, are places where there are concentrations of people who are poverty-prone, in a society that has otherwise solved its basic social problems. A more recent formulation of this kind of view has been put forward by Murray (1990), who refers to an **'underclass'**. This underclass, in his view, is not the poor in general but those who are poor from their own choice and depend on state benefits, and carry an underclass culture, because they do not want to work, do not want to live in nuclear families and are habitually delinquent and criminal. Taylor-Gooby and Dale (1981) argue that one of the weaknesses of this kind of argument is that there is stronger evidence to suggest that the wealthy in society transmit privilege than that the poor inherit poverty (see also Brown 1990; Walker 1990; Abbott and Wallace 1992). Concepts of 'problem families' and 'inadequate parenting' have been criticized by feminists, who argue that such a view of poverty is not only individualistic but embodies a particular view of women and of the role of women in perpetuating poverty.

If poverty is seen as the outcome of individual or subcultural failures, social policy must be geared to the correction or prevention of such failures. In general, such explanations lead to minimal social intervention, with often deterrent and/or paternalistic policies directed at sub-groups identified by the theory.

A problem of management and planning: Reforming society

In this perspective, poverty is seen as the outcome of the ways in which society is organized. In capitalist societies such as Britain, there are inequalities and some people must fall to the bottom; there are losers as well as gainers. Society can ensure that the losers do not find themselves in poverty by providing adequate income maintenance and other services and by ensuring equal life chances – that is, equality of opportunity. This is a view clearly associated with the Fabian socialists (see, for example, Titmuss 1968).

This standpoint, then, focuses on the efficacy of welfare agencies in fulfilling their objectives. Reformists point to administrative decisions which result in the low take-up of benefits (the sheer complexity of the system, for example, or lack of information, or obstructive professionalism and social stigma). Underlying these contentions is the implicit view that the welfare state *could* succeed in overcoming poverty if it could be made to function more effectively and/or if there were the political will. Forrest and Murie (1988) refer to this approach as 'the problem of management and planning'. Referring specifically to the housing problem in inner cities, they point to the role of planners in the exacerbation or creation of urban problems; in particular, the effect of planning decisions on land values, which has serious implications for the provision of low-cost housing. Other work points to the role of housing managers (people who allocate council housing, for example, or mortgages) in rationing resources and determining the housing choices of large numbers of particularly vulnerable people.

While it is important to rectify institutional malfunctioning, Taylor-Gooby and Murie and Forrest, among others, point out that such institutions are located within a system which constrains and determines the nature, size and distribution of the 'social surplus'. Council house management, for example, may leave a lot to be desired, but moratoria on building, the imposition of sales, the relaxation of house-building standards, etc., all constrain the role of housing authorities. The view that administrative deficiency lies at the root of social malaise therefore implies that administrative reform could conceivably provide a solution in the long term. Ambrose and Colenutt's (1975) study of Brighton, however, delved deeper into the issue of planning and urban problems and demonstrated the determining role of power elites within the local council. Many councillors, for example, were building society managers or estate agents with vested interests in particular policy developments. Taylor-Gooby concludes that, 'Institutional accounts of social problems rest on a view of society that claims there are no fundamental obstacles to the resolution of problems' (1994: 32).

Box 4.6 Differing explanations of poverty

Theoretical model of problem	Explanation of the problem	Location of the problem	Key concept	Type of change sought	Method of change
Social pathology and culture	Problems arising from the pathology of deviant groups	In internal dynamics of deviant groups	Poverty	Better adjusted and less deviant people	Social education and social work with groups
	Individual psychological handicaps and inadequacies transmitted from one generation to the next	In relation-ships between individuals, families and groups	Deprivation	More integrated self-supporting families	Compens-atory social work, support and self-help
Management and planning	Failures of planning, management or administration	In relationship between disadvantaged and the bureaucracy	Disadvantage	More total and coordinated approaches by the bureaucracy	Rational social planning
Resources	Inequitable distribution of resources	In relationship between under-privileged and formal political machine	Under-privilege	Better allocation of resources	Positive discrimina-tion policies
Structural	Divisions necessary to maintain an economic system based on private profit	In relationship between working-class and political and economic structure	Inequality	Better distri-bution of power and control	Changes in political conscious-ness and organization

Source: Adapted from Community Development Project (1977).

A structural problem: Poverty as an inherent factor in capitalist society

Accounts such as the foregoing, however, fail to take into account the *recurrent* nature of disadvantage; others have argued that a structural explanation is required to make sense of this recurrence. Structural approaches identify the underlying causes of inequalities in the way society is constituted as a whole and suggest that major barriers lie in the way of satisfactory solutions, although they do not necessarily imply that such solutions are impossible. Structural accounts make two claims:

1 The way in which society is organized militates against the eradication of poverty; inner-city decline, for example, is seen as a specific manifestation of the uneven development of capitalism.
2 While certain 'states of affairs' may be recognized as 'problems' by some individuals or groups, their continuance may actually serve the interests of other, often more powerful groups in society.

Poverty, then, is seen as the inevitable result of the operation of a particular form of social organization. The final report of the Community Development Project's study of poverty in Britain indicated that 'the inescapable outcome of the private ownership of the means of production', and concluded:

> The spatial concentration of such problems in a small geographical area is not an isolated phenomenon to be tackled by special remedies; nor even a small pocket left behind by the tides of industrialisation and urbanisation. It is a product of the very same processes which have brought growth and prosperity to other areas and interest groups.
>
> (CDP 1977: 64)

'Underclass' theories

In the 1980s, the term 'underclass' came to be used by a range of commentators and social scientists from both the right and left of the political spectrum to refer to the poor. The common element of these accounts is that there is said to be a group who are trapped outside of and below society, effectively excluded from the mainstream. Westergaard (1992) has indicated that the term is used in at least three different ways: the 'moral turpitude' version, the 'outcast poverty' version and the 'rhetorical' version.

The 'moral turpitude' version to which we have referred above is most clearly associated with the arguments of the US social scientist Charles Murray, whose arguments have influenced Conservative governments in Britain (Abbott and Wallace 1992). According to Murray, the underclass is a specific sub-group of the poor – those who share a culture of dependency and bring poverty on themselves because of their chosen lifestyle.

Conversely, the 'outcast poverty' version of the underclass idea sees the causes of poverty as structural: the poor are the victims of market relations, the enterprise culture and the vagaries of public policy. The underclass is made up of the retired and other groups dependent on state benefits and the lowly paid. It is seen as excluded, by its poverty, from participation in society. Society is seen as increasingly polarized into a marginalized underclass segregated from a majority society which is itself increasingly 'classless' and incorporated into a growing prosperity. Halsey (1987), for example, sees the emergence of an increasingly polarized society with the majority securely attached to a still prosperous economy and the minority finding themselves economically and socially marginalized.

The 'rhetorical' version uses the term to highlight the plight of the poor. The notion of an underclass used in this way emphasizes social exclusion and the structural difficulties of moving out of poverty. The term is used to call attention to the plight of those who are permanently excluded from enjoying an income that enables them to participate in the normal day-to-day activities of the society in which they live. This analysis shifts attention to the structure of the labour market and away from the individual characteristics of the lowly paid, the unemployed and the elderly. Unequal changes in the labour market are seen as a major factor in creating the underclass.

The concept of underclass is valuable in drawing attention to the existence of a 'truly disadvantaged' segment of the population and to the structural factors which created it and mitigate its members climbing out of it. However, as Westergaard (1992) has pointed out, in its more sociological usage (that is, when seen as a social class in relation to the relative classlessness of the rest of society) it tends to over-emphasize the prosperity of those not seen as part of the underclass. Westergaard points out that there are continuing inequalities in society and that the major beneficiaries of the tax cuts and economic growth in the last 15 years have been a relatively small proportion of top wage-earners (see also Abbott and Wallace 1992). While social security reforms, employment policies and growing divorce rates may have created a group at the bottom of society, financial policies have consistently advantaged the highest paid workers. Westergaard indicates that the bottom half of households gained by 10 per cent at best during the 1980s, less than half the nominal rate of 'rising affluence'. He concludes that:

> 'At least half' is quite plainly not a minority . . . it has not made for a new and distinctive divide between outcast 'underclass' and incorporated 'middle mass'. There is no such sharp, single line towards the bottom of the pile.
>
> (Westergaard 1992: 580)

Implications for policy

The competing explanations of poverty are not mutually exclusive, nor do they necessarily result in completely different kinds of policy outcomes. Nevertheless, there is a relationship between seeing poverty as the result of individual characteristics on the one hand or structural ones on the other and the type of social policy advocated. Those who attribute poverty to the laziness and attitudes of poor people are likely to argue that poor relief must be accompanied by measures to change the behaviour of the poor. Conversely, those who view poverty as the outcome of an unequal society in which the poor are disadvantaged in economic, social and political terms would argue that it is inappropriate to structure the relief of poverty through systems that indicate moral responsibility. An example of this is 'Workfair', the notion that the unemployed should have to work for their benefit even if the work they do is meaningless and the rate of benefit they receive is considerably lower than would be paid for the job under normal circumstances. Workfair programmes are often justified on the basis that they enable the poor to learn habits of industry; less often do they teach skills that will lead to secure employment.

Conversely, structural problems imply that some change in the social structure is desirable. This, however, is often difficult to achieve. The consequence is that the policies adopted by governments tend to rely on the redistribution of income, income maintenance, **fiscal policy** and social work. The emphasis placed on different forms of policy initiative will depend on the political ideologies of the government in power, but the basic outcome is that the vast effect of structural disadvantage is unchanged by social policies.

Conclusions

Poverty still exists in modern Britain and significant groups of the population are living in poverty. Being poor prevents people participating in the normal day-to-day activities of the society in which they live; in effect, they are socially excluded. While there are debates as to the causes of poverty, social changes – increased unemployment, the growing number of elderly people (especially *very* elderly people) and lone-parent families – have resulted in an increase in the number of people who live in poverty, including the number of children. Benefit levels are inadequate to enable people to participate in society, and it is doubtful if they enable people to live even at subsistence level (Walker 1993). The increased targeting of benefits has exacerbated the problem, especially given the low take-up rate of means-tested benefits. It has been argued that the social security system could be reformed, given the political will, to reduce the extent of poverty. However, the Conservative governments in power since 1979 have tended to argue that low levels of benefit are necessary to induce the poor to take the available jobs and encourage parents (especially fathers) to take responsibility for the welfare of their families (Abbott and Wallace 1992). In other words, they see the solution to poverty as in the hands of the poor themselves rather than as necessitating state action. Debates about poverty, inequality and social justice are contentious, not just because of the debates surrounding the definitions of poverty and its causes, but because those who most strongly advocate state action to combat poverty are generally concerned to reduce inequalities in society, while those who see poverty as a residual problem tend to believe that inequalities act as an incentive to hard work and self-reliance. They argue that high levels of state benefits result in a dependency culture.

Summary

- The previous chapter summarized a variety of explanations of health inequalities. This chapter has broadened the area of study to a more general discussion of poverty and inequality and the implications for welfare systems.

- Before we can measure levels of poverty in any society we first have to define it. Three different definitions of poverty have been discussed here: that of absolute, subsistence and relative poverty. In the British context there is general agreement on the need for a relative concept which is both historically and culturally sensitive and takes account of the need to enable citizens to participate in society.

- Having established the need for a relative definition we then have to find a means of measuring poverty in order to establish some form of poverty line as the basis for social policy. Three approaches are discussed here: the public opinion or 'social consensus' approach; the income/expenditure approach and the professional definition approach.

- Evaluations of poverty in the UK show that poverty is not evenly distributed across social groups but is concentrated within certain populations including the retired, the unemployed, lone-parent families, the low paid, families with children and women.

- Policymaker's understanding of the causes of poverty/inequality shape the policy response and these are very much influenced by ideology. Where poverty is seen as a reflection of individual failure, for example, the policy response will be aimed at individuals. We have outlined three alternative perspectives on the causes of poverty: as a result of social pathology, of institutional malfunctioning and as a reflection of wider structural features of society.

- Finally, all aspects of social policy intervention may result in certain unanticipated effects – otherwise known as 'unintended consequences'. This is also true of anti-poverty measures which may induce dependency, erode the work ethic and threaten the fiscal sustainability of welfare.

Further reading

George, V. and Howard, I. (1991) *Poverty Amidst Affluence*. London: Edward Elgar.

Oppenheim, C. (1990) *Poverty: The Facts*. London: Child Poverty Action Group.

Townsend, P. (1993) *The International Analysis of Poverty*. Hemel Hempstead: Harvester Wheatsheaf.

Transport and General Workers' Union (1994) *In Place of Fear: The Future of the Welfare State*. London: TGWU.

Walker, C. (1993) *Managing Poverty*. London: Routledge.

STATE INCOME MAINTENANCE AND WELFARE BENEFITS

Introduction

This chapter will consider state policies designed to ensure that everyone's **basic income** needs are met. In Britain, we generally refer to the major policies directed to ensure at least a minimum income as 'social security', and the majority of social spending in Britain is by the government (CSO 1995: 136). In 1992–93, 21 per cent of gross domestic product (GDP) was spent on social protection (cash and benefits in kind), while about a third of all government expenditure went on social security (CSO 1995: 148). This represents about 10 per cent of GDP and is the single largest item of public expenditure. Forty-four per cent of the funding comes from general taxation, 30 per cent from employers' national insurance (NI) contributions, 24 per cent from employee's NI contributions and 2 per cent from investment income from the National Insurance Fund (DSS 1991b: 8). All the available evidence suggests that social security spending will continue to rise. This follows an increase in social security expenditure of 44 per cent between 1978–79 and 1991–92. This increase in expenditure can be explained partly by the ageing of the population and partly by an anticipation by the government of increased expenditure on lone parents and sick and disabled people (DSS 1991b). Currently, 51 per cent of social security expenditure goes on benfits for the elderly, 18 per cent on disabled and long-term sick people, 18 per cent on females, 9 per cent on unemployed people, 2 per cent on the short-term sick and disabled people, and 2 per cent on widows and orphans (DSS 1991b: 6). Expenditure in Britain is lower than in most other EC countries; only Spain, the Irish

Republic, Portugal and Greece spend less per head, with Denmark, for example, spending twice as much in 1992 (CSO 1995: chart 8.3). (Social security systems function to sustain incomes through the distribution of cash benefits. There is, however, little agreement as to whether the objective is to *prevent* or to *relieve* poverty.)

Social security

Social security is concerned with financial support, from the cradle to the grave. Beveridge's plan was tied to a policy of full employment, whereby employees and employers paid insurance contributions to provide for men and their families in times of unemployment, sickness, disability and old age. In addition, there was to be maternity benefit, widows' benefit and death grants. These **insurance benefits** were intended to support individuals and families at subsistence level. As a safety net, a non-contributory social assistance scheme was to be financed from taxation. Its aim was to meet the needs not covered adequately by insurance, but it was to be seen as less desirable than insured benefits and to be based on a means test.

A clear distinction was drawn between **universal benefits** and means-tested (targeted) benefits. State benefits were to provide a national minimum, people being free to make private arrangements; there continued to be a mixed economy of provision. State insurance was compulsory, but individuals and their employers could still provide additional protection (e.g. employer pensions, sick pay, health insurance, private pensions, mortgage protection, permanent disability income). Indeed, in the last 15 years, the government has tried to encourage people to make private provision (see Chapter 6).

Social security benefits have a number of different facets, the four most important of which are compensation, personal insurance protection, employment protection and integrated social and economic development (TGWU 1994). Compensation is provided, for example, for disabilities and industrial injuries. Personal income protection is based on the insurance principle; regular weekly contributions paid while in employment provide for protection in old age, sickness, disablement and unemployment.

The social security system in Britain was changed incrementally in the 1950s, 1960s and 1970s (e.g. the option for women to pay lower contributions was withdrawn in 1975) and a number of new benefits introduced (e.g. **mobility allowance** and **attendance allowance**). In the 1980s, the Conservative government carried out a major review (the Fowler Review), resulting in the 1986 Social Security Act, implemented in 1988. The government argued that the benefits system had become too complex with the mixture of insured and targeted benefits, and that the poverty trap provided a major **disincentive** for people to come off benefit and take available jobs. However, it is not clear that the new system is any less complex or that it has removed the poverty trap (Johnson 1990). The Conservatives were also concerned that the system did not target benefits sufficiently and that it was too costly to administer. The aim of the new system of benefits introduced in 1988 was, then, to target payments at those most in need and to provide incentives to individuals to take the available jobs and provide for their old age. A further concern of the Conservative Party has been to reduce 'dependency' and to do so by changing people's behaviour – to make them more self-reliant.

As a field of study, social security is a wide one, embracing the distribution of income, the taxation system, private insurance provision and the system of income transfers organized by the state. To understand the implications of social policy fully, we must consider not only the contribution of statutory provision but also the role of the commercial sector and of occupational welfare. This is particularly important in relation to social security and recent developments in pensions policy (see Chapter 6).

The social security system has been reformed in a number of significant ways since the Conservatives came to power in 1979. The reforms have been aimed at reducing costs, targeting benefits, reducing dependency and simplifying the system. The most significant of these changes have been:

1 An attempt to cut expenditure by: uprating most social security and pension benefits by inflation rates rather than rises in average annual earnings; the replacement of grants for single items by loans from the cash-limited **Social Fund**; and the reduction in the future value of the state earnings-related pension and the promotion via subsidies of personal pension plans and new occupational schemes.
2 Changes in regulations for claiming unemployment benefit, intended to increase work incentives.
3 The transfer of the administration of statutory sick pay and statutory maternity pay from the national insurance scheme to employers.
4 The freezing of universal child benefit in 1987, with poor families in employment targeted by family credit (a means-tested benefit).
5 The administrative devolution of most social security benefits to a semi-autonomous executive agency, the Benefits Agency, of national insurance contributions to the National Insurance Contributing Agency, of hostel provision for single homeless people to the Resettlement Agency, and of responsibility for operational strategy in the DSS to the Information Technology Services Agency (note: there are separate child support and social security agencies in Northern Ireland).
6 The establishment in 1993 of the Child Support Agency to administer new arrangements for the enforcement of child maintenance payments by absent parents; this measure was intended, at least in part, to reduce the cost of income support for lone parents.

The British social security system

The British state systems of income support fall into three categories: (1) contributory benefits; (2) **non-contributory** benefits which are not means-tested as such, but are allocated according to some 'needs' criterion (e.g. age or disability); and (3) means-tested benefits (see Box 5.1). It is important to stress that a person or a family may depend on both contributory and non-contributory support simultaneously. Indeed, one of the most significant recent trends has been to displace contributory schemes with means-tested ones. The Beveridge Plan envisaged that contributory benefits would provide the main source of support in old age, sickness and unemployment, although in fact the actual insured benefits were paid at much lower rates than those recommended by Beveridge. In addition, the limited period for which sickness and unemployment benefits are paid has meant that the idea of insurance was compromised from the start, with a significant number of people dependent on means-tested benefits for topping up inadequate insured benefits. However, government policy in recent years has been to argue for the targeting of benefits to those most in need, and this has meant an increasing emphasis on means-tested income support as opposed to contributory and universal benefits by, for example, making the contribution requirement for entitlement to retirement pension more stringent.

A major concern about means-tested benefits has been lack of 'take-up'; that is, people failing to claim benefits to which they are entitled. As Spicker (1995: 155–6) points out:

> For many years this was described as a problem of **stigma**, because some claimants felt humiliated by claiming, but the problem is rather more complex than this suggests. Reasons for **non-takeup** include ignorance about benefits, the complexity and difficulty of the process, previous problems in attempting to claim, limited marginal benefits and the costs to the claimant of proceeding.

A good example is welfare policies designed to help families with children. Child benefit is universal and has virtually 100 per cent uptake. However, since 1971, successive governments have introduced benefits – family income supplement, replaced by family credit in 1988 – targeted at helping poor families with children where at least one parent is in employment. However, the take-up of these benefits is very low, and even lower among Black communities (Cook and Watt 1992; Marsh and Macky 1993). Furthermore, there is the problem of the poverty trap; that is, an increase in earnings can leave a family little better off or even worse off. Hills (1993) calculated, for example, that a cohabiting couple with two children living in a rented home could double their gross income from £100 to £200 and see little difference in the cash in their pockets.

Contributory benefits

Contributory benefits are those for which employees make weekly or monthly payments through their wages, on an **earnings-related** basis, to the national insurance scheme. Employers also have to make contributions on behalf of their employees. These contributions go towards a range of benefits covering sickness, maternity leave, unemployment and pensions (see Box 5.1). Widows' benefits is dependent on the contribution record of their late husbands. In 1990–91, contributory benefits accounted for 55 per cent of spending on social security (DSS 1991b: 8).

In relation to these benefits, employees who have made adequate contributions are therefore *entitled* to a benefit, for a period at least. Un-

---

Box 5.1 Main social security benefits

Contributory *(paid only to those who have paid insurance contributions)*	Non-contributory *(and not means-tested)*	Means-tested *(paid only to those on limited means)*
• Statutory maternity benefit • Retirement pension • Unemployment benefit • Widows' pension • Widowed mothers' allowance • Incapacity benefit	• Children's allowance • Mobility allowance • Attendance allowance • Disabled living allowance • Invalid care allowance • War pensions	• Income support • Income maintenance • **Supplementary pension** • Death benefit • Social Fund • Family credit • **Housing benefit** • Council tax rebate • Free prescriptions • Free dental treatment • Free eyesight test • Disability working allowance

---

employment benefit, for example, is available to those who have made adequate national insurance contributions, after three days of being out of work. After a year on this benefit, however, entitlement is 'exhausted' and recipients have to rely on a means-tested benefit. This also applies to sick pay, which covers an employee for 28 weeks, after which anyone still unfit for work moves on to incapacity benefit, a **flat-rate benefit** without additions for children until the claimant has been incapable of work for 52 weeks, and with age-related additions being paid only to workers who become ill before the age of 45.

Social security retirement pensions are paid until death, and a widow may be entitled to a pension based on her late husband's contributions. Entitlement to a **state retirement pension** is based on age (men must be over 65 and women 60) and a contribution record. To qualify for a full pension, a person must have paid or been credited with contributions for about nine-tenths of his or her working life – normally 44 years for a woman and 49 for a man. Those with a lower level of contribution may be entitled to a reduced pension. Women often have a reduced entitlement to pension because they have spent periods outside the labour market (although they are now credited with contributions while caring for dependent children or other dependants in receipt of attendance allowance/**disability living allowance**) and/or periods of low-paid part-time work where they did not reach the lower limit of earnings for paying contributions. In addition, married women in the past often opted not to pay full contributions and rely for a pension on their husband's contribution record. On retirement, then, many women are not entitled to a pension, or to a full pension, in their own right. Instead, they depend on their husbands' entitlement if they are married and on means-tested benefits if they are divorced or single. Women who are widowed before retirement age may not be entitled to a full pension when they reach 60 if they do not have a contributions record of their own. Many Black Britons who came to this country in the 1950s and 1960s will also be entitled to only a reduced pension on retirement. Pensioners who are entitled to only a reduced pension, who are often those who do not have an employer's pension or a **private pension** and have not earned sufficient to be entitled to an earnings-related pension, have to rely on means-tested benefits to raise their income to subsistence level (see Chapters 4 and 7).

Various 'rules' exist for the various benefits, ostensibly to prevent abuse of the system. We focus on the rules as they apply to unemployment benefit here, by way of illustration (see Box 5.2 for the rules relating to incapacity benefit).

Box 5.2   Conditions for receiving incapacity benefit

In order to be found incapable of work, an individual must score 15 or more on the physical test or 10 or more on the mental health test. (A score of more than 6 on the mental health test can be added to the score on the physical test.)

The physical test

Examples of conditions that will score 15 points:

Walking: cannot walk more than 50 yards without stopping or
    suffering discomfort
Sitting: cannot sit comfortably for more than 10 minutes without
    having to move from the chair
Standing: cannot stand for more than 10 minutes without having to
    sit for a rest
Lifting: cannot pick up and pour from a saucepan with either hand
Sight: cannot read a large-print book
Continence: loses control of bowels at least once a week
Fits: has a *grand mal* attack at least once a month

Examples of conditions awarded 7 points:

Walking: cannot walk 200 yards without stopping or suffering
    discomfort
Sitting: cannot sit comfortably for more than half an hour without
    having to move from the chair
Standing: cannot stand for more than half an hour without having to
    move from the chair

Examples of conditions awarded 8 points:

Lifting: cannot pick up and carry a 5-lb bag of potatoes with either hand
Sight: cannot recognize a friend across the street
Fits: has at least one *grand mal* fit in 6 months

Example of conditions awarded 6 points:

Lifting: cannot raise an arm to put on a hat

Example of conditions awarded 3 points:

Continence: loses control of bladder at least once a month

Mental health test

Examples of conditions awarded two points:

Cannot answer the telephone and reliably take a message
Often sits for hours doing nothing
Needs encouragement to get up and dress
Needs alcohol before mid-day
Feels scared and panicky for no obvious reason

Examples of conditions awarded 1 point:

Cannot concentrate to read a magazine article or follow a radio programme
Cannot use a telephone directory to find a telephone number
Prevented by condition from doing leisure activities enjoyed before becoming ill
Gives up things because feels there is so much to do and feels tired or disoriented

Two of the more contentious aspects of unemployment benefit are the **'actively seeking work'** rule and the 'disqualification' rule:

1 *Actively seeking employment*. This test requires that a person take steps, within a week, to find work, for example making written or oral application for employment, seeking information from advertisers, agencies or employers. Claimants are given a leaflet which asks them to keep a record of any visits to job centres or interviews, etc., with copies of any letters sent. This activity is checked at 'restart interviews' and through random periodic checks. If it is thought a person is 'not trying hard enough', he or she will be asked to attend an 'Actively Seeking Review'. In considering a case, the 'adjudications officer' will look at all circumstances, including, for example, qualifications and the availability of vacancies, but apparently not at family/domestic commitments (although

crewing a lifeboat, taking an outward bound course or undertaking voluntary work will be given consideration!).

2 *Disqualifications.* Employees can be disqualified from eligibility for unemployment benefit by (1) dismissal for misconduct (negligence, etc.), (2) voluntarily leaving employment or training without just cause, (3) failing to take up employment or training opportunities, or (4) taking part in strikes or other trades disputes. Disqualifications can last for up to 26 weeks. A person may, therefore, be disqualified for refusing to apply for or accept the offer of a place on a training scheme notified to them by the Job Centre, or refusing the offer of a job. Similarly, a person will be disqualified for losing employment by reason of a stoppage of work due to a trade dispute at the place of employment (with some exceptions, including those people who are 'not directly interested'). If a person is disqualified from unemployment benefit, he or she may nevertheless be entitled to income support (a means-tested benefit) for dependent members of the household.

Additional rules that are seen as discriminating particularly against women are the requirement to state a willingness to take up available employment anywhere in the country and the need to demonstrate that adequate child care is available for those with children younger than school age.

The Social Security Act 1986, although primarily concerned with the system of means-tested benefits, introduced some important changes in contributory benefits, most notably the phasing out of the state-earnings related pension scheme (SERPS). The government justified this policy on the grounds that the value of contributions was far outstripped by the number of beneficiaries (partly as a result of the increasing proportion of elderly people). Workers were encouraged to take out personal pension plans, especially when their employers did not have a pensions scheme.

Non-contributory benefits which are not means-tested

A small number of benefits exist which require neither contributions nor means-testing. They are, strictly speaking, 'universal' benefits, available to all individuals who fall within certain needs categories, irrespective of means. The most important feature of these benefits is that by removing the need to qualify by work record, some of the worst obstacles to more comprehensive coverage are also removed. The major reason that few have been introduced is that, because they are financed from general taxation, they are difficult to justify in terms of **redistribution**, because they do not necessarily redistribute income from the better off to the poor. When such benefits have been introduced, as with the disability living allowance, the eligibility criteria have been very stringent, because the cost of non-contributory benefits is difficult for governments to justify. In 1990–91, these benefits accounted for 16 per cent of government spending on social security.

A distinction can be made between non-contributory benefits which depend on some kind of qualifying test and those which are available with no test of contributions, need or means. The latter generally depend on membership of a demographic category, for example children or old people. Benefits of this type are paid universally to certain classes of people, providing them with a minimum income level. The major advantages of such benefits are that they are easy and inexpensive to administer and take-up is high. The best known and most hotly debated of them is child benefit, available to all parents or guardians of children under 16 and children aged 16–19 who are still in full-time non-higher education. The only qualifying condition is a residence one (the child must 'generally' live within the UK, and either he or she must live with the applicant or the applicant must pay maintenance at the rate of at least the amount of child benefit). In addition to child benefit, one-parent benefit is available for lone parents and is paid with child benefit, subject to some limitations for those in receipt of certain other benefits.

The major argument for child benefit is that it protects families against poverty. It is also suggested that it is a visible acknowledgement of a social responsibility for child-rearing and it provides an income for mothers; for many mothers, it is the only independent income they have. However, it does not in practice prevent family poverty for the poorest. Families on **income support**, for example, do not benefit, as it is counted as part of their income in determining entitlement to benefit. The redistributive effect of child benefit is best seen as a transfer from people without children to those who have them and as an evening out of income over the lifetime.

Child benefit in Britain is less generous than in other countries:

> Austria ranked with the United Kingdom, Denmark and Germany in providing relatively parsimonious child support; Belgium, France, Luxembourg and the Netherlands were the most generous in their level of support.
>
> (Cass 1983: 42)

The Beveridge Plan envisaged a high level of support for families with children, but this has been eroded. Originally, families were supported both by allowances (a child benefit paid for second and subsequent children, which was taxable) and fiscal welfare (a tax allowance for children). In 1946, the combined value of the two, for a family with three children, was 27 per cent of average male manual earnings. By the 1980s, with the abolition of the tax allowance and the introduction of child benefit, a non-taxable allowance paid for all children, the value of state support had fallen to 13 per cent (Deacon and Bradshaw 1986).

Disability living allowance is an example of a benefit which is non-contributory and not means-tested but has a qualifying test. It is paid where a person under the age of 65 is so severely disabled physically or mentally that he or she requires frequent attention or constant supervision during the day and/or night and/or is unable to go out of the house unaided and without supervision. This benefit replaces, for those below retirement age, community care allowance and mobility allowance. (Those over retirement age continue to get community care allowance.) These benefits are intended to cover the additional costs of severe disability/long-term illness and enable disabled people to get out of their homes.

Means-tested benefits

Means-tested benefits are paid only to those who have limited capital and earnings. Assessment for eligibility involves an investigation by the authorities into 'means' – a 'means test'. In 1990–91, means-tested benefits accounted for 24 per cent of government spending on social security (DSS 1991b: 8). The Social Security Act (implemented in April 1988, following the Fowler Report) radically altered the structure of means-tested benefits. In setting out the objectives for reform, in the White Paper which proceeded the Act, the government stated:

> We believe that resources must be directed more effectively to areas of greater need, notably low-income families with children. We want a sensible co-operation between the social security and tax systems. And we want a system which is consistent with the government's overall objectives for the economy.
>
> (DHSS 1985)

The Act replaced supplementary benefit and family income supplement with new benefits and changed the housing benefit scheme (for further details, see CPAG 1995).

Supplementary benefit was replaced by income support, which scrapped all special needs payments and introduced a simpler system of personal allowances enhanced in some case with 'premiums' (such as lone-parent premium and family premium). The government's objectives were to streamline benefits, to reduce cost, to target public money more accurately and to reduce/eliminate the poverty trap. In 1990, one in seven people in Britain depended on income support; this included 17 per cent of pensioners, 24 per cent of disabled people and the long-term sick, 68 per cent of lone parents and 77 per cent of the unemployed (Bradshaw 1991: 25).

Family income supplement was replaced by family credit, a means-tested benefit available to low-paid workers with children, working at least 16 hours a week. (Families who were on family income supplement were entitled to free school meals for their children. This benefit was removed and replaced by a cash allowance. The advantages of this are that it is paid every week – unlike school meals, which are not usually available during school holidays – and it removes the stigma from children of visibly receiving free school meals. The major disadvantage is that the cash sum allowed per child is less than the charge for school meals in most areas.) A central objective in reforming support to those in employment on low incomes was to ensure that they would not be less well off than comparable families on income support.

Housing benefit provides support for rent and rates for those on low income but does not assist people to purchase their own homes (though owner-occupiers on income support have their mortgage interest paid after 6 months on benefit). It is means-tested and paid automatically to people on income support.

The 1986 Act also swept away discretionary single payments under the supplementary benefit scheme and set up instead the Social Fund, administered by DSS officers. There are two types of grant available from this

Fund, as of right, to people on income support or family credit: a lump-sum maternity needs payment and a funeral needs payment (depending on funeral costs), which were previously contributory benefits of near-universal availability. There is also provision for grants to be made from the Social Fund to assist in the promotion of community care, to help in establishing people in the community or help with travel expenses, etc. **Community care grants** have received some publicity recently, as their availability and scope has been questioned. Apart from these grants, all other help from the Social Fund comes in the form of loans, normally repayable by weekly deductions from benefits. One particularly contentious aspect of the Social Fund, however, is its cash-limited nature. In practice, loan officers have an annual budget, and once it is exhausted, no further loans can be made. In addition, repayments on loans cannot be used to regenerate the loans fund. The implication of this is that, if serious needs are presented once the fund is exhausted, they cannot be met. There is no formal right of appeal against decisions.

Evaluation of the reforms – that is, research undertaken since their implementation to determine if they have achieved their objectives – has explored the declared aims of targeting money to those most in need, eliminating the poverty trap and reducing complexity and dependency on state benefits. It does not suggest that the government's objectives have been achieved (see, for example, Abbott and Wallace 1992).

Universalism, selectivity and social security

Assuming that the role of social policy in general is to meet need and reduce poverty, it is possible to argue endlessly about the efficacy and desirability of different modes of provision. The debate over the balance of selective and universal services has a long history within social policy. Since 1979, however, the dominance of the ideology of the New Right has sharpened this debate, with increasing emphasis placed on notions of freedom, choice, **efficiency** and the elimination of dependency. On balance, the shift in the 1980s has been away from contributory schemes and towards an increase in selectivism and means-testing, on the grounds that targeting benefits reduces the cost and at the same time meets needs more effectively. The major problems with this kind of policy are low take-up and the poverty trap.

Reddin (1979) developed definitions of universalist and selectivist services that go beyond party political dogma to consider the real issues at stake and the implications for equity in social policy. In particular, he noted that one can have a very generous system of **selective benefits**, or conversely a very miserly universal benefit (such as child benefit or the old maternity grant of £25), their existence being more symbolic than a real benefit to the recipient. Reddin defined universal services as those which provide for a category of citizens, such as children or disabled people, without any direct regard for their incomes. Typically, such programmes are financed collectively and administered by government agencies. Universal services may discriminate on the basis of 'needs', but not on the basis of ability to pay. They are relatively inexpensive to administer and have a high take-up rate.

Selective services, on the other hand, are characteristically only offered to those individuals who are in some demonstrable need, usually defined by some form of means test. Selective services tend to be posed in the context of private market arrangements for the majority of citizens, with the provision of selective public services for a minority of definably poor people. (This comparison fits neatly into Titmuss' residual and institutional welfare model.) They are relatively expensive to administer and tend to have a low take-up rate, partly because of the stigma associated with them and partly because of the complexities of claiming. The British Attitude Survey in 1992 found that 55 per cent of respondents felt that people receiving social security benefits are made to feel like second-class citizens, with only 22 per cent of respondents denying this (Jowell *et al.* 1994a).

Reddin argued, however, that there is some blurring at the edges of these definitions and, further, that there are no truly universal services in Britain. In particular, he pointed to the fact that we all *contribute* unequally through rates, taxes and wage-related contributions (we need to consider the financing of the system) and also that very few services are actually *received* equally. Seeing a doctor, for example, is ostensibly free, but escalating prescription charges may introduce inequalities in outcome. In relation to social security, there are serious questions about the information available to the public about benefits, and questions about take-up rates.

One issue raised continually by the Conservative government in support of selective services concerns the flexibility of social policy in responding to changing needs. It has been argued, for example, that one of the reasons why the NHS is in difficulties over funding is that Bevan failed to anticipate the increase in demand for health care as a result of increased expectations and technological change. In other words, universal services have proved too much of a fiscal burden.

Reddin also argued that we must take account of the changing values of the wider community if we are to understand the impact of policies. This might include: attitudes towards the recipients of services by non-recipients (are they seen as scroungers, for example?) resulting in stigma and low take-up; the attitudes of the recipients themselves and their experience of means-testing (an estimated 60 per cent of family credit goes unclaimed); and, finally, the attitudes of the population as a whole towards taxation and the funding of services. Reddin concluded that what we have in practice is 'selectively financed universal services, selectively used'.

The debate surrounding the balance of universal and selective provision, then, takes place on two levels: first, on an ideological level and, second, in terms of administrative feasibility and **effectiveness**. Collectivists have typically favoured universal services as an important instrument in the achievement of equality through redistribution, while anti-collectivists have been fierce advocates of a residual model of welfare provision with an emphasis on non-intervention, the promotion of choice and the remedial treatment of poverty. For many proponents on the Right, universalism discourages thrift and erodes incentives to work.

We use the term 'Right' here loosely, as the Social Democrat MP David Owen (1981: 7) argued in similar vein that 'blanket subsidies breed complacency and undue financial indiscipline'. Owen went on to argue that we should abandon universality as the overriding principle and support the notion of 'portable private pensions', in order that existing public resources can be more effectively targeted at the central problem of poverty in old age. His position reflects the pragmatism often associated with the Social Democratic tradition, particularly in terms of affordability. Titmuss (1987), conversely, argued that this, in itself, *is* ideological, as it fails to raise questions about existing use of resources (such as tax relief to owner-occupiers) and is more concerned with issues of political expediency than with social justice.

However, accepting for the moment that we have a finite 'pot of money', some of the arguments in favour of selective services bear consideration. The principal arguments are as follows:

1 The selective approach enables existing money to be focused on the needy (targeted).
2 It prevents money being squandered on the already well-off (an argument often used in relation to child benefit).
3 It reduces public expenditure and stimulates the commercial sector, thereby increasing consumer choice.

One of the most problematic aspects of selective approaches, however, concerns the administrative difficulties of identifying and defining 'the poor'. Titmuss (1987) suggested that selective services operate as a form of **social control** and deliberately discourage take-up through the imposition of stigma, the denial of information and the sheer complexity of procedures. As such, they reinforce the work ethic and induce a sense of personal failure in their recipients. Jones (1992: 46), however, stressed that not all selective services are stigmatizing (giving the example of selective benefits for disabled people), while some universal services, such as the NHS, actually stigmatize in the way people are treated. As Abel-Smith and Titmuss (1987: 189) argued:

> The challenge that faces us is not the choice between universal and selective services. The real challenge resides in the question: what particular infrastructure is needed to provide a framework of values and opportunity bases within and around which can be developed socially acceptable selective services able to discriminate positively with the minimum risk of stigma in favour of those whose needs are greatest? There can, therefore, be no answer in Britain to the problems of poverty, ethnic integration and social and educational inequalities without an infrastructure of universalist services.

Conclusions

Social security is concerned with income maintenance across the life course and is not intended only as a measure for preventing or alleviating poverty.

The insurance principle means that citizens are required to provide for certain contingencies when in employment. However, the level of insured benefits is low and those entirely dependent on them have a very low standard of living compared with the majority of the population, as do those dependent on means-tested benefits. Those who are not insured by their employers and/or do not, or are unable to, make provision for old age, sickness and so on in addition to the state social security system are likely to suffer poverty and hardship. Only those who are themselves making additional provision or whose employer is doing so on their behalf are able to maintain an acceptable standard of living.

As indicated at the beginning of Chapter 4, there continue to be debates as to whether or not poverty exists in contemporary Britain as well as over ways to combat it. On the one hand, there are those who argue that low levels of benefit will encourage the poor to stand on their own feet and provide for themselves, and that the associated low level of taxation will encourage the better-off to work harder. Conversely, there are those who argue that there is little evidence that low taxation encourages more creation of wealth and that not only does poverty often mitigate against initiative, but lack of jobs is a major factor preventing the poor overcoming their poverty. The 1995 British Attitudes Survey found that only 25 per cent of respondents thought that if benefit levels were less generous more people would learn to stand on their own feet, and only 27 per cent thought that most of the unemployed could get jobs if they really wanted to do so. Conversely, 58 per cent thought the government should spend more on welfare benefits even if this led to higher taxation, while only 20 per cent disagreed (see CSO 1995: table 8.32).

If we accept that poverty is defined by an inability to enjoy a socially acceptable standard of living, then there remains considerable poverty in Britain. The major *immediate* cause is the inadequacy of social assistance to provide claimants with a high enough standard of living, as the majority of those in poverty are dependent on state benefits; for example, in 1993, those in the bottom fifth of households obtained 70 per cent of their income, on average, from such benefits. Additionally, the hard application of the means test and the way it is administered deters large numbers of people from claiming. At a local level, some councils have attempted to develop strategic approaches to poverty to alleviate the plight of the poor (see, for example, Box 5.3). However, if any significant impact is be to made on the problem, then central government needs to lead the way. The single most effective way of reducing the numbers of people in poverty would be to provide the unemployed with jobs. An effective employment and training programme combined with a minimum wage policy, a fair tax and national insurance system and restoration of child benefit could help substantially to alleviate the problem.

Three kinds of strategy have been advocated in the last few years to reform the social security system:

1 Negative income tax: a means of combining the tax and benefit systems in one.
2 Basic income as a right for everyone: every citizen would have a

---

Box 5.3 Strathclyde's strategic approach to poverty

1 Maximization of the provision of direct financial assistance to people living in poverty from sources under the council's own control (e.g. public transport concessionary fares and clothing and furniture grants).
2 Prioritization in favour of people living in poverty for the delivery of council services of benefit to them.
3 The provision of a money advice service for those in debt and combating illegal money-lending.
4 The provision of a welfare advisory service to help people to get the state welfare benefits to which they are entitled.
5 The promotion of community initiatives, including credit unions, as well as the support of voluntary and community organizations involved in initiatives to address poverty.
6 All departments and committees of the council are required to carry out an assessment of the impact of their policies on people living in poverty during the annual budgetary process.
7 The collection and dissemination of information on poverty in Strathclyde, to inform policy making.
8 The making of representations to central government about the need to reduce poverty by policies aimed at reducing unemployment and **low pay**, changing the taxation system and reforming the criminal justice system.

Source: Adapted from Strathclyde Regional Council (1993).

---

universal entitlement to a tax-free basic income from the state and would pay tax on the whole of income from other sources.
3 Major reform of the social security system to ensure a basic adequate income and the gradual elimination of the need for means-tested benefits.

Negative income tax proposals have been criticized for not solving the problems of the present system (e.g. Lister 1989), and basic income is seen as costing too much to attract support (Atkinson 1989). The third option is seen by many commentators as feasible, although the politics of the Conservative government over the last 15 years have been in the opposite direction (Lister 1989; Walker 1990). Government, it is suggested, is unwilling to reduce the benefits of the better-off to improve the living conditions of the poor (Walker 1993). The key issue is adequacy of benefits; benefits must be sufficient to enable those who receive them to participate fully in the society in which they live, if poverty is to be eliminated.

Summary

- Building on the previous chapter, this chapter has examined in more detail the structure of the social security system in Britain. Demographic changes have had a major impact on public expenditure, an increasing proportion of social security payments going to elderly people.

- Benefits can be categorized according to the method of financing them and the forms of entitlement. Some benefits are contributory (depend on a contribution record) whilst others are non-contributory (universal). The latter can be sub-divided into means tested (selective) and non-means tested benefits.

- Even contributory benefits may involve complex systems of entitlement which may function to reward/sanction certain forms of behaviour. An example of this would be the 'actively seeking work rule' which is applied to unemployment benefit.

- The debate over whether benefits should be provided on a selective or universal basis has long dominated discussion about social security. The former is supported on the grounds of economy and efficiency (in that they can be targeted on certain groups most in need) whilst proponents of universal benefits argue that problems of non-take-up and stigma reduce the effectiveness of means-tested benefits and involve excessive incursion into private lives of recipients.

Further reading

Child Poverty Action Group (annual) *National Welfare Benefits Handbook*. London; CPAG.

Spicker, P. (1993) *Poverty and Social Security*. London: Routledge.

Walker, C. (1993) *Managing Poverty*. London: Routledge.

PRIVATIZATION AND SOCIAL WELFARE

Introduction

This chapter focuses on the impact of **privatization** on welfare provision both in terms of the development of commercial provision (purchased by individual consumers and by employers) and also in terms of its impact within existing state-provided services. It considers in some detail two areas in which privatization has had a large impact in recent years. The first is the impact of privatization and consumer-oriented practices within the state sector itself; here the focus is on changes within the NHS. We look at public attitudes towards privatization and raise questions concerning the implications of privatization for the changing role of the state. The second reflects the growth of parallel private provision in the area of pensions policy. This section considers **occupational pensions** as one dimension of private provision.

The election of the Conservative government to power in 1979 led to a renewed emphasis on the role of the commercial sector in the provison of welfare. Not only have the Conservatives argued for a reduction in the role of the state sector, but also that commercial sector management practices and the 'discipline' of the market should be introduced into the state sector. Thompson (1992) has identified seven themes underpinning the government approach to the role of the **public sector**: privatization, delegation, competition, enterprise, deregulation, service quality and curtailment of union powers (see Box 6.1). We would also add to the list tighter control and regulation by the government, with the imposition of spending limits and of standards.

Box 6.1 Main themes of government policy and the privatization of welfare

Main themes	Characteristics	Evidenced in
Privatization	Privatization of state monopolies	Privatization of gas, water, rail, telephones
Delegation	Delegation of budgeting authority	NHS reforms
Competition	**Competitive tendering**	Community care reforms Reforms in education
Enterprise	Encouragement of social markets	Reforms in social services Creation of TECs Creation of city technology colleges
Deregulation	Deregulation of some public services	Local government reforms
Service quality		Citizens' Charter
Curtailment of trades union powers	Trades union reforms	

Underlying principles
Efficiency
Effectiveness
Value for money
Managerialism

Source: Adapted from Thompson (1992: 24).

The role of the commercial sector in the provision of welfare is by no means new; indeed, the commercial sector has dominated social provision in some areas. The levels of both political and public support for privatization indicate a broad consensus in some areas (such as housing) co-existing with fierce dissension in others (such as health care). This chapter focuses on developments in commercial welfare defined as the purchase of social goods in the marketplace by consumers. It is important to distinguish between two forms of commercial provision at this stage: that selected and paid for by individuals and that provided and paid for by employers. The latter category was termed 'occupational welfare' in Titmuss' (1955) social division of welfare.

Welfare provision by employers, for their employees, is similar in many respects to commercial provision. Indeed, it is purchased from the commercial sector by the company concerned and has the effect of shifting responsibility away from the state as primary provider. Both forms of commercial provision have also been recipients of state subsidies and both serve the goal of promoting private industry and profit. Occupational welfare does, however, differ in important respects, because membership of any such scheme does not imply a conscious choice, as such, on behalf of consumers. Such occupational benefits typically form part of a broader package of employment-related **remuneration**. Membership of a private health care scheme, for example, may 'come with the job', and may not otherwise have been selected by the employee concerned. The employer may either offer such benefits as a form of paternalism, as a 'perk' or incentive to their employees, or they may receive fiscal benefits from the state as an incentive to provide such benefits – perhaps even as a substitute for increased remuneration. Recent developments in the area of occupational and personal pensions are discussed later in this chapter.

In addition to the purchase of alternative or additional welfare services in the commercial sector by individual consumers and employers, privatization has brought about broader changes in the way statutory bodies and the voluntary sector work. The introduction of commercial sector management techniques, case management and contracting-out of functions in these sectors has changed the ways in which many public services operate. For example, the introduction by the Education Reform Act 1988 of local management of schools and procedures enabling individual schools to opt-out of local government control and become budget-holding bodies funded directly by central government, illustrates the broader impact of privatization within the public sector. Here the government has promoted the development of what have been termed **'quasi-markets'** as a means of increasing efficiency and effectiveness by introducing the discipline of the market into former public monopolies. The implementation of the community care reforms in 1993 has created a social market in domiciliary and day care, with local authority social services departments being required to purchase services from the commercial and voluntary sectors (see Chapter 9). The establishment of five semi-autonomous agencies to administer social security is part of the same process. The impact of privatization on the internal operation of the NHS is dealt with in more detail later in this chapter.

The political context of recent privatization

Political developments in the last decade or so have resulted in some major policy shifts away from universal statutory provision towards greater reliance on the commercial sector. Such shifts have been brought about by a range of factors, some of which reflect ideological commitments and others matters of expediency. Examples of the former can be seen in the commitment of the New Right to reinforce the 'traditional' role of the family (and of patriarchal social relations) in society, reduce public dependency and promote individualism. On the other hand, demographic pressures and changes in family structure have led to concerns about the fiscal sustainability of the post-war Beveridgean welfare state founded on principles of universalism and social citizenship. The key concern here is often said to be the need to contain public expenditure, but linked to this concern is a particular view of the market and the price mechanism as the superior means of allocating social goods and facilitating consumer choice.

The principle of universal provision was introduced in the post-war welfare state as a means of ensuring a broad equality of entitlement to fundamental social resources, by virtue of citizenship or membership of that society, irrespective of wealth and occupational status. Thus the health status and educational opportunities of post-war British citizens were no longer dependent upon their ability to pay for services. This system was based upon principles of social justice and not egalitarianism however: the persistence of income and wealth inequality was acceptable and socially just once the principle of merit was preserved and citizens could be genuinely said to have equal life chances.

To some extent, this system of broad equality in welfare resources was able to co-exist with a small commercial sector restricted to a minority of very wealthy individuals without calling into question the legitimacy of the underlying framework (although the compatibility of private education with equality of educational opportunity was undoubtedly questioned). The best way to preserve the goals of universalism was not to prevent private provision (which may be interpreted as an unreasonable restriction on individual freedom) but to ensure that the quality of state services was of a sufficiently high level to restrict the growth of commercial provision (as in the Swedish system; see Esping-Anderson 1990). This balance was maintained in many services, at least, until fairly recently. In the post-Thatcherite welfare system, however, the positive encouragement of the middle classes, through incentives and welfare retrenchment, to buy into commercial welfare schemes and opt-out of state-provided services, increases the risk of a tiered system of welfare entitlement and threatens to destroy the foundations of social citizenship. In the context of health care, for example, the government has increasingly intervened to actively promote private health care through fiscal subsidies to both individuals and employers at the same time as the public have witnessed the closure of NHS wards and hospitals across the country. It could, of course, be argued that by encouraging those who can afford to pay for private care to opt out of state provision, it is possible to target state resources more effectively on those in real need. The problem with this approach, however, is that the development of two-tier systems of welfare provision can lead to **socially stigmatized** services and the haemorrhaging of highly trained staff into more lucrative and attractive posts in the commercial sector (as has been recently argued in the context of opted-out hospitals).

The simple retention of a framework of universal benefits (such as the

NHS, child benefit, the state pension and state education) does not in itself, however, safeguard citizenship when equality of access is no longer matched by equality in use. The growth of a commercial sector, complemented by the residualization of statutory obligations, may result in hierarchies of welfare entitlement co-existing within a theoretically universal system. Thus, while universal entitlement to a basic contributory pension exists in the UK, a very high level of supplementation by occupational and private provision, and a reduction in the value of the basic pension, suggests a marked deviation from the citizenship principle. The same could be argued in relation to the NHS, where the combination of real cuts in quality of service with public perceptions of reduced quality has led to the expansion of commercial sector alternatives (subsidized by the state). Where this takes place and a significant proportion of the population either possess or aspire to possess commercial services, to describe state services as universal is to make a theoretical point and not to describe the reality of differential entitlement.

The impact of New Right ideology appears to have brought about a shift from a tolerance of parallel private provision to a view of private provision as inherently better and morally superior to statutory provision. The introduction of financial incentives and subsidies to both employers and individual 'consumers' has led to the expansion of the commercial sector ideal to the point of undermining the solidaristic foundations of the welfare state itself. This can be seen most clearly in the promotion of home ownership as the morally superior form of **housing tenure**, which encourages individual and family responsibility. Such ideologically motivated pressures to extend home ownership to all households including those on low incomes have, in recent years, been tempered by economic reality, as the recession – and in particular house-price deflation – have left this flagship of privatization sorely shaken and the public more reticent.

In addition to the impact of the New Right on domestic politics, Taylor-Gooby (1994) further argues that accession to the European Community has increased pressure for policy convergence across European welfare systems. These, he argues, are dominated by Bismarckian, insurance-based welfare systems and not by the British 'universal state safety-net model' (p. 26). These systems of welfare provision tie social entitlement much more closely to employment status, with benefits closely linked to insurance-based contributions by both employees and employers.

This chapter begins by reviewing evidence from recent surveys of public attitudes towards welfare policy and then focuses on the development of privatization in two areas of social policy: health care and pensions policy. The impact of privatization on social inequality and the changing role of the state form two key themes in the ensuing discussion.

Privatization and the public

The Introduction to this chapter suggested that the impact of privatization has been uneven. Nowhere has the commercial sector dominated welfare policy more, for as long, and with apparent public approval, than

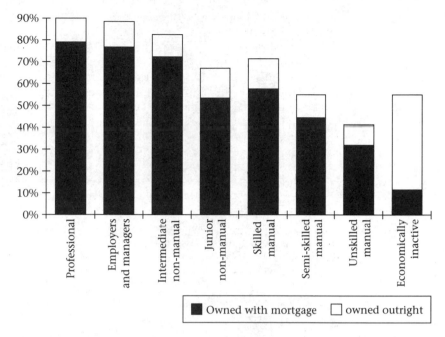

Figure 6.1 Housing tenure by socio-economic group, 1994.
Source: Derived from CSO (1995: 182) Table 10.19.

in the housing field. Indeed, some 70 per cent of households in Britain either own or are buying their own homes. This figure does, however, conceal some variation between different socio-economic groups (see Fig. 6.1). On the other hand, the proportionate use of commercial sector educational services is still relatively small, accounting for less than 7 per cent of all pupils in 1992–93 (CSO 1995: 48). The proportion of people covered by commercial health care schemes also remains small; although the number of people with private medical insurance increased sharply between 1971 and 1990, it fell back slightly to 6.8 million in 1993 (CSO 1995: 141).

We now consider the extent of public support for the privatization of welfare services. The important thing to come out of this review is that, in the minds of the public – and those politicians with an eye to their electoral vulnerability – it is dangerous to generalize about privatization. Indeed, the findings suggest that the public responds differently to the prospect of privatization depending on the service in question.

Public attitudes to privatization

The 1993 British Social Attitudes Survey (Jowell *et al.* 1994b) sought to assess the extent to which the recent restructuring of welfare provision in the UK has been supported by the public. In an article in the report Taylor-Gooby (1994) notes that the main motivation, at present, for choosing to use private provision is the belief that individuals can purchase superior

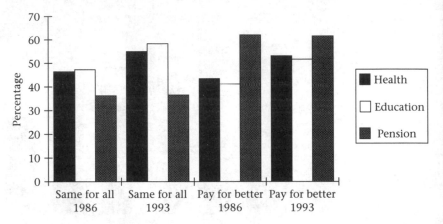

Figure 6.2 Attitudes to private provision: Percentage of respondents saying that provision should be the same for everyone as compared with those saying that people should be able to pay for better provision, by sector.
Source: Taylor-Gooby (1994: 31).

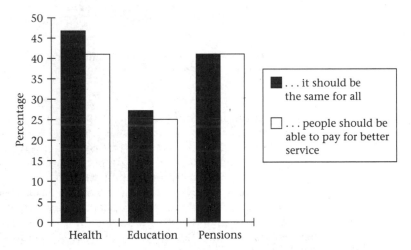

Figure 6.3 Percentage of respondents claiming which service should be the government's top priority (i.e. support for the private compared with the public sector).
Source: Taylor-Gooby (1994: 32).

provision. The survey therefore asked respondents whether people who are able to afford commercial provision should be able to pay for a better service. The results are shown in Fig. 6.2.

The survey further found that, even for those who expressed support for the right of people to purchase commercial services, they regarded this as supplementary to statutory provision and not as a substitute. In other words, they still felt that the state should provide basic services. Indeed, the results showed a remarkable consensus regarding priorities in government spending (Fig. 6.3). On the basis of these findings, Taylor-Gooby (1994: 32) concludes:

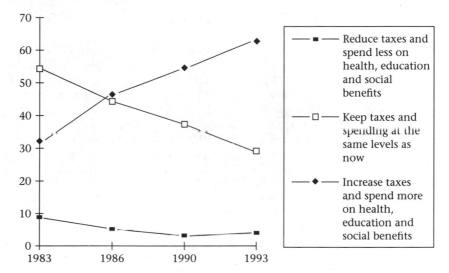

Figure 6.4 The 'spending consensus'.
Source: Derived from Jowell *et al.* (1994).

There is every indication then that those who want privilege in the **private sector** are almost as likely to want good basic state services as the rest of the population. Private provision is not seen (yet, at least) as an alternative to the welfare state.

In the areas of health and housing, public support for the view that those able to afford it should be able to buy better quality commercial services has fallen sharply since 1986. Only with respect to pensions do the majority of the public continue to support the principle of purchasing better provision in the commercial sector.

This 'spending consensus' (Lipsey 1994), evident in every British Social Attitudes survey since the series began in 1983, holds even when the prospect of increased taxation is raised (see Fig. 6.4). Lipsey concludes on the basis of the most recent survey that, 'The British people want more state spending even if it means more taxes' (p. 1).

Privatization and health care

Since 1979, successive Conservative governments have been concerned both to encourage the development of private health care, including the commercial sector, and to encourage the public sector to behave more as if it were commercial. While there has been no renunciation of a commitment to the availability of comprehensive health care, questions have been raised about the legitimate scope of state activity. Despite this, public support for the concept of the NHS remains high (Jowell *et al.* 1995 a, b).

Public expenditure on health care

The proportion of total health care spending by the state in Britain has been one of the highest in the developed world and remains so despite a decline in its proportionate contribution, from over 90 per cent in 1979 to 85 per cent in 1991 (Ginsburg 1992; Abbott and Giarchi, in press) and 83.6 per cent in 1995 (CVCP 1995). *Total* health care expenditure in Britain in real terms is lower than the OECD average, and the gap has increased since the 1960s. In 1995, the annual expenditure on health care per head of population was $914, compared with $1765 in The Netherlands, over $1400 in France and Germany and $1542 in Switzerland (CVCP 1995). In fact, most OECD countries, including the United States, have a higher level of *public* health care spending per head of population than Britain (Ginsburg 1992).

The lower level of spending is compensated for by the lower administrative and labour costs of the NHS compared with other health care systems, although the number of doctors and hospital beds per 10,000 citizens is also lower. For example, Germany provides 30 doctors per 10,000 population and 108 hospital beds, compared with 14 doctors and 64 hospital beds in Britain (CVCP 1995). Until the implementation of the National Health Service and Community Care Act 1990, about 5 per cent of total health spending in Britain went on administration, compared with about 25 per cent in the United States (Ginsburg 1992). There is some evidence that the 1990 reforms have increased administrative costs and necessitated an increase in the number of administrators (Ham, 1994). For example, for every 100 hospital administrators and clerical staff in 1980 there were 130 in 1992, with the major growth between 1989 and 1992 (Department of Health 1993: fig. 16). The Institute of Health Management (1994) has indicated that since 1989 an additional 12,000 managers and 26,000 clerks and administrators have been appointed. In the same period, the number of nurses employed has dropped by 26,000.

As LeGrand and Robinson (1994a) have suggested, privatization is a reduction of the state's activity in one or more areas of providing, subsidizing or regulating health care. The Conservatives have tried to encourage growth in the private health care sector on the one hand, and on the other to reduce the costs of the NHS. There has been a modest increase in private health care, and while there has continued to be a real increase in public expenditure, this has not been sufficient even to keep pace with the demands made by the increasing number of elderly people. Between 1960 and 1975 government spending on health care grew twice as fast as real GDP, but between 1979 and 1988 this declined to a factor of 1.7. It is probably fair to say that spending on the NHS has been sufficient to keep it going, but no more (House of Commons Social Services Committee 1986, 1988).

The commercial sector is seen by the Conservatives as being more efficient, better managed and more responsive to the needs of the consumer than the public sector, which is insulated from competition, dominated by the trades unions and therefore inefficient, wasteful and unresponsive to patients. On the one hand the Conservatives have sought to reduce the public cost of health care by encouraging more people to use commercial services, and on the other to introduce greater efficiency into the NHS by 'managed' competition – arguing that competition among providers will not only reduce costs but increase effectiveness and responsiveness. Conservative policy in relation to health care thus covers a range of different elements, including:

1 The encouragement of the growth of non-NHS provision, including the commercial and voluntary sectors.
2 Encouragement of employer-provided health care.
3 Increased charges for NHS services.
4 Competitive tendering and contracting out of NHS ancillary services.
5 The introduction of private sector management styles and methods into the NHS.
6 The introduction of managed markets and the purchaser/provider split in health care.
7 An increased emphasis on informal care.

The next subsection looks in more detail at developments in some of these areas.

The development of private and commercial health care

The underlying philosophy of the NHS was that health care should not be a commodity provided and consumed in a market. The main principle informing the funding of the service was that only public provision of health care could deliver an acceptable level of equity in access to and use of resources, as well as making the most effective use of the resources available for health care.

However, private and commercial health care were not completely eliminated when the NHS was introduced in 1948. When the NHS was founded, about 270 hospitals remained outside it, which often treated NHS patients on a contractual basis. Apart from the commercial sector, consultants employed by the NHS were also permitted to undertake private practice, and there were private (pay) beds in NHS hospitals. The NHS has nevertheless played the dominant role in the supply, control and financing of health services in Britain, and until the Labour government began the phasing out of pay beds in NHS hospitals in the mid-1970s, the majority of private patients were treated in NHS facilities. One consequence of the reduction in NHS facilities for treating private patients was an increase in privately run facilities.

The Conservative administration elected to power in 1979 was ideologically committed to the expansion of private health care, although there has been a marked reluctance on behalf of the British people to move even to a partial, let alone a total, reliance on private care. The government has had to step back from any radical reforms that change the basic right to free treatment based on need and funded out of general taxation. Any attempt to change the nature of the NHS has met with strong opposition, and the administration has been forced on a number of occasions to reiterate a commitment to retaining the NHS. It was clearly an intention of the Conservatives, for example, to encourage more people to take out private health insurance, and although there has been an increase, it has not reached the 25 per cent coverage rate the government had once hoped to achieve. A perception that there has been a reduction in services has not resulted in people turning to commercial treatment, but in demands for improvements to health services provided by the state. Opinion surveys have consistently demonstrated that there is considerable support for increased taxation specifically designed to increase health care spending. This does not mean that some people are not paying privately for some health care needs, and there is some evidence of an increase in the number of people paying for **alternative/complementary medical care** (Leadbetter 1990; Saks 1994). Saks, for example, suggests that one in seven of the population go to practitioners of alternative health care for treatment. This move is often made, however, when **conventional medical care** provided by the NHS has proved ineffective. People may also be prepared to pay for some forms of treatment if these are not available on the NHS, especially if they see themselves as having caused the problem. A good example here would be physiotherapy treatment for sports injuries. A lack of available NHS facilities may also result in people turning to commercial treatment (e.g. terminations and infertility treatment).

The percentage of the population relying totally on private health care is extremely small. The majority of the population have an NHS general practitioner (family doctor). Indeed, access to private hospital (consultant) health care is most frequently obtained through a GP, as is access to NHS consultant health care. The main growth in commercial health care provision has consequently been in hospital care. Although the Conservative government abolished the Health Services Board charged with closing down pay beds in NHS hospitals, the number of such beds has been drastically reduced. The main growth in commercial facilities has been in for-profit-making acute hospitals and nursing homes for the elderly. In particular, there has been a significant increase in the number of hospitals owned by US companies. In 1979, there were three US-owned hospitals with a total of 366 beds; by 1986, however, there were 31 acute hospitals with 2239 beds (Higgins 1988). Between 1979 and 1985, there was a 35 per cent increase in commercial acute hospitals and a 54 per cent increase in the number of beds they provided. In 1979, 72 per cent of all private beds were in non-profit private hospitals such as those run by the Nuffield Hospital Trust; by 1987, this had fallen to 49 per cent. In 1981, the government stressed the need for health authorities' planning to take into account existing and planned private provision (DHSS 1981b).

The reforms of the Conservatives have been aimed at encouraging more people to take out private health insurance and enabling consultants to undertake more private work. In 1971, only 2 per cent of the population were covered by private health insurance, and this rose to a peak of just under 8 per cent in the mid-1980s; in 1993, it stood at just under 7 per cent (CSO 1995: table 8.12). Only about a fifth of private patients have no health insurance (Nicholl et al. 1989). The 1981 Budget introduced tax relief on private health insurance premiums for those on low incomes and permitted employers purchasing health insurance for employees to set the cost against corporation tax. The 1989 Budget introduced further tax relief on health insurance premiums for those aged 60 or over.

The contracts of hospital consultants were changed in 1980 so that they could engage in private practice without losing the advantages of working within the NHS. A full-time consultant can now earn up to 10 per cent of his or her gross NHS salary from private practice. A consultant on maximum part-time contract can make unlimited earnings from private practice and only forfeit an eleventh of the NHS salary, as opposed to two-elevenths previously. The consequence of this change has been on the one hand to increase the number of consultants accepting full-time and maximum part-time contracts, and on the other to increase the amount of private practice.

The commercial sector benefits in a number of ways from the existence of the NHS. The NHS is forced to accept all patients who seek help; the commercial sector can select whom they choose to treat, leaving the state to provide for the chronic sick and those needing expensive treatments. Private health insurance premiums increase with age, making it difficult for older people, with an increased risk of ill health and developing chronic medical conditions, to afford to continue paying premiums or indeed to take over the cost from their employers on retirement. Health insurers limit the amount available to cover the cost of treatment and the length of time over which they will cover treatment. Health checks to screen out those with pre-existing conditions, and premium rates based on actuarially calculated risk factors designed to keep claims low and prevent premiums from rising unduly, mean that private health insurance tends to be held mainly by middle-class people in employment (Higgins 1988). The commercial sector also benefits from the fact that the NHS trains medical and nursing staff and the professions allied to medicine. The commercial sector makes virtually no contribution to the training of staff. The services of NHS general practitioners are also an important element in supporting private health care. The majority of private patient cases come via their NHS general practitioner; indeed, a condition of health insurance is that the patient be referred by their GP. The commercial sector also benefits from the state because health and local authorities purchase services from them, especially beds for older people in nursing homes. Finally, the commercial sector benefits from being able to use NHS facilities – especially 'high-tech' ones – that the sector could not afford to purchase. The main concern, however, has been that the existence of private health care not only enables the purchase of treatment superior to what is available on the NHS, but also breaches the principle of equity. Being able to pay for treatment enables people to obtain it earlier than they would on the NHS, and in some cases this increases the waiting time for those who cannot afford to pay.

Charges for NHS treatment

The NHS was intended to be free at the point of delivery and based on need, not ability to pay. The principle of free treatment was first breached in 1949, when it was decided to levy charges on visitors and subsequently on people not ordinarily resident in Britain. The latter provision was not widely used until 1982, when the government introduced complex rules

for charging overseas visitors. These rules were seen as racist and in particular as linked to immigration controls.

In 1951, the Labour government introduced charges for spectacles,
dentures and NHS prescriptions. These charges remained modest until
1979, accounting for less than 2 per cent of NHS income. Since 1979,
charges for NHS treatment have increased dramatically, and income from
this source has risen to over 4 per cent of total expenditure. Dental,
optician and prescription charges have all increased. Those not exempt
from payment (children and young people in full-time education and
those on low incomes) now frequently have to pay the full cost of dental
treatment and of spectacles, while the cost of an NHS prescription can
actually be greater than the cost of the medication prescribed. Indeed,
changes to the payments made to dentists for treating NHS patients mean
that many are prepared to take on new patients only if they are 'private'.
This makes it especially difficult for those who cannot afford to pay to get
dental treatment if they have to leave the list of the dentist who has been
treating them or have not been registered with a dentist in the past.

Contracting out of NHS services

The contracting out or purchasing of services from commercial companies, as opposed to providing them 'in house', has always been possible
within the NHS. However, until the return of the Conservative government in 1979, the norm was for services to be provided by NHS employees.
In 1979, 2 per cent of NHS domestic cleaning, 14 per cent of laundry and
far less than 1 per cent of catering was provided by the commercial sector.
Since 1979, there has been a push to privatize ancillary services, the
government arguing that the commercial sector can provide more efficient and effective services than those provided by employees. On the one
hand, the government was concerned about the power of trades unions
among ancillary workers and the way in which they disrupted hospital
services in 1978–79, and on the other they argued that the commercial
sector could provide the services more cheaply. Competitive tendering in
particular was seen as a way of ensuring that an adequate service was
provided at lowest cost. However, Ascher (1987) has argued that the need
to economize played only a small part in the decision to introduce compulsory contracting out of services, and it is not clear that the claimed
savings of £1000 million pounds per annum (Independent, 15 June 1988,
p. 6) have been put back into patient care.

The government instituted compulsory competitive tendering for NHS
services in 1983: health authorities were required to put hospital cleaning, catering and laundry out to tender. The full implementation of the
requirement was delayed, and the process was also undermined by resistance from health authorities and ancillary workers' trades unions. In the
first round of competitive tendering, only a small percentage of contracts
went to private firms, and the Ministry of Health put pressure on health
authorities to award more. Health authorities were also forced to remove
'fair wage' clauses from service contracts (they had already been prevented from tying contracts to the minimum terms and conditions of
employment of NHS staff; see Ascher 1987).

By December 1985, 40 per cent of contracts had been awarded to the commercial sector (Ascher 1987); however, this percentage had declined to 23 per cent by 1990 (Joint NHS Privatisation Unit 1990; MacGregor 1990). One in four private contracts had not been adequately fulfilled, and 5 per cent of private contracts had been withdrawn. By the late 1980s, health authorities were awarding fewer contracts to the commercial sector and renewing fewer of those already held there (Joint NHS Privatisation Unit 1990). However, between 1981 and 1988, the number of NHS ancillary staff fell by 33.5 per cent and the pay and conditions of employment of those remaining in employment also fell (Joint NHS Privatisation Unit 1990). Pollock and Whitty (1990) argue that poor conditions of work, poor wages and inadequate staffing levels are likely to have adverse consequences for patient care, whether the services are provided by commercial contractors or 'in house'.

Employer-provided health care

The extent of employer-provided health care is difficult to determine, as it has not been the subject of research in Britain (May and Brunsden 1994). Titmuss (1955) has pointed to the 'hidden' welfare benefits received by those in employment. We do know, for example, that some 45 per cent of private health care insurance is paid for by employers (Higgins 1988). May and Brunsden (1994) argue that within an individualistic, risk-minimization, self-help and lifestyle modification framework, there has been an increase in corporate health care in the last 10 years. They suggest that the major aim is to increase work performance, with an emphasis on individuals taking responsibility for their own health and regulating their own behaviour. Balcombe *et al.* (1993) estimate that 75 per cent of British employers provide some form of 'wellness intervention', such as single-factor screening and/or specialist responses to health issues such as alcohol abuse, substance abuse and HIV/AIDS. An increasing number of employers are providing specialist screening for female employees, and health promotion measures such as 'healthy eating', 'no smoking' or 'no alcohol' policies. Many employers provide sport and recreational facilities for employees. However, apart from paying for the premiums for private health insurance, few employers provide direct health care, although an increasing number are providing counselling, including personal counselling.

The introduction of commercial sector management styles and methods

The Conservative government elected to power in 1979 was convinced that the problems of funding in the NHS were at least in part due to inefficient management, that the NHS was over-administered and under-managed (Hunter 1980). As Hunter (1994: 2) has indicated:

Strengthening management, raising its profile and status, developing management skills and competencies, investing in management information systems and so on are seen as crucial to the success of policies directed towards securing value for money and improved quality of care for a given budget, while holding individuals and organisations accountable for what they do.

The concern was that the NHS was bureaucratic, paternalistic, unresponsive to the needs of patients and organized to meet the needs of doctors; that is, it was a service dominated by administrative hierarchies and professionalization. A need was perceived for general managers to be introduced to manage the NHS.

Following a review by Griffiths (1983), general managers were introduced in 1983, with the intention of bringing about a cultural change in the NHS with the introduction of commercial sector management practices. These included planning, target setting, monitoring performance against pre-set targets, stricter control over the professional and manual labour force costs and performance, ensuring greater consumer satisfaction, and rewarding good performance. General managers were introduced at all levels of the NHS, appointed on short-term contracts with **performance-related pay**.

The new managerialism that underpinned the creation of the new management structures emphasized excellence and leadership rather than technical expertise in management science – or, indeed, knowledge of health or the NHS. The government had intended that a significant number of general managers should be recruited from the commercial sector to infuse the NHS with industrial and commercial managerial talent. However, a majority of those appointed in the first round were former NHS administrators, nurses, community physicians, consultants and former officers from the Armed Forces. Indeed, Pettigrew *et al.* (1992) suggest that the most effective management occurred when the managers understood the health service, and that the 'best' managers were former NHS administrators.

Cox (1991), summing up the impact of the introduction of general management prior to the implementation of the National Health Service and Community Care Act 1990, argued that there was little evidence to indicate that greater control than previously was exercised over medical decision-making. However, at ward level, nurses had felt an increased managerial pressure on productivity and on the skill mix. The most radical change (discussed above) was the contracting-out of services, and this had tended to create a more marked feeling of an 'us' and a 'them' among ancillary workers.

The new general managers were encouraged by the government to develop income-generation schemes to help fund NHS activity. The Health and Medicines Act 1988 facilitated this development and, in 1989, the Department of Health issued guidelines on the scope of income-generation schemes. As a consequence, schemes such as renting shop space in hospitals, renting advertising space in casualty departments and the selling of land for car parks developed rapidly. The income from such schemes is, however, very modest compared with the overall cost of the NHS.

There was also a growth in the internal NHS market in the late 1980s, advocated by Enthoven (1985). By 1987, some London teaching hospitals were charging directly for services for out-of-district patients rather than waiting to be compensated 2 years in arrears through adjustment to their district financial allocation. By 1988 in East Anglia, such an internal market within the national health system had been established (Timmins 1988).

In 1987 and early 1988, there was a funding crisis in the NHS and considerable concern that people, especially young children, were not getting the emergency treatment they needed. The Conservative government argued that this was a result not of under-funding but of inefficient use of resources and poor management. Following a review, a White Paper – *Working for Patients* (Department of Health 1989a) – was published, to be followed by the National Health Service and Community Care Act 1990. The major objectives of these reforms were that doctors would be held accountable for their actions, that there would be a real shift in power from doctors to managers and that a consumer-oriented service would result. Hunter (1994) has indicated that the 'new public management' introduced into the NHS in the 1980s and early 1990s had eight distinct features:

1 An emphasis on patients as customers.
2 Commercial sector management styles.
3 Competition 'created' through the use of managed markets and contracting.
4 Explicit standards and measures of performance.
5 A greater emphasis on outputs and results.
6 Disaggregation of public bureaucracies into agencies operating on a user-pay basis.
7 Stress on performance indicators for managers.
8 Stress on discipline in resource use and unit improvement.

Cox (1991) has suggested that policies designed to introduce good management and limit the power of the medical profession should be welcomed. However, he argues that the government has not always been prepared to give NHS managers the independence to manage and has not provided an adequate funding base. Furthermore, he suggests that some reforms have been motivated more by an ideological commitment to a 'small-business' approach than by the aim of securing a planned and rationalized corporate provision. This, he indicates, has on the one hand lowered the income and morale of ancillary staff and on the other prevented general managers from taking the control over standards they feel could have been achieved if they had employed their own staff.

NHS managed markets

In the 1990s, the Conservatives carried out the first major reform of the NHS since its introduction in 1948. The National Health and Community Care Act 1990 legislated for internal/managed markets with a split between the purchasers of health care on the one hand and the providers on the other. There seems to have been a general acceptance that changing the basic principles on which the NHS had been founded would be extremely unpopular. Nevertheless, the government were intent on making the NHS more effective and less inefficient. They maintained that it was wasteful of public money, that too much was spent on administration and not patient care, and that the NHS was not responsive to the needs of customers. They argued that this was because it was not subject to the discipline of the market – that is, to competition. The 1989 White Paper, the recommendations of which were implemented in the 1990 legislation, was heavily influenced by reforms that had been introduced in the United States, which had proved effective in reducing spiralling costs there, but the main source of finance for health care in Britain continued to be general taxation. The NHS was also to remain the main provider of health care for the vast majority of the population, with commercial provision acting as a supplement to the NHS rather than a substitute.

There were five key elements contained in the legislation in relation to health care:

1 A separation of purchasers and providers of health care.
2 **NHS Trusts** were to be established which were to be responsible for providing services.
3 District health authorities were to be responsible for the purchase of services from providers on behalf of their populations.
4 Larger GP practices were to have the opportunity to become **fund-holders** and purchase health services on behalf of their patients.
5 The use of contracts/service agreements to link purchasers and providers.

The intention was that the reforms would establish competition among providers of health care services. As the finance would follow the patients, it was assumed that providers would become responsive to the demands of patients and those purchasing services on their behalf.

District health authorities were to become responsible for purchasing health care services to meet the needs of their populations from a variety of providers, including the commercial sector. Also, GP practices with more than 11,000 patients could become fundholders and take on responsibility for purchasing the majority of health services for their patients. The health authorities could continue to run services (district managed units) or units could form NHS Trusts and 'sell' services to district health authorities and GP budget-holders.

By 1995, the purchaser/provider split had been fully implemented – all NHS services are now provided by self-governing Trusts. By 1993, there were 1682 **GP fundholders**, covering 36 per cent of the population. East Anglia and Oxford had the highest proportion of patients in fundholding practices (44 per cent) and NE Thames the lowest (19 per cent) (see Department of Health 1995). District health authorities and FHSAs have merged, in the main, and had been completed by 1996 (see Figs 6.5 and 6.6). The number of regional authorities, and their role, has been reduced in an attempt to reduce administrative costs. The government did not feel that it was necessary to evaluate the reforms. However, some evaluation has been undertaken. Clearly, the provider/purchaser split has been achieved and competition is reasonably well developed, at least in some parts of the country. Appleby *et al.* (1994), for example, indicate that three-quarters of the hospitals in the West Midlands were operating in a competitive market by 1994. However, there is likely to be less

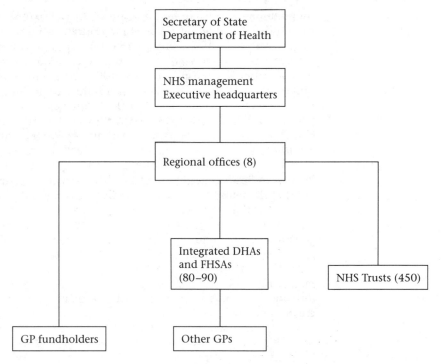

Figure 6.5 The structure of the NHS with effect from April 1995.

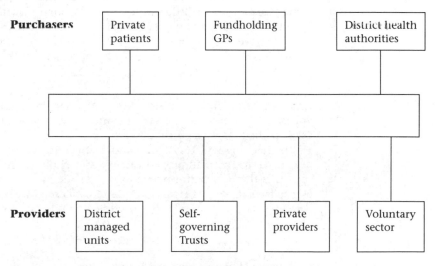

Figure 6.6 The purchaser/provider split in the NHS.

competition in less populated regions; to the extent that it does exist, patients will be expected to travel long distances (Abbott and Payne 1990). Glennester *et al.* (1994) suggest that GP fundholders can ensure a more rapid and responsive service for their patients, but there is concern about equity. A BMA survey in December 1993, for example, indicated that four in ten hospitals allowed patients of fundholders to jump queues for treatment (quoted in Institute of Health Management 1994). Mahon *et al.* (1994) found that patients were not consulted about hospital referrals, but that most patients were happy for their GP to make the choice. Jones *et al.* (1994), examining the experience of health of older people before and after the reforms in terms of accessibility, choice, communication and quality, indicate that they had felt little benefit. LeGrand (1994) points out that the reforms will ultimately be judged by the extent to which they improve quality, efficiency, choice, responsiveness and equity. He questions whether they will bring about the desired improvements and suggests that the prerequisites for an efficient and equatable market were not met when they were introduced.

Ham (1994), in summing up the gains and losses, suggests that the main gains have been providers being more accountable for their performance and purchasers being able to focus on health needs, attaching greater priority to action designed to improve health. The losses, he suggests, are increased management costs, the threat posed to equity due to the ability of GP fundholders to buy preferential treatment and services for their patients, and the fact that money is not following the patient:

> This is because most of the contracts negotiated by purchasers are *en bloc* contracts in which providers receive a sum of money each year to deliver a range of services to a local community... These contracts are not sensitive to changes in productivity during the year and they therefore represent little improvement, from a provider's perspective, on the old system of global budgets. To this extent the efficiency trap which gave rise to the reforms still exists and the rhetoric of patient choice is confronted with the reality of patients following the money rather than vice versa.
>
> (Ham 1994: 4)

Ham is reasonably optimistic, however, that competition between providers will intensify as purchasers and providers of health care become used to their new responsibilities.

Whether this will result in a more efficient, responsive and equitable health service with improved quality and choice is not certain. What is certain is that the performance tables on the Patients' Charter published by the Department of Health are more concerned with the throughput of patients than quality of service, choice, equity or effectiveness of treatment (see Table 6.1).

The impact of private provision on income in old age

We have already demonstrated the high level of public support for increased government spending on pensions, second only to support for the

Table 6.1 League tables: The position of Derby City Hospital NHS Trust

Indicator	Derby (%)	England average (%)
Outpatient appointments	94	88
Cancelled operations (actual number)	—	7
Day surgery		
Inguinal hernia repair	44	29
Laparoscopy with sterilization	71	73
Waiting times (selected disciplines)		
Number seen within 3 months		
General surgery	82	72
Trauma and orthopaedics	91	50
Gynaecology	79	76
Ear, nose and throat	32	55
Number seen within 12 months		
General surgery	98	95
Trauma and orthopaedics	100	90
Gynaecology	99	98
Ear, nose and throat	96	94

Source: Derby City Hospital NHS Trust (1995).

NHS. On the other hand, these surveys also reflect some support for the view that the public should be able to purchase 'better' provision in the commercial sector if they wish. Although the majority of respondents see pensions as a top priority for increased government spending, many also support the idea of additional (as opposed to alternative) compulsory occupational schemes. Faced with the problem that 'pensions are taking up a larger and larger part of government spending', the most popular option, supported by over 75 per cent of respondents, is the further development of occupational welfare, making it compulsory for employers to set up pensions schemes.

This section considers in more detail the issue of income support for pensioners. It examines the sources of income support within the mixed economy of welfare and outlines some of the pressures on existing structures, which have led to calls for increased levels of commercial contribution and restructuring of the state provision.

Sources of income in old age

The main sources of income for retired persons in Britain at present include, in rank order:

- state social security
- occupational and personal pensions
- investment income
- earnings from employment.

In this area of social policy, the contribution of the informal and voluntary sectors is either less significant or effectively concealed by available

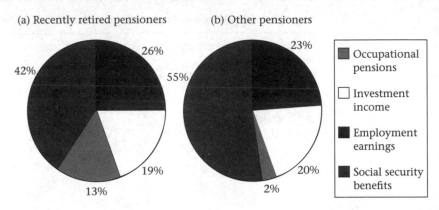

Figure 6.7   Sources of income among (a) the recently retired and (b) 'other' pensioners.
Source: CSO (1995).

data. We do not know, for example, the level of income support given to pensioners by family and friends, although this may, in reality, amount to a significant contribution. Figure 6.7 indicates the different sources of income for two broad groups of pensioners: those 'recently retired' (defined as single women aged 60–64, single men aged 65–69 and retired couples where the husband is aged 65–69) and 'others'.

More recently retired pensioners are considerably less likely to be dependent on the state pension alone than those who have been retired for some time. This is partly due to increased income from investments and occupational pensions among recently retired pensioners, but also due to substantial reductions in earnings from employment for those people who have been retired for some time. These figures indicate the high level of dependence upon state social security payments as the main source of income in old age.

In April 1995, the value of the state pension was as follows:

- basic pension for a single person: £57.60 per week or £2995.20 per year;
- basic pension for a married couple: £92.10 per week or £4789.20 per year.

While these sums can hardly be said to be generous, the very large number of claimants results in pensions forming a major and growing component of social security expenditure.

The implications of demographic pressures on pensions spending

Population ageing over the next 50 years is predicted to lead to substantial increases in the number of elderly people and in increases in the average amount of time a person survives in retirement both in absolute terms and as a proportion of the total population. For although the state pension is theoretically 'contributory', in that workers contribute throughout their working lives through national insurance payments, these contributions are insufficient to meet the costs of retirement. This has led to

Table 6.2 Projected population in Britain aged 65 and over, 1990–2030.

Year	Number (millions)
1990	8.5
2000	8.3
2010	8.4
2020	9.5
2030	11.3

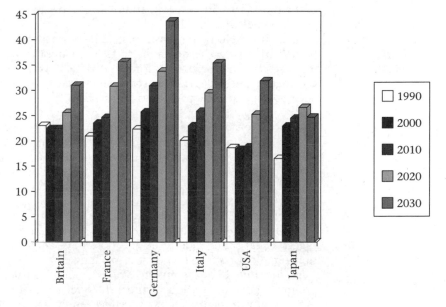

Figure 6.8 Age dependency ratios in selected countries, 1990–2030.
Source: OECD (1988: 29).

concern regarding the increasing 'burden' the elderly will place upon the population of working age. This 'burden' can be expressed by means of 'dependency ratios' (a measure of the number of dependent elderly persons per 100 paid workers). Table 6.2 shows the projected increases in the population of retired persons in Britain and Fig. 6.8 the dependency ratios in selected countries.

The future of the state pension

The basic state pension in Britain was established in 1948 as part of the Beveridgean welfare state and provided a universal flat-rate benefit for all individuals who reached pensionable age (60 for women and 65 for men) and who had made adequate national insurance based contributions during their working lives. Until recently, the value of the basic state pension remained fairly stable at around one-fifth of average male earnings.

The Social Security Pensions Act (SPA) 1975, which was passed following a national debate regarding the appropriate balance between state and employer responsibility for pensions, retained the basic national insurance based pension and required employees to contribute to a new State Earnings-Related Pension Scheme (SERPS) or to an approved employer's pension scheme which would pay a guaranteed minimum pension (GMP) and widow's benefits at least as generous as SERPS (Groves 1991: 39). SERPS represented an attempt to extend earnings-related pensions to all payers of national insurance. With entitlements based on the 'best twenty years' of earnings, it was designed to meet the needs of the lower paid and intermittent employees. In recent years, the desirability and sustainability of the universal state pension, and of SERPS, has been called into question on a number of grounds.

First, the value of the basic pension, in real terms, has been eroded, particularly since the decision in 1980 to uprate the state pension by increases in prices alone (before that date it was uprated in line with earnings or prices depending upon which was higher). There is also evidence to suggest that pensioner households experience a higher rate of price inflation than other households, further reducing the purchasing power of the state pension (Oppenheim 1990: 69). Second, there is concern over the impact of demographic pressures on public expenditure as the number of dependent elderly people in society increases. In 1990, people over retirement age numbered 10.5 million in Britain, or 18 per cent of the population (Oppenheim 1990: 68). The 1995 issue of Social Trends (CSO 1995) reported that nearly half of all social security payments in 1993–94 were made to the elderly. Third, there is evidence of increasing affluence among some sections of the retired population, which suggests that many elderly people now have adequate individual provision for themselves and therefore no longer require welfare support.

By the mid-1980s, concern over the fiscal sustainability of SERPS prompted its modification in the 1986 Social Security Act. Through this Act, the government sought to 'reduce public expenditure as well as to increase labour mobility and self-reliance: SERPS was seen as a disincentive to building up individual provision' (Field and Owen 1993: 5). The Act introduced measures which severely diminished benefits accruing from SERPS, replacing (with effect from 1999) the 'best twenty years' rule with 'lifetime average earnings', and introduced new financial incentives for those who 'opted-out' of SERPS and/or certain employer's schemes into individual personal pensions. These reforms widened the range of schemes eligible for contracting out and, for the first time, provided financial incentives for people to contract out of SERPS and into occupational and private pensions (Fry et al. 1990: 36).

Conservative government legislation has thus 'conceptualised the state retirement pension merely as a "foundation" on which more adequate financial provision for old age can be based therefore considerably increasing the complexity of the pensions' (Groves 1991: 42) and increased the range of 'options'. People now have the 'choice' of supplementing their basic state pension entitlement with an occupational pension, SERPS, the purchase of a private pension or a permitted combination of these. While, arguably, this choice has always existed, a new framework of fiscal subsidies has been put in place to influence and facilitate choices, effect-ively subsidizing the commercial sector.

Taken together, these trends have led to the suggestion that univer-sal provision might be supplemented or even possibly replaced by more effectively targeted, selective, state benefits, providing those in need with a higher rate of support and complemented by increasing use of com-mercial and occupational schemes (Fry *et al.* 1990: 7). The following subsection considers the effect of these changes on social inequality in old age.

Privatization and inequality in old age

The impact of increasing commercial provision in the pensions field on standards of living and levels of social inequality among the pensioner population is more difficult to assess than in many other areas of social policy, as it has a less immediate effect. Changes in policies implemented today may take some 20 or more years to come into effect as people buy in commercial provision or opt out of SERPS. Under the present legisla-tion, it is not possible to be a member of both a personal pension scheme and an occupational pension (unless the person has more than one job). Figures on membership in 1992 (OPCS 1994) indicate a gender imbalance with more male employees belonging to a pension scheme. Eighty-nine per cent of professional men working full-time were members of either an occupational or personal scheme, compared with 75 per cent of pro-fessional women working full-time and only 32 per cent of professional part-time women (OPCS 1994). For all social groups, the likelihood of belonging to a scheme increased with age, although male and female part-time workers aged over 55 were less likely to belong to a scheme than those in younger age groups. These figures cause some concern given the high level of female part-time working in Britain and the projected expan-sion of 'atypical' work, for both sexes, across Europe.

Analyses of membership of schemes by employee characteristics also in-dicated a relationship between pay levels and membership: the higher the gross weekly income, the more likely are both men and women to belong to employer's schemes or to have a personal pension. Among those work-ing full-time, then, 80 per cent of men and 82 per cent of women who earned more than £300 per week belonged to a scheme, compared with only 35 per cent of men and 26 per cent of women earning between £100 and £150 per week. People working in larger undertakings were also more likely to belong to an occupational scheme. Figures 6.9 and 6.10 look at membership of schemes by sex and socio-economic group.

In order to interpret Figs 6.9 and 6.10, it is important to remember that, under existing legislation, one can belong to either an occupational or personal pension, but not both (except in particular circumstances). The graphs show considerable variations in levels of membership between socio-economic groups. Seventy-six per cent of professional full-time men and 67 per cent of women belonged to employer's schemes and 25 and 23 per cent, respectively, to personal pensions schemes. For unskilled workers,

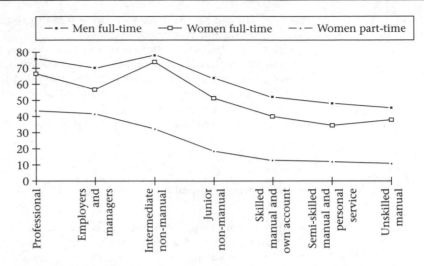

Figure 6.9 Membership of current employer's pension scheme by sex and socio-economic group (employees aged 16 and over excluding Youth Training and Employment Training).
Source: OPCS (1994: 100).

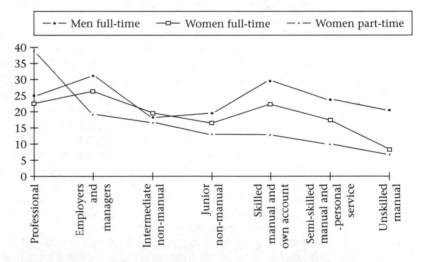

Figure 6.10 Membership of personal pension schemes by sex and socio-economic group (employees aged 16 and over excluding Youth Training and Employment Training).
Source: OPCS (1994: 101).

however, only 45 per cent of full-time men and 37 per cent of full-time women had occupational pensions, and only 21 and 8 per cent, respectively, had personal pensions. Men and women in the intermediate group were most likely to have occupational pensions with employers, and managers most likely to have personal pensions schemes.

It is somewhat difficult to assess the relative merits of either occupational or personal pensions schemes in terms of the benefits received on retirement. With the former, payments are typically based on the number of reckonable pensionable years' contributions and favour employees who have worked in the same employment or industry for long periods. These schemes may therefore penalize more mobile workers who could end up 'acquiring a string of "frozen" occupational pensions, the real value of which deteriorates as they approach retirement age' (Fry et al. 1990: 41) In the face of flexibilization and casualization of the European workforce, it is to be expected that occupational schemes, as they stand, may prove dysfunctional to wider structural changes and an increasingly unreliable source of income in old age. The transferability of these pensions to other undertakings in Europe is uncertain and is currently under discussion by the European Union.

With personal pensions, on the other hand, payments are typically based upon the financial performance of the pension fund. This clearly involves greater risk – particularly given the poor performance of investments in recent years – but may suit those who have to wait a relatively long period before retirement or wish to have more flexibility over their working lives, perhaps moving between careers or organizations. Members of personal pensions schemes may also make proportionately higher contributions.

What is clear, however, is that in the future – even more so than today – levels of income in retirement will mirror the distribution of income during working life. For those whose experience of the labour market has been one of unemployment, low pay, unskilled and part-time work, are likely to suffer from poorer quality pensions and lower standards of living in old age.

Women make up around two-thirds of the elderly population and are far more likely than men to experience poverty and dependency in old age because of their lower earnings, interrupted work patterns (due in part to caring responsibilities and unpaid work) and greater life expectancy. The Child Poverty Action Group recently reported that, in 1991, 'even adjusting for different retirement ages, there were over three times as many women pensioners as men dependent on income support' (Oppenheim 1990: 68). Groves (1991: 39) concluded her analysis of the impact of pensions policies on women by expressing concern that:

> The principles underpinning current government policies on financial provision for old age and, especially, the respective roles and responsibilities envisaged for the state, the employer, the private insurance market and the private individual in making such provision, call into question some very important aspects of female financial dependence and independence within and outside marriage.

The projections for elderly Black people suggest a similar picture of social polarization and inequality. Disadvantage in the labour market and high levels of unemployment are compounded by contribution-based benefits which tend to discriminate against those in intermittent and/or low-paid work. A Child Poverty Action Group report came to the following conclusions:

The State Earnings Related Pension Scheme (SERPS) was weakened and is to be based on a lifetime's earnings instead of the best 20 years rule. This will indirectly discriminate against ethnic minorities: people who have come to this country in their thirties and forties and will have a shorter working life and thus a lower retirement pension.

The inducements to take up private pensions will merely reinforce existing inequalities in the labour market and thus not benefit the majority of people from ethnic minorities.

(Oppenheim 1990: 71)

Glennester's analysis of policy developments leads him to suggest that the Conservative government's 1986 reforms represent a move in the direction of a 'compulsory private model' where:

The state would provide a basic flat-rate pension, but there would be no guarantee that it would be preserved. By not uprating it in line with inflation, the state pension could be phased out. Everyone would have to be a member of a private occupational or a personal private pension scheme. Income support would remain for existing pensioners, but in order to ensure that people did not simply rely on it, membership of an occupational pension scheme would become compulsory.

(Glennester 1992: 260)

Such a system of state-regulated occupational and commercial pensions, he contends, is closer to the practice of many other European countries, but

... without very stringent regulation tend[s] to perpetuate or even exaggerate the inequalities of working life. Those who have been healthy and had a fortunate employment history, as well as getting better pay, get much better retirement terms.

(Glennester 1992: 261)

Privatization: Reducing the role of the state?

So while shifts in the responsibility for income support in old age may reduce public expenditure on the basic state pension, and possibly enable the funds available to be targeted more effectively on the poorest pensioners, they imply increased statutory responsibility in the regulation of employers and commercial provision. Without such regulation, those people who fail to make provision for their old age will fall on to the state for support.

Since 1986, every full-time employee earning over a certain basic minimum wage must technically be a member of either SERPS, an occupational or personal pensions scheme. In addition, the government also sets the minimum level an employee must contribute. Individual 'choice' is thus restricted by the state to three alternative forms of pension contribution:

- direct taxation by the state (SERPS);
- indirect taxation by an employer (occupational pensions); or
- direct payment into a commercial scheme (personal pension).

The state further intervened in 1986 to require all new pensions in the commercial sector to provide limited inflation-proofing for private pensions so that their real value does not decline so steeply over time.

Shifting the responsibility on to employers and individuals thus calls for increased state regulation in the pensions field. It has also resulted in *increased* public expenditure, mainly through fiscal incentives and subsidies. Precise and accurate figures on state subsidization of private and occupational pensions are difficult to obtain. The following figures do, however, indicate the financial implications of some of these fiscal subsidies to the Exchequer (Glennester 1992: 258):

- Employees do not pay tax on that part of their income they pay as contributions to pension funds (total cost in 1989–90: £31,800 million).
- Employers' contributions are treated as an expense and are not taxed (total value in 1989–90: £3100 million).
- Investment income from superannuation funds is not liable for tax (total value 1989–90: £4100 million).
- Lump sum payments up to certain limits at retirement are not liable for tax (total value 1989–90: £1000 million).

In addition to these costs, there were 'special incentive payments' to encourage people to opt-out of SERPS, and those who did so paid the lower amount of 7 per cent of earnings (instead of the 9 per cent required under SERPS). The government then pays the private scheme a sum equal to the 2 per cent difference, a form of direct subsidy to the commercial sector.

Glennester (1992) argues that tax allowances on pension funds should be abolished on grounds of both efficiency and equity. In relation to efficiency, such subsidies divert funds away from other forms of investment (because of the higher rate of return), which may damage the economy in the long term. Higher income groups also benefit disproportionately from this form of government subsidy where tax relief is based on the highest rate of tax payable by the contributor. The system is thus inequitable, as higher rates of subsidy accrue to those in higher tax brackets.

The next section shifts the focus from pensions policy to housing and considers the implications of privatization in the area of housing policy for both public expenditure and local autonomy. Housing has been chosen as an example here because it is the area in which private provision has dominated. Home ownership has also received cross-party support as the bedrock of a stake-holding society.

The costs of private housing

If we look at privatization in the area of housing and the promotion of owner-occupation in the UK it is clear that policy changes in favour of increased owner-occupation have resulted in some major shifts in public expenditure. Malpass and Murie (1994) note that, although housing cut-backs accounted for over 75 per cent of all public spending reductions in 1980, with capital spending falling to less than a tenth of its 1976–77 real level:

> To see the pattern of housing public expenditure solely in terms of cuts is however misleading. On top of expenditure cuts there has been a transfer in the balance of effective public expenditure away from the public sector and direct investment and towards the support of owner occupation.
>
> (Malpass and Murie 1994: 107)

What appears at first sight as a net reduction in public expenditure, may, when subjected to more rigorous analysis, amount to simply a trans-fer of subsidy. The public expenditure implications of shifts in housing policy have been obscured by problems with statistics. The government's view of what constitutes public spending as set out in the annual White Paper on Public Expenditure excludes two important areas of spending on housing: housing benefit appears in figures on public spending but not as housing expenditure, while mortgage interest tax relief is not defined as public spending at all.

These two components of housing expenditure have dominated the pattern of housing finance in the 1990s as the general subsidy to local authority housing (through the Housing Revenue Account) has been vir-tually eliminated (Willis and Cameron 1993: 51). The cost of housing benefit for council and private tenants in 1992–93 was some £7.5 billion and the cost to the Exchequer of mortgage tax relief amounted to three times the cost of other housing expenditure in 1990–91 (Malpass and Murie 1994: 108). If we add to these subsidies the costs of the govern-ment's 'Right to Buy' policy and discounts on council house sales and the increasing costs of supplementary benefit help with mortgage costs for those people who have lost their jobs or are unable to keep up their mortgage payments, a picture emerges not of public expenditure cuts as a result of privatization, but rather of a massive transfer of housing re-sources. This situation has been described by Malpass and Murie (1994: 109) as:

> . . . a transfer, from the public sector to the support of owner occupa-tion, from investment to subsidy, and from the subsidisation of the production of public housing to the subsidisation of individual con-sumption reflect[ing] other priorities which have tended to override public expenditure considerations.

The role of the state in relation to housing policy has not, therefore, declined but shifted and public expenditure has increased. These policy shifts reflect a broader ideological commitment to owner-occupation as a preferred form of tenure, one which promotes independence, individual responsibility and profit. In the process, we have witnessed a marked centralization of responsibility and control as local housing departments have seen their autonomy cut (with the imposition of council house sales, a moratorium on new building and changes in the financing of council housing).

Conclusions: Privatization or changing state role?

We have seen that the role of commercial provision has increased in many areas of social policy. Public support for the commercial sector varies depending upon the service in question, with private housing – and, to a lesser extent, pensions – receiving public support, while the expansion of private health care receives little public support. Even where there is public support for the growth of private 'options', these are seen principally as a means of supplementing state provision and not as a replacement.

One of the key arguments used to support the growth of the commercial sector has been the perceived need to contain public expenditure on universal state provision during a period of demographic change and escalating costs. While this remains an important factor, the evidence suggests that this is only one consideration and broader, ideologically motivated considerations often assume priority. In practice, privatization or the introduction of commercial sector management practices often increases the overall costs of service provision. In addition, the shifting balance also implies a stronger role for central government in the regulation and financing of provision coupled with important restrictions on local autonomy (and the role of local government) in some areas.

Summary

- The election of the Conservative government to power in 1979 led to a renewed emphasis on the role of the commercial sector in welfare provision.

- The proportionate contribution of the private sector varies depending on the type of service. In the field of housing, for example, the private sector has long dominated provision whilst in the area of healthcare it has, until recently, played a very limited role.

- Public support for privatization similarly varies with strong support for owner-occupation and private pensions but much weaker support for the erosion of public sector health and education services.

- The privatization of welfare has taken a number of forms including both the encouragement of alternative, parallel, private provision: the contracting out of certain services and the introduction of fees and private sector management techniques within the state sector.

- The growth in privatization policies both within the NHS and in relation to income support in old age will lead to increased levels of social inequality and polarization.

- Progressive privatization in some areas has not resulted in the anticipated reduction in public expenditure but simply a transfer of resources from the state to the private sector. This is most clearly seen in the case of private residential care.

• High levels of regulation will be required if the transition from state
social security to reliance on personal private provision is to prevent
people from falling on to the state for subsistence support.

Further reading

Clarke, J., Cochrane, A. and McLaughlin, E. (eds) (1994) *Managing Social
Policy*. London: Sage.
Field, F. and Owen, M. (1993) *Private Pensions for All: Squaring the Circle*.
London: Fabian Society.
Forrest, R. and Murie, A. (1988) *Selling the Welfare State*. London: Routledge.

THE CHANGING ROLE OF THE VOLUNTARY SECTOR IN THE PROVISION OF SOCIAL WELFARE

Introduction

This chapter considers the changing role of the voluntary sector in the provision of welfare. We are talking here about a sector that provides welfare, not volunteers who give their time to provide help. Volunteer labour is an important element in many voluntary organizations, but volunteers can also work in the state sector and are an important element in the informal sector. Although the role of the voluntary sector predates the welfare state, its proportionate contribution within the welfare state has, until recently, been relatively limited, but the provision of welfare was dominated by the voluntary sector until the founding of the welfare state in the 1940s. Recent renewal of interest in the voluntary sector reflects rapid expansion both in service provision in some key areas of social policy and in political support for the concept of voluntarism as a morally superior form of provision. Strong support for voluntary action comes from across the political spectrum. In many ways its ideological importance has been as important as its contribution to welfare provision.

However, a distinction needs to be made between volunteering and the voluntary sector, concepts which tend to get muddled together in the current political/moral rhetoric of active citizenship. What is discussed in this chapter is the role that the sector does and could play within the mixed economy of welfare and the welfare state. On the one hand, there are those who see a minimum role for the sector, seeing voluntary aid as patronizing and outdated; on the other, there is the view that the sector should play a central role. Those who hold the former view tend to see the sector as mainly concerned with the giving of charity to others, while those who take the latter view tend to stress the role of mutual aid (or self-help). A rather different view is to see the sector as one provider of welfare among others, part of a welfare partnership. These different views relate not only to different political perspectives but also to different understandings of what the sector is and what it can contribute.

The Victorian legacy

For many, especially on the left of the political spectrum, the founding of the welfare state in Britain in 1948 meant that there was no longer a need for a voluntary sector in the provision of welfare. It was assumed that, to the extent that the sector persisted, its role would be minimal and marginal. Welfare state services made philanthropic organizations redundant, and national insurance and social housing did away with the need for mutual aid. The universal, comprehensive provisions made by the state, it was assumed, would replace the patchy, patronizing and peculiarly selective provision made by the voluntary sector.

In the nineteenth and early twentieth centuries, voluntary organizations had played a central role in meeting welfare needs, often in areas where the state made little or no provision. Davies (1987: 182), for example, has indicated that in the nineteenth century

> . . . most people were involved in an array of voluntary organisations which met the needs of most for education, leisure, assistance or simple conviviality. The common response to any social problem, personal or collective, was mutuality and co-operation.

Waine (1992), similarly, has pointed out that by the beginning of the twentieth century, the key social services were provided by voluntary organizations, including unemployment benefits, health insurance and beds in the voluntary hospitals.

The voluntary sector was important both in providing services where the state provided none and in providing services alongside those provided by the Poor Law. In Victorian Britain, the sector was comprised of two main elements: philanthropy and mutual aid. Philanthropy was concerned with charitable giving and the provision of services, mainly by the middle classes to the working classes. Volunteering was often seen as a Christian duty, and one goal was the 'civilizing' of the working class.

Originally the labour was provided by the middle classes themselves, as in the Visiting Movements, but by the end of the nineteenth century voluntary organizations often employed working-class women to do the actual visiting, while middle-class women gave their voluntary labour to management and fund-raising. Services were often patronizing. In Chapter 2 we discussed the Charity Organizations Society, which was founded in the late nineteenth century to regulate charitable giving 'in the best interests of the poor' and in society's best interests – that is, to ensure that charity did not destroy the motivation to take paid employment nor encourage the worst habits of the poor such as excessive drinking.

Not all voluntary work patronized and regulated the poor in this manner, however. The majority of hospitals founded in the nineteenth century for treating acute illnesses were paid for by subscriptions from the wealthy. The 'child saving movement' of the late nineteenth century, exemplified by Dr Barnardo's, was influenced by evangelical Christian values. It played a vital role in bringing to attention the abuse and neglect some children experienced and provided homes for orphaned and abused children. The philanthropic voluntary organizations of the nineteenth century were often involved as much in campaigning as in provision; they acted as pressure groups on behalf of the disadvantaged. Prison reform and health reforms, for example, were heavily influenced by voluntary organization campaigns.

Mutual aid, which also developed in Victorian Britain, is based on voluntary collective efforts, which both serve self-interest and support the interests of others. The most common mutual aid schemes were voluntary assistance for income maintenance and health care, but other examples include cooperative associations (both for goods and for labour), self-help groups, trades unions and building societies.

Mutual aid is therefore to be strictly distinguished from philanthropy; mutual benefit associations are not run by one set of people with the aim of helping another, but as an association of individuals pledged to help each other (a form of reciprocal altruism). Assistance was not a result of charity but of entitlement, earned by regular contributions paid by all members. The Foresters, a leading Friendly Society, indicated that:

> For certain benefits in sickness . . . all the Brethren in common subscribe to one fund. That fund is our Bank; and to draw therefrom is the independent and manly right of any Member, whenever the contingency for which the funds are subscribed may arise, as freely as if the fund was in the hand of their own banker; and they had but to issue a cheque for the amount. These are not BENEVOLENCES – they are rights.
>
> (quoted by Green 1993: 50)

Modern voluntary organizations can also be divided into philanthropic institutions and mutual aid associations. Taylor (1991) has identified three phases in the development of the voluntary sector in Britain since the 1940s. During the first phase, in the 1950s and 1960s, she suggests that voluntary organizations played on the whole a marginal role, many finding it difficult to establish a niche for themselves, though some succeeded in doing so. The Women's Voluntary Organization, for example, played a central role in supplying meals on wheels, although these were paid for by local government. Others continued to provide a service alongside state provision, for example Dr Barnardo's and the National Society for the Prevention of Cruelty to Children; others disappeared (e.g. the voluntary hospitals were nationalized).

The second phase, beginning in the late 1960s, saw the development of campaigning groups, influenced by the Civil Rights Movement in the United States, both for and of disadvantaged and marginalized groups. Major voluntary organizations such as Help the Aged, the Child Poverty Action Group and Shelter were founded in this period, as were the disabled rights movement and other self-advocacy groups. The last of these, often regarded as new social movements, are self-help and populist, concerned with mutual aid and political campaigning (Oliver 1990).

The most recent phase, beginning in the 1980s, has been the encouragement of voluntary organizations to take a strong role in the mixed economy of welfare. This has been encouraged by the New Right on the basis of both economic and moral arguments. While New Right commentators have often stressed the moral case for voluntary organizations, and especially for mutual aid (see, for example, Green 1993), it is the economic case that has dominated (see Abbott and Wallace 1992). Many on the centre and left of the political spectrum have also stressed the important values of mutual help and communality that voluntary organizations can engender, stressing the value of communitarianism. However, feminists have been critical of the renewed emphasis on volunteering and voluntary organizations, pointing out that these often rely on the unpaid and often unrecognized labour of women (Finch and Groves 1983).

The voluntary sector in the welfare state

Since the foundation of the welfare state, the 'values and virtues' of the voluntary sector have received support, in particular, from a tradition referred to as the 'middle way' in British political thought, encompassing the ideas of conservatives such as Macmillan, Butler and Gilmour, but also 'reformists' such as Keynes and Beveridge (George and Wilding 1994: 46). According to this tradition, the voluntary sector was not competing with the welfare state, as such, in providing welfare; the two were mutually supportive. Beveridge himself saw the health of the voluntary sector as an index of the general health of society (Beveridge 1948, cited in George and Wilding 1994: 56). Within the context of universal income maintenance, the NHS, state education provision and the greatly expanded role of the social services, he saw the voluntary sector as performing a quite specific range of tasks – giving advice, organizing leisure, pioneering and experimentation (Beveridge 1948: 9). The Beveridge model of the relationship between the state and the voluntary sector went virtually unchallenged until the late 1970s, when advocates of welfare pluralism suggested extending the role of the voluntary sector (e.g. Gladstone 1979; Hadley and Hatch 1981).

Richard Titmuss (1968), in perhaps the first major study of voluntarism in British social policy in the 1960s, envisaged a symbiotic relationship developing between the voluntary sector and the state with the growth of the welfare state actually encouraging the voluntary ethic in society. Indeed, Titmuss saw the development of the welfare state itself as a civilizing force, an instrument of social justice that could promote the 'art of giving' in society. Social welfare constituted 'a major force sustaining the social conscience' (Abel-Smith and Titmuss 1987: 113). Titmuss saw the development of state responsibility in welfare as a necessary response to increasing levels of complexity and specialization in modern capitalist societies to the point at which personal bonds of family, kinship and community were no longer able to meet the needs for social welfare. Some form of formally organized system of social support was therefore required, to be administered by strangers and paid for collectively by strangers: 'Altruism by strangers for strangers was and is an attempt to fill a moral void created by applied science' (Abel-Smith and Titmuss 1987: 115). Titmuss' own research involved a comparison of systems of blood doning in Britain and the United States. In the United States (in the 1960s at least), blood was treated as a consumption good to be traded in the marketplace; donors and recipients were 'prisoners of commerce'. This was contrasted with the system in Britain where blood was (and still is) given by volunteers in a 'social services institution' answering the 'conscience of obligation' (Abel-Smith and Titmuss 1987: 191). The system of blood doning in the United States has changed in recent years as a result of concerns over the quality of 'purchased' blood, particularly following the spread of AIDS. This case study was used to demonstrate Titmuss' profound belief that state welfare encouraged voluntarism. For Titmuss, voluntary associations and volunteering by individuals should provide only a supplementary role within terms set out by the state and should not provide charity that was in any sense demeaning (Pinker 1993). Titmuss did not believe that anybody should have to rely on voluntary organizations for basic welfare: this should be provided for all, as a right, by state services.

In contrast to this view of social welfare as a civilizing force, the New Right in British politics have presented a view of the welfare state as creating a 'dependency culture' of welfare-reliant individuals which undermines not only the private sector and the family, but also the spirit of voluntarism and collective self-help. They have argued that state welfare is 'demoralising and contains perverse incentives which encourage dependency' and has undermined the voluntary sector. Appealing once again to the concept of altruism (or helping the unknown stranger), but this time as the preserve of Christian values, the Institute of Economic Affairs (1995: 2) argued that:

> Christian philanthropy, like the Good Samaritan, stands beside the suffering person, but charitable bodies founded by Christians as an expression of faith now find themselves 'crowded out' by universal state welfare, or acting as its agents.

Conservative governments since 1979 have advocated the growth of the voluntary sector. In a speech in 1981, Margaret Thatcher indicated her belief that the volunteer movement is at the heart of all our social welfare provision and that the statutory services are there to underpin when necessary, fill gaps and help the helpers (Thatcher 1981). In the last decade, the Conservative government has backed up its moral support with a series of policies, including both incentives and pressures, aimed at a significant expansion in the overall contribution of the voluntary sector. The area in which this policy has met with most success has been in relation to community care, especially with the implementation of the National Health Service and Community Care Act 1990. Here, it has been argued, voluntary organizations are more flexible, closer to the community and hence to need, and more cost-effective because they employ volunteers. Thus a range of opportunities for independent care providers have opened up with the introduction of a market in community care. Local authorities are being encouraged to reduce their role in service delivery, becoming instead purchasers of services contracted from the commercial and voluntary sectors (and with the use of informal carers). New arrangements for the funding of community care under the National Health Service and Community Care Act 1990 have thus involved the transfer of large sums of money from state provision to the voluntary sector. Under the provisions of this Act, local authorities must spend 85 per cent of the element of funding transferred from the Department of Social Security (£399 million) on the independent sector, defined as any provider organization which is not owned, managed or controlled by a local authority.

The government has been less concerned with supporting mutual aid associations, which would arguably most encourage self-reliance, than with creating competition in service provision with the aim of reducing costs. However, some New Right commentators, in advocating the encouragement of the voluntary sector, have been concerned to focus not on the economic argument – support for the market economy – but on the self-reliance engendered by mutual aid. They have been critical of large charities and voluntary organizations that are professionalized and exhibit little or no relationship between the members/donors and the recipients (Davies 1987). Professionalization has not only reduced individual responsibility and self-reliance but also community responsibility.

Despite the strength of its appeal in political manifestos and cross-party support for the voluntary sector, public opinion does not fully support the endeavours of the present government in shifting responsibility on to voluntary effort, especially the increased reliance on charitable giving rather than paying for services out of general taxation. The 1994–95, British Social Attitudes Survey (Jowell *et al.* 1995) asked a series of questions to assess the degree of public support for government policies which placed greater emphasis on the voluntary sector as a key provider of basic welfare services (see Fig. 7.1). In response to a question which asked where money should come from for a range of different needs, the survey found that:

> ... the public clearly expected the government to take responsibility for the core areas of welfare provision which meet basic needs for health, shelter and survival in this country... In contrast the needs

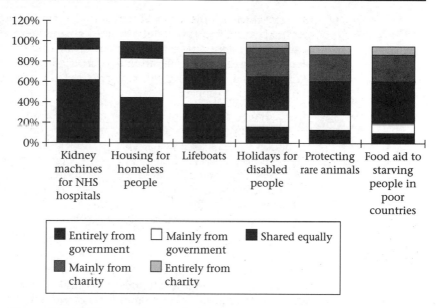

Figure 7.1 Public attitudes to voluntary provision in areas typically associated with voluntary sector activity.
Source: Taylor-Gooby (1995).

of animals and those who live abroad are regarded as more peripheral. Charity begins abroad.

(Taylor-Gooby 1995: 29)

The survey found little evidence to suggest that there is public support for the replacement of statutory services by voluntary provision in the core areas of social policy. On the contrary, Taylor-Gooby (1995: 30) concludes his analysis with the comment that:

... our survey suggests that the public is less attached to the voluntary principle in areas where it has traditionally applied than it is to the principle of state responsibility for its traditional core areas, such as health and education. This is hardly a pattern of attitudes which is conducive to a transfer of responsibilities from government to charities.

The public, it seems, prefer the co-existence of voluntary and statutory provision with the former supplementing, rather than replacing, the latter.

What is the voluntary sector? Problems of definition

A recent publication entitled *Researching the Voluntary Sector* (Saxon-Harrold and Kendall 1994) talks about the difficulty of conveying a coherent image of the voluntary sector to the public. This difficulty stems from the fact that there is no universally accepted definition of the sector, which results

in a lack of available official statistics. The absence of any clear definition makes it difficult not only to research the voluntary sector, but also
to assess its contribution to the provision of social welfare. The problem
of definition, argues the National Council for Voluntary Organisations
(NCVO), results from the sheer diversity of the sector:

> These organisations and groups vary greatly in their size, structure,
> legal status, financial assets, use of paid staff and/or volunteers, and
> the geographical scope of their work. At one end of the scale are the
> smallest of local community groups and self-help groups. Such groups
> tend to have an informal structure, either through choice or as a
> result of problems associated with becoming formalised. At the other
> end of the spectrum are the large, well-known national, and indeed
> international, bodies such as Oxfam, which invariably adopt one of
> a range of formal structures. Some organisations which have adopted
> a formal structure also have the legal status of a charity, which pro-
> vides a range of fiscal and legal benefits.
>
> (NCVO 1993a: 5)

However, the essential features of voluntary organizations which set
them apart from the other components of welfare provision are that they
are non-governmental, non-profit-making and benefit from voluntarism.
The voluntary sector is heterogeneous, varying from local playgroups to
large formal organizations such as Dr Barnado's. Voluntary organizations
can provide services directly (e.g. tea trolleys run by 'Friends of the Hospital'), coordinate the efforts of other voluntary organizations (e.g. the
Housing Corporations) or lobby for change (e.g. the Child Poverty Action
Group). There is also the distinction we made above between philanthropic and mutual aid organizations. Many voluntary organizations,
especially the larger ones, carry out more than one of the functions we
have identified. Age Concern, for example, is a philanthropic organization which, as well as campaigning on behalf of older people, provides
day centres, home helps and other services for the elderly. The Child
Poverty Action Group is a philanthropic group that campaigns on behalf
of the poor. 'Friends of the Hospital' are philanthropic groups that are
mainly concerned with fund-raising and providing help to hospitals by
buying equipment. Credit Unions, by contrast, are mutual aid groups
designed to help people save and borrow money. Organizations like MIND
are both philanthropic and mutual aid organizations, both campaigning
and providing services. It is therefore difficult to define or classify voluntary organizations. Religious bodies also provide voluntary services (e.g.
hostels provided by the Salvation Army) and at least this element of their
work is part of the voluntary sector. The independence of voluntary organizations from government distinguishes them from state welfare and
the lack of profit-making – or, more specifically, profit distribution – distinguishes them from the commercial market. And, finally, the dominance of a voluntary ethos (and non-remunerated contribution) sets the
voluntary sector apart from both statutory and commercial provision. The
term 'non-governmental organization' (NGO) is increasingly used in place
of 'voluntary organization' in the European Union; these are defined as
non-governmental, non-profit-distributing and non-private.

The distinction between the voluntary sector and the informal sector is achieved in the above definition by the requirement that the organization or group is 'formal'. This definition, however, excludes an estimated 300,000 informal community groups (Chanan, cited in NCVO 1993a: 9). Although 'informal' in terms of structure, these are still a type of organization or 'group', and can be distinguished from informal care on that basis alone. Another means of differentiating between the voluntary and informal sectors has been in terms of an individual carer or volunteer's motive. The concept of voluntarism is often associated with altruism, defined by Ware and Goodin (1990: 187) as 'behaviour that benefits another (unrelated) actor and which imposes some cost on the originator'. The motive for informal care is not altruism as such, but typically kinship obligation or particular obligations to close friends or neighbours. Voluntarism, then, stems from broader citizenship obligations as opposed to family, kinship or neighbourhood bonds.

In practice, however, as we shall see in the following discussion, it is very difficult to maintain such hard and fast distinctions.

The voluntary sector and housing: A case study

Rather than talk about the voluntary sector in general, we focus on the expanding role of the voluntary sector in the provision of social housing. We consider how this sector has developed as a source of welfare supply and how provision by the voluntary sector differs from that provided by the state, the commercial sector and informal care. In this context, we consider the impact of new liaisons between voluntary sector bodies, the commercial sector, informal care and the state (particularly with increasing reliance on state funding and accompanying regulation) on the independence and character of the voluntary sector and the 'voluntary ethic' itself. In doing so we highlight both the way in which the voluntary sector has become involved in state welfare, for economic and political motives, and the ways in which it can be utilized for mutual aid. It becomes clear that any static notion of the mixed economy of welfare is problematic. In practice, we are witnessing the development of mixed institutional forms. In this vein, a recent text comments on the 'increasing fuzziness of the boundaries between the public and private sector and the expansion of a "murkier third terrain" that is both public and private' (Taylor *et al.* 1994: 129).

In this context of blurred boundaries and purchaser/provider arrangements, the final section of the chapter returns to the notion of voluntarism and voluntary work. It raises some concerns about the increased use of unpaid workers in welfare provision and discusses the growth of paid volunteering.

The housing association movement

The voluntary sector's contribution to housing is mainly through the provision of social rented housing by housing associations. In practice, housing associations provide housing both for rent and for ownership, with some schemes promoting low-income owner-occupation (including, for example, shared ownership and Tenant's Incentives Schemes). In 1993–94, the total gross expenditure of the Housing Corporation was £1828.4 million, 83 per cent of which went on housing for rent and the remainder on housing for sale schemes. In addition, local authorities sponsored housing association schemes costing £616 million in 1992–93.

A housing association is a non-profit-making organization which provides and manages homes for people who cannot afford to buy a suitable home on the open market. An association may be a charity, a registered industrial **provident society** or both. In 1993, some 85 per cent of central government funding to the voluntary sector consisted of payments to housing associations (NCVO 1993a: 29). Murie (1993: 137) has noted that

> . . . since 1988 a new financial regime and new assured tenancies have made [Housing Associations] the acceptable face of social rented housing for a government previously reluctant to acknowledge the need for such housing.

Government support for voluntary housing effort is by no means new and can be traced back to the passing of the Labouring Classes Dwelling Houses Act of 1866. The Housing Corporation was set up by Parliament in 1964 to fund housing construction by registered housing associations using central government finance. Although some associations obtain funding from private sources and charitable trusts, the majority provide housing with public money either from the Housing Corporation or from a local authority. The sector had, however, remained very small, until recently accounting for a tiny proportion of housing stock. The growth of the housing association movement since 1974 has come about as a result of increased state intervention, mainly in the form of subsidy. The Conservative government, especially since 1988, has recognized the need for rented housing and for subsidized housing for the less well off (Ridley 1988). It has seen housing associations as the major agency for supplying these, both because borrowing by housing associations is not counted as part of public sector borrowing and because the Conservatives have sought to reduce the role of local government. The Conservatives have been especially critical of local authority housing departments, seeing them as being unresponsive to the needs of tenants and encouraging passivity; that is, tenants not being prepared to take on responsibility for the up-keep of their houses and neighbourhoods because they feel no sense of ownership.

Housing association stock

In terms of the overall proportion of housing stock, housing association properties constitute only 3 per cent of the total (CSO 1995: 173). The housing association sector has, however, experienced expansion during a period of overall retrenchment and has been the only sector to increase the construction of new houses in recent years, with all other sectors

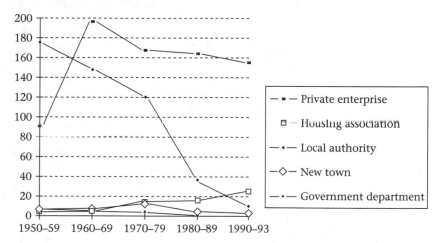

Figure 7.2 Average annual change in dwelling stock in Britain (thousands).
Source: CSO (1995: 174).

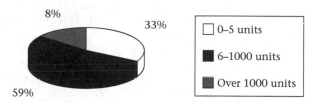

Figure 7.3 The size of housing associations by number of housing units, 1993.
Source: Housing Corporation (1993).

declining – two and a half times more dwellings were constructed in this sector in 1993 than in 1988 (CSO 1995: 174) (see Fig. 7.2).

Most associations are involved in managing a housing stock of less than 1000 units (Fig. 7.3). Of the 2165 housing associations registered with the Housing Corporation in 1993, 33 per cent managed fewer than five housing units; the majority of associations managed between six and 1000 units and only 8 per cent managed more than 1000 units. These figures are a little misleading, however, as although only 8 per cent of housing associations managed large stocks, these 8 per cent provided over 84 per cent of total housing association dwellings (Fig. 7.4). Indeed, some of the larger associations, such as the North British and Anchor Associations, control over 22,000 units.

The policy context

Housing policy over the last 40 years has been dominated by policy measures aimed at increasing home ownership (commercial provision). Cross-party consensus has supported the growth of a 'property-owning democracy'. What has distinguished policy since 1980, however, has been a shift in strategy from one of providing incentives for home ownership

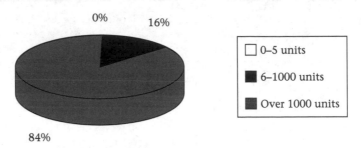

0%   16%

□ 0–5 units

■ 6–1000 units

■ Over 1000 units

84%

Figure 7.4 Housing association stock by size of units, 1993.
Source: Housing Corporation (1993).

(the 'carrot' approach) to the deliberate policy of residualization in the public sector (the 'stick'!). Since 1979, the Conservative Party has sought to extend owner-occupation to lower income groups through the introduction of a statutory 'Right to Buy' for council tenants (in the 1980 Housing Act). Sales of council properties were encouraged by a generous system of discounts which were extended by the Housing and Building Control Act 1984 to a maximum of 60 per cent of market value and again, for flats, in January 1987 to 70 per cent. This policy, accompanied by the imposition of a moratorium on new council house building and tight controls on local government expenditure, resulted in the transfer of a large proportion of public stock into the private sector. Council house sales reduced considerably the ability of housing authorities to house people on their waiting lists; as a result, many people who would have preferred to rent a council house were forced to buy in the commercial sector. This twin policy of incentives and residualization resulted in substantial 'successes' in terms of shifts in patterns of housing tenure in favour of the commercial sector. Economic recession in the 1980s, however, resulted both in a record number of mortgage repossessions as a result of mortgage arrears and a substantial decline in investment in new commercial house building as house prices plummeted.

This trend is likely to continue and possibly accelerate as the effects of changes in housing policy introduced in the 1988 Housing Act begin to take effect. The Act was introduced after it became evident, as sales figures declined after 1992, that sales of council houses alone were not going to achieve the long-term objective of removing general needs housing from the responsibility of local government. The Housing Act 1988 provided further 'legislation for demunicipalisation' (Malpass and Murie 1994: 105). The 'Tenant's Choice' provisions gave tenants (other than those in sheltered housing or others excluded from the Right to Buy) the right to 'choose' an alternative landlord. At the time, the response by tenants and prospective landlords was negligible, but local authorities did use the provisions of the Housing and Planning Act 1986 to transfer their housing stock to housing associations voluntarily. Cole and Furbey (1994: 173) explain that the main impact of this legislation was

. . . to persuade local authorities to make use of provision under the 1986 Housing and Planning Act to seek a 'voluntary transfer' of their entire housing stock to new landlords, usually housing associations, often as a defensive measure to prevent the fragmentation of social housing in their localities... Initially, the proportion of transfers blocked by tenants was very high. It was only after the financial implications of the Local Government and Housing Act 1989 became apparent, with their indications of a further erosion in the relative quality of public housing, that more ballots produced majorities in favour of block transfers.

A new direction was thus taken to further reduce the stock of public sector housing, but this time the transfer was to be directly from the state to the voluntary sector. Since 1988–89, over 30 local authorities have transferred all or part of their housing stock to housing associations and, by May 1994, 140,000 dwellings had been transferred under this procedure, the majority in the south-east. The largest transfer took place in 1992 when over 12,000 dwellings were transferred by the London Borough of Bromley (CSO 1995: 175). However, Treasury concern about the costs to the housing benefit bill of the higher rents charged by housing associations compared with local authorities has inhibited the progress of further transfers (Murie 1993).

Housing associations as voluntary organizations

We have already noted that three characteristics of voluntary organizations are that they are independent, non-profit distributing and rely on volunteers. The advantages of voluntary organizations are also said to stem from their relatively smaller size, their ability to identify and respond to local needs in a flexible and non-bureaucratic fashion. The information given above, however, suggests that the overwhelming majority of housing association stock is provided by very large organizations with a regional, as opposed to local, base. Indeed, many cover substantially larger geographical areas than local authority housing departments and are unlikely to provide a sensitive, local or uncomplicated service (Malpass and Murie 1994: 174). National figures also tend to mask large regional variations in housing association provision (see Fig. 7.5). In England, housing association activity is concentrated in the London area, particularly inner London. This level of concentration in urban areas and the capital city, in particular, can also be seen in Northern Ireland, where 30 of the 47 associations registered with the Northern Ireland Housing Trust operate principally in the Belfast area (McGivern 1989, cited in Malpass and Murie 1994: 174).

The role of volunteers in this sector is also restricted. In 1991, for example, 32,996 full-time staff were employed by housing associations in England. As with many voluntary organizations, in practice the label 'voluntary' applies only to the management committees and not to service delivery. In relation to housing associations, even fund-raising, which forms the major occupation of all volunteers, is insignificant. The administration of associations is therefore likely to mirror that of statutory agencies.

Housing associations' reliance upon central and local government finance

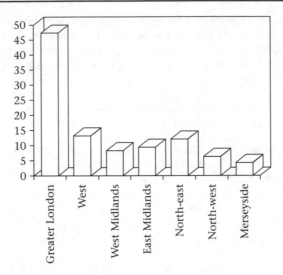

Figure 7.5 Regional distribution of housing association stock (percentage of national bed spaces) in England, 1993.
Source: Housing Corporation (1993).

raises important questions. Recent changes have further modified the financial position of housing associations with implications for their autonomy and independence. In order to encourage new partnerships between the commercial and voluntary sectors and to reduce the reliance on public expenditure, the government introduced 'challenge' funding initiatives in the 1980s which offered additional funds to those associations initiating projects involving an element of commercial finance. These projects were set up to demonstrate that commercial finance could be raised for social housing schemes. Whitehead (1993), however, argues that many of the initial schemes involved elements of additional state subsidy, such as land provided at below-market rates by local authorities. Furthermore, 'if the system were to work for social housing overall, grant rates would have to be significantly higher' (p. 88). The system also appeared to favour larger asset-rich housing associations, which found it easier to raise loans in the commercial market. The 1988 Housing Act laid down the financial framework by which commercial finance was to be introduced into all new housing association developments.

The replacement of fair rents with assured tenancies enabled housing associations to set rents at market levels, thus increasing their attractiveness to commercial financiers. What this implies, in effect, is a transfer of state financial responsibility from capital funding via Housing Corporation grant to means-tested housing benefit. Figures for 1993 showed that 69 per cent of housing association tenants were in receipt of housing benefit (Housing Corporation 1993).

Although the proportion of state finance via the Housing Corporation has declined with the introduction of 'mixed funding', the majority of funds still come from central government through the Housing Corporation. Associations are thus still subject to heavy state regulation. Projects or programmes must be agreed in detail by the Corporation, which regularly monitors the operation of housing associations. The Housing Corporation's Annual Report 1993–94 refers to the 'great strides we have made in adding to our regulatory armoury' with the introduction of a new 'Performance Review System' to include both financial and non-financial indicators of associations' performance.

In addition to strict financial regulation by the Housing Corporation, local authorities are also involved in funding housing associations. In return for this support, local authorities are able to 'nominate' a proportion of people from their waiting lists for housing association dwellings. Indeed, in 1993, the main source of referral for housing association lettings (accounting for 46 per cent of all lettings) was by local authority nomination. This combination of close working relationships between housing associations and local housing departments, coupled with financial dependency on the Housing Corporation – and, increasingly, on commercial financiers – threatens to damage housing associations' image as small, community-based, independent organizations responding flexibly to local need.

While housing policy since 1979 has been led by considerations of public expenditure and a drive to promote the commercial sector both as provider and financier of housing, this policy has not resulted in the withdrawal of government from housing; rather, we have witnessed a shift in the nature and complexity of state intervention. An important component of this shift has been the increase in control by central government and the declining autonomy of local authorities in the housing field. The rate of growth and development of policy in the housing association movement is highly dependent upon state policy. Malpass and Murie's (1994: 173) assessment of the changes affecting housing associations sums this up well:

> In this rediscovery of voluntary effort ... and the subsequent development of policy towards housing associations, central government has used the voluntary sector to increase its direct control over housing programmes and by-passed local authorities with which it has a less simple relationship. This development of housing associations can consequently be seen as part of the wider centralising tendency evident in housing policy in recent years.

Voluntarism and community self-help: The Black voluntary housing movement

The distinction between philanthropic and mutual aid groups – those concerned with 'helping others' and those which are user- or community-based (in other words, forms of community self-help) – is particularly useful for understanding developments in the housing association movement. While numerically the movement is dominated by the former (philanthropic) bodies, which we have seen are similar in many respects to large local housing authorities, it is important not to overlook the contribution and character of many smaller organizations which are, in many ways, closer to the communities they exist to support. This section focuses on one particularly successful development in the Black, self-help, voluntary housing movement.

Research by Taylor *et al.* (1994: 133) found that 'Voluntary organisations are developing fast in the minority ethnic communities', particularly in user-based activities. Malcolm Harrison (1994) documents the achievements of the Black voluntary housing movement and, in particular, the struggles of Black-led housing organizations in overcoming the 'victim-oriented' approach of much welfare provision. Although the material gains of this movement have been limited in terms of its ability to improve substantially the housing standards of Britain's Black population, it has provided an important means of empowerment for the Black community to counter the often paternalistic and racist approach of many housing authorities. Harrison traces the evolution of this movement from the early 1980s when, in the context of urban disturbances, attention was increasing focused on racial disadvantage in key urban areas. In 1986–87, the Housing Corporation began a 5-year programme to 'encourage and sustain separate black-run organisations as a channel for delivering social rented housing' (Harrison 1994: 23). Such organizations were already in existence and supported by an umbrella group, the National Federation of Black Housing Associations. The movement sought to improve housing standards for Black people through:

1 Involvement of community organizations reflecting a variety of cultural and religious groupings, thereby enabling the development of more culturally sensitive solutions.
2 Empowerment of users via self-management and needs-led objectives.
3 Increased participation in the wider housing association movement.

During the 5-year period, some 44 new ethnic housing associations were registered with the Housing Corporation, bringing the total to 66. Although the overall stock remains small, these organizations have targeted particular communities, often identifying needs overlooked by mainstream organizations. The schemes have included, for example, homes for Asian elders, a client group with particular language and cultural needs. In contrast to the associations we looked at in the previous section, the largest Black housing association provides just over 600 units and most others are much smaller than this.

One particular example of developments in voluntary sector housing in response to a specific social need can be seen in the Refugee Housing Association. This organization aims:

• To provide high quality affordable housing to refugees in need.
• To provide culturally appropriate and responsive services to meet social, emotional and other needs of refugees.
• To facilitate opportunities for the tenants to participate fully in the national life of this country.
• To work with community groups, refugee organisations and any other bodies concerned with the welfare of refugees, so as to be responsive to the needs of the wider refugee community. (Annual Report 1994)

This association has over 400 units in its reception centres to meet the needs of people newly arrived in Britain and 500 units of permanent housing to enable refugees to move out of temporary housing. It also manages a programme of private sector leases for less vulnerable refugees. In addition to housing needs, it provides support services to enable tenants to successfully regain independence and facilitate their integration into British society. Three tenants sit on the association's management committee and a tenant's association is being set up to encourage participation in the management of the association. An indicator of its ability to respond quickly to meet newly identified needs can be seen in the proportion of Bosnian tenants, who amounted to some 19 per cent of the total in 1993. The Refugee Housing Association is funded by the Housing Corporation (10 per cent) and by local authorities (0.6 per cent), but the largest proportion of its income comes from rental payments, the majority of which comes from housing benefit payments.

The success of these small associations is, however, under threat from the changes in housing association finance discussed above. These changes, particularly increases in rents and the requirement to raise commercial sector finance, are expected to place considerable pressure on smaller associations with limited assets. The continued viability of some of the smaller schemes has been called into question and Harrison (1994) predicts the survival of only the largest black-run organizations. Their independence is also under threat due to proposals for closer cooperation with large white-run organizations. The Housing Corporation initiative itself, welcome as it was for the necessary injection of cash, nevertheless represented a threat to the independence of organizations. Harrison for example, argues that the:

> ... funding arrangements and priorities at the Corporation have directly shaped the programmes of new associations, possibly distorting development strategies in the direction of lower risks, pragmatism and growth (with less regard for the original preferences of the organisations).
>
> (Harrison 1994: 29)

To the extent that voluntary activity is dependent upon state or commercial sector funding, it runs the risk of becoming funding-led as opposed to needs-led as organizational bids for funds are required to meet the specific criteria of the funding body.

The future of voluntarism

In the introduction to this chapter, we saw that one of the hallmarks of the voluntary sector was its reliance upon voluntary effort, both philanthropic and mutual aid. This is seen to be important both in terms of reducing costs but also promoting active citizenship and community self-reliance. In the discussion about housing associations, we indicated that the contribution of volunteers in some organizations is very limited – here it was restricted to involvement in management committees. By far the most common form of voluntary activity is fund-raising (accounting for some 75 per cent of volunteers; Hedley and Davis Smith 1992: 78), but many volunteers are also involved in care and support-giving roles. This is particularly true of women and volunteers from lower socio-economic groups (with men and higher socio-economic groups concentrated in committee and advice-giving work; Hedley and Davis Smith 1992: 78).

The discussion now moves away from the nature of voluntary organizations to consider the issue of volunteering in more detail and, in particular, to address some recent debates about voluntarism. These issues concern the potential exploitation of unpaid work and its impact on paid workers, the development of paid volunteering and the relationship between voluntarism and informal care (the subject of the next chapter).

Safeguarding volunteers and paid workers

While the idealism associated with voluntarism supports the notion of 'employing' volunteers in care-giving (and in advocacy schemes), in reality there are concerns over the level of training of volunteers and their reliability, and also about the exploitation of volunteers as a source of 'cheap' (free!) labour, which may undermine the jobs of paid workers – not only by volunteers substituting for paid workers, but by voluntary organizations, using voluntary labour, being able to undercut the charges of state and commercial organizations and thereby win contracts to provide services. Hedley and Davis Smith (1992: 33) document the uneasy relationship between the voluntary movement and the British Labour Movement, which traditionally associated voluntarism with nineteenth-century charity, philanthropy and dependency and as a threat to paid jobs. Particular concern has arisen in the past over the use of volunteers during strikes. Hedley and Davis Smith conclude that tensions have eased in recent years partly as a result of a shift in thinking on the left away from the notion of state welfare and in favour of the mixed economy of welfare. The Labour Party, in particular, has expressed a commitment to raising awareness of the role of the voluntary sector. Concerns remain over the implications of the use of volunteers in 'contracted out' services which are already low paid areas of work. The introduction of paid volunteering schemes similarly raises issues concerning the boundaries between paid and unpaid work and fears that such developments herald a new form of exploitation. With these issues in mind, the Greater London Council, prior to its abolition by the government in 1986, increased its support for the voluntary sector and developed a series of guidelines on policy and practice towards volunteers in organizations funded by itself. This policy attempted to deal with the difficult political and social issues surrounding volunteering, including the respective roles of volunteers and salaried workers, the importance of guaranteed standards of service and the need to promote equal opportunities for volunteers in training and employment and to prevent exploitation.

Voluntarism, altruism and 'paid volunteering'

The very term 'voluntarism' and its close association with notions of altruism implies that time and effort is freely given, without the need for remuneration. Since the 1980s, a new form of relationship has developed, further blurring the boundaries between the voluntary sector and the state. The phenomenon known as 'paid volunteering', which involves cash payment to individual volunteers, raises interesting questions about the future compatibility of altruism or 'active citizenship' in the face of an increasingly market-oriented welfare system. This contradiction led Baldock and Ungerson (1991: 140) to refer to paid volunteering as 'the mongrel progeny of this curious 1980s melange of money-making and altruism'. Paid volunteering has been associated typically with innovative and experimental schemes aimed at providing care 'in the community'. Such schemes include good neighbour schemes, where a neighbour is paid to care for a dependent person living in their own home, and respite schemes, where a volunteer is paid to relieve a carer for a given period of time. The growing tendency of local authorities to contract out work to large voluntary organizations, resulting in considerably larger budgets combined with contractual pressure to guarantee service delivery, has increased the use of paid volunteer workers. This may have resulted from the need to increase the sheer numbers of volunteers (as a form of incentive), to secure continuity of service and, where necessary, to pay for the higher levels of skill required.

Baldock and Ungerson consider the implications of paid volunteering for women in the face of evidence that the overwhelming majority of paid volunteers are women. On the one hand, they argue that paid volunteering 'thrives on the disadvantages that define the subordinate position of women in our society' to the extent that the levels of payment are tiny and highly exploitative. The authors raise the crucial question as to whether paid volunteering is simply 'a mechanism for engaging women in extremely low-paid work while presenting their work as something other than work and more akin to pleasure and leisure' (Baldock and Ungerson 1991: 143), a form of 'quasi-volunteer'. On the other hand, the fact that women are paid, however little, represents a break with a tradition in which women were expected to undertake similar tasks with no expectation of remuneration whatsoever. As such, paid volunteering goes some way towards recognizing the work involved in caring and may 'eventually develop into a more conventionally organised form of properly paid work, not just for volunteers but for informal carers as well' (Baldock and Ungerson 1991: 137).

The introduction of more market-oriented criteria in both the financing of large voluntary organizations, like housing associations, and in providing incentives and financial rewards for volunteers, raises interesting questions about the future character of this sector and the distinctiveness of its contribution. Alan Ware (1990) addresses precisely this issue in a chapter concerned with the compatibility of markets and 'altruistically inspired voluntary action'. Individualism associated with free market philosophy leads to the pursuit of narrow self-interest and a cost–benefit mentality which eventually undermines altruism – giving to an unknown stranger and expecting nothing back in return. In this context, Ware argues that only reciprocal altruism can survive ('altruism' practised within a wider reciprocating group as a form of social insurance). Ware (1990: 204) concludes by saying that 'the general effect of the expansion of the market system has been to corrode altruism'.

Voluntary activity, obligation and informal care

The voluntary sector provides an important source of support for the millions of people involved in caring – on an unpaid basis and usually in the home – for dependent relatives and friends, although voluntary organizations that provide services for dependent groups of people have been criticized for offering inappropriate services or working in an oppressive way, as have the statutory services (Oliver 1990). They have, however, been important in raising awareness of informal care and applying pressure on central and local government to provide increased levels of support, both in terms of services such as day-care or respite care and cash benefits for carers. Schemes such as sitting services for elderly people suffering from senile dementia, transport schemes and carers' support groups have provided important sources of support for isolated and exhausted carers. It is perhaps in this area that the voluntary sector has demonstrated its ability to come up with new and innovative forms of service, some of which subsequently become incorporated within statutory schemes (sitting services, for example, have been taken on in some local authorities). Although there is clearly an important relationship between the voluntary sector and informal care and, in many ways, recent policy initiatives in community care have further blurred the boundaries between these sectors, the act of caring for a dependent relative, friend or neighbour must be distinguished from voluntary work. In one sense, people do volunteer to undertake these caring tasks, but an act can be considered to be truly voluntary only when the person has freedom of choice. We have already seen how Titmuss defined altruism as the gift to an unknown, or unrelated, stranger.

Many people providing services in the informal sector have little or no genuine choice, either because of the lack of alternative services or because of their sense of duty or obligation. We shall see in the next chapter how statutory services themselves can be organized around certain assumptions about the role of the family and the apportionment of roles within the family, with implications for the degree of 'choice' available to carers. Heginbotham (1990: 15) argues that evidence of the disproportionate pressure brought to bear on women to undertake informal care prevents such a role being defined as 'truly voluntary':

... often statutory services make tacit assumptions that a male spouse or a son will not be in a position to, want to, or be able to look after a frail or dependent relative, whereas no such inhibitions normally attend their attitude towards wives or daughters.

The sexism inherent in these decisions is reinforced by social attitudes which bring further pressure to bear on men and women to comply with assigned gender roles. Fielding *et al.* (1991: 98) conclude their book on active citizenship with a 'word of warning':

> The pure theory of volunteering is easily confused by its entanglement with the dilemma of women today which sets them free to move in the world outside the family without releasing them from the bonds of domestic tradition. We have a long way to go before we can talk of volunteering as a universal experience, freely available to all.

Conclusions

This chapter has raised some general points about the viability of increased reliance upon the voluntary sector in the provision of welfare. It has noted the enormous diversity of provision and the problems of definition and measurement of the voluntary contribution. Focusing on one aspect of the voluntary provision, that of social housing, it has demonstrated the nature of the voluntary sector and the pressure it is under. The voluntary sector faces a dilemma: in order to become a major player in the delivery of social welfare, it cannot rely on philanthropic donations but must demand substantial financial support from both the state and the commercial sector. While such support greatly increases the potential for development, it also increases dependency on funding-led organizations, which may pose a threat to the sector's independence and diversity. Increasing political commitment to the notion of voluntarism has not been met by increased philanthropy. Indeed, donations to voluntary organizations have fallen. Voluntary Organizations are under pressure to become larger, more bureaucratically organized, bodies and managing agents. Even the supply of voluntary effort is under question, as organizations are forced to consider the possibility of offering financial incentives to bolster the supply of volunteers.

Summary

- The voluntary sector dominated formal welfare provision in Britain until the 1940s.

- There is no universally accepted definition of the voluntary sector. The type of organizations involved vary greatly in size, structure, legal and financial status, their use of paid and unpaid staff and the geographical scope of their work.

- Voluntary organizations can be loosely grouped into two categories; those based on philanthropy and those based on mutual aid and self-help.

- Since the 1980s the government in Britain has sought to encourage the development of this sector and increase reliance on voluntary provision within the mixed economy of welfare.

- The development of housing associations is used to illustrate the growth of this sector and the increasingly complex interactions and alliances between the state and other providers of welfare and, in particular, the impact of substantial statutory funding and regulation.

- The chapter has also considered the problems of territorial justice – or unevenness in provision – and the impact of a shift from public to voluntary provision on local autonomy.

Further reading

Davis Smith, J., Rochester, C. and Hedley, R. (1995) *An Introduction to the Voluntary Sector*. London: Routledge.
Fielding, N., Reeve, C. and Simey, M.C. (1991) *Active Citizens, New Voices and Values*. London: Bedford Square Press.
Saxon-Harrold, S.K.E. and Kendall, J. (eds) (1994) *Researching the Voluntary Sector*, 2nd edn. London: Charities Aid Foundation.

THE ROLE OF INFORMAL CARE

Introduction

This chapter looks at the increased awareness of informal care as the dominant service provision in western welfare systems. It examines some of the processes leading to this recognition, including concerns about public expenditure and ideology as well as the increased awareness, brought about by feminist research, of the gender implications of the reliance placed upon this sector for welfare provision. Carers have of course always been central to the support of disabled and older people, but over the last 10–15 years this fact has increasingly been recognized both within the policy statements of the government and within the academic research agenda. The chapter considers what is distinctive about informal care, who is actually doing the caring and how carers are supported by the state via domiciliary services. Finally, it assesses developments in payments for informal care both in terms of the changing role of the state and the implications of such schemes for carers. The debate about informal care raises important questions about the relationship between men and women in society, the family and the state, and formal and informal care.

Formal and informal care

At its simplest, informal care is the regular physical and/or personal assistance given to people (adults or children) with disabilities or illnesses, by people (generally adults, but sometimes children) who are not paid to provide such care. The last chapter discussed the close relationship between voluntarism and informal care and showed how the voluntary sector has provided important support for informal carers. The two sectors can be distinguished on both conceptual and empirical grounds, however. In conceptual terms, it could be argued that volunteers and informal carers have different motivations, drawing on the distinction between altruism and kinship obligation. On empirical grounds, the sectors differ in terms of the specific tasks undertaken. We saw in the last chapter, for example, how the majority of volunteers are involved in fund-raising, administration and committee work, often within large voluntary organizations, with less than 25 per cent involved in some form of direct service provision. All informal carers, on the other hand, are providing some form of personal and/or domestic service, typically in isolation. However, the boundary between the two is fuzzy, especially when we move beyond the care provided by relatives to care provided by friends and neighbours.

It is also important to recognize the ambiguous relationship between *formal* and *informal* carers. Assumptions about the roles and responsibilities of informal carers shape the response of formal service providers to 'the cared-for' and determine the support given by front-line services to informal carers. Although over the last 10–15 years the government has indicated that informal carers should be supported, there has been little explicit guidance. Policy for carers remains vague, and the situation of informal carers remains uncertain and ambiguous. Graham (1984) has pointed out that formal carers devalue the expertise and experience of informal carers in providing appropriate care and their knowledge and understanding of the needs of the cared-for person (see also Abbott and Sapsford 1987a). It has also been argued that carers are expected to undertake the bulk of caring and that services are provided only when they are clearly unable to cope (see, for example, Abbott 1992a; 1992b).

However, Twigg and Atkin (1995) argue that the situation is more complex than this and that the services demanded and received by carers also depend on their own perception of their role. (This may of course be mediated by their understanding of what services are available and the attitudes towards them of service providers.) Twigg and Atkin outline three responses of carers that influence their relationship with formal care providers. First, there are those who are engulfed by their role (mainly women and spouses), see the responsibility of care as theirs and do not ask for services. Others adopt a 'boundary setting' response, detaching themselves from the situation and making a separation between themselves and the person for whom they care. They define what they see as their responsibility and demand services for tasks they see as lying outside their role. Finally, there are those who adopt a 'symbiotic' approach; they gain in a positive way from their caring role and do not want the responsibility and its consequences to be taken away from them. Their response is typical of parents caring for offspring with mental health problems or learning disabilities, and where the burden of care is not great. Service providers, although not making these distinctions, are aware that services are provided to those carers who are most demanding and assertive.

Service providers also maintain that it is the right of the cared-for person to determine the nature of service provision. This means that the needs or the wishes of the carers are frequently marginalized or ignored if they are not the same as those of the cared-for person. Furthermore, the relationship between the carer and the cared-for may influence the provision of formal services – they are less likely to be offered if the carers are spouses or parents than if they are children or more distant relations. Services are also more likely to be offered if the cared-for person has moved to live with the carer or vice versa than if they have always been co-resident. Gender, social class, age and race also influence service provision. Men, especially if they are in employment, are more likely to be offered services than non-employed women. Older carers are similarly more likely to be considered as needing formal help than younger carers. Middle-class people are more likely to know their entitlement to services than working-class people and to demand these services. Care-service provision to Black people is often unsuitable and inaccessible.

What is 'informal care'?

Claire Ungerson (1995: 32) defines informal care as:

> ... activities that provide personal services within the domestic domain for people with special needs; most importantly within the British convention, the provision of services is unwaged. The assumption is that the supply of these domestically based caring services is forthcoming, not because it is paid for, but because its provision fulfils certain norms and obligations arising out of the operation of affect, biography and kinship.

In terms of the nature of work involved, Willmott and Thomas (1984) identified five categories of task undertaken by informal carers:

- *Personal care*: washing, bathing, dressing, toileting and general attention to bodily needs and comforts.
- *Domestic care*: cooking, cleaning and laundering.
- *Auxiliary care*: baby-sitting, child-minding, shopping, transport, odd-jobbing, gardening, borrowing and lending.

- *Social support*: visiting and companionship.
- *Surveillance*: 'keeping an eye on' vulnerable people.

These distinctions are important as the nature of the 'task' is often linked to the relationship of the carer. Wives, mothers and daughters, for example, are more likely to provide personal care, and neighbours more likely to provide surveillance.

The role and contribution of informal care in the provision of welfare has until recently been largely neglected both by policy-makers and Social Policy academics – 'hidden from history'. Indeed, when Richard Titmuss (1955) wrote his seminal essay on 'The social division of welfare', he failed to acknowledge the contribution of this sector despite the fact that 'care by families and within communities has long provided the cornerstone of Britain's welfare system' (Graham 1993b: 124). The contribution of informal care to the support of the elderly, disabled people and children has dominated service provision both before and since the development of modern welfare systems. It is only in the past two decades, however, that this contribution has begun to be recognized by government and academic research – most importantly feminist research, which has highlighted the unrecognized, unremunerated work that women do in providing informal care. This has become even more evident with the development of explicit policies of community care.

A powerful argument for the expansion of this sector, or at the very least for its continuing role, is that family care is 'quality care' and that it respects the wishes of 'dependants'. Part of this concern reflects a very negative image of residential or 'institutional' care in Britain. Thus the policy of welfare retrenchment and the development of care in the community gained support from the critique of institutional care. However, the idea of community care, which in reality has generally meant care by the family, has been part of government rhetoric since the 1950s and has always been the dominant mode of care. Much of the government's recent emphasis on community care and the role of informal carers must be seen as rhetorical; the evidence available indicates that the majority of people do care for their dependent relatives and want to do so (Abbott and Sapsford 1987a; Finch 1990), although with the support of formal services (West *et al.* 1984).

Caring for and caring about

It is important to distinguish between 'caring for' and 'caring about'. The former refers to the actual tasks of caring and does not require an affective or emotional bond. Both formal and informal carers may care *for* someone. 'Caring *about*' is to be concerned and can be expressed in a caring relationship and by taking care of someone. It is often assumed that informal carers care about the cared-for person as well as caring for him or her. This is not always the case; care may be undertaken out of a feeling of obligation or even resignation. Alternatively, someone may be cared *about* but not cared *for* by relatives; there is some evidence that men may, for example, buy in services rather than provide them themselves.

Present government thinking about the family and its role in society, according to Dalley (1988), fuses these two aspects for women so that in order to demonstrate genuine 'care' they have to both care *about* and also care *for* dependent people. Many women (and child carers) are therefore not free to choose 'not to care' for a dependent relative without either putting that person at risk or damaging their own identity. It is for this reason that Land (1991: 18) refers to women's assigned caring roles as an example of 'compulsory altruism'. Men, on the other hand, are more often able to demonstrate that they 'care about' dependent family members by taking financial responsibility, perhaps by providing the family home or buying in services. They are not expected to 'care for' the personal and domestic needs of the dependent person to the same extent. In other words, a male relative (particularly when he is not an elderly spouse of the dependent person) is not expected to do the 'hands on caring', such as toileting or bathing, nor to give up his work role to care for a dependant on a full-time basis. Men, far more than women, have the choice of whether or not to be involved in informal care and, for men, involvement in such caring roles 'translates most visibly and immediately into the loss of male privilege . . . the privilege of being uninvolved' (Saraceno 1987: 200). Dalley (1988: 13) concludes her study thus:

> Whenever policy documents talk about the responsibility, willingness and the duty of families to provide care – and [the government white paper] Growing Older [DHSS 1981a] is a good example – the substance of these statements is that they mean WOMEN will do the physical and emotional providing for, whilst men should underwrite this effort financially.

The costs of informal care

Politicians and other policy-makers are well aware of the ways in which community care depends on the work of informal carers and assumes that families should and will want to take on these responsibilities:

> The family is the place where we care for each other, where we feel our responsibilities for each other, where we practise consideration for each other. Caring families are the basis of a society that cares.
>
> (James Callaghan to the Church of Scotland
> Assembly, quoted in *The Guardian*, 23 May 1978)

Indeed, it is explicitly recognized that if the care of dependent groups provided by families and other informal carers were to be fully costed, it would be extremely expensive:

> The 'cost effectiveness' of these packages [of community care] depends on not putting a financial value on the contribution of informal carers who may in fact shoulder considerable financial, social and emotional burdens.
>
> (DHSS 1981c)

The government's recent policy developments enacted in the National Health Service and Community Care Act 1990 continue to assume that much care will be provided by families, but also recognizes that informal carers need support:

> The Government acknowledges that the great bulk of community care is provided by friends, family and neighbours. The decision to take on a caring role is never an easy one. However, many people make the choice and it is right that they should be able to play their part in looking after those close to them. But it must be recognised that carers need help and support if they are to continue to carry out their role.
>
> (Department of Health 1989c)

The financial benefits and allowances available (e.g. disability living allowance) are unlikely to be sufficient to compensate for the extra cost of caring. Research by Judith Buckle (1984) and Caroline Glendinning (1983) certainly indicates that the additional financial costs of caring for a mentally handicapped child are not compensated for by benefits. In addition to this are the wages often foregone by a female carer who is not able to take on paid employment (Nissel and Bonnerjea 1982).

The burden on women

However, one may go beyond the simple lack of finance to argue that community care necessarily imposes a special burden on women (see, for example, Bayley 1973; Wilkin 1979; Abbott and Sapsford 1987a). The actual implementation of the policy means, for example, that the mother of a handicapped child is expected to take on the main burden of caring for that child. The policy has not in practice meant a shift of resources from hospitals to the local community, but a shift in the type of labour employed; paid, trained, professional labour (or, at the very least, paid) is replaced by unpaid, untrained, seemingly cheap labour. The burden is much greater than that experienced by the mother caring for a 'normal' young child: the 'child' goes on requiring fairly intensive and regular care long past the time when 'normal' children have become relatively independent. The mother may in fact become tied to a life-long 'child'. She will no longer be able to enjoy the normal life experiences of other women – relative independence when the children have grown up, possibly returning to paid employment – and this will affect not only her but also the rest of the family, including siblings of the handicapped child. For example, research (e.g. Abbott and Sapsford 1987a; from which the quotes below are taken) has shown that mothering children with severe learning difficulties presents three special kinds of problem which mitigate against normal employment.

First, depending on the degree of the child's difficulties, more intensive childcare may be required than would be the case with a 'normal' child, and this may make it difficult to find babysitters or childminders or to persuade relatives to share the childcare. Second, timing has to be very precise; for example, as one mother said, 'I mean, you can't really leave a handicapped child really on its own', and there is little or no leeway in the schedule. Such children must be met from school or the school bus and cannot be left to their own devices during the school holidays. In the end, school times come to dominate the lives of such mothers even more tyrannically than is normally the case. In the words of one mother, 'My life has been run by the school bus for fifteen years now. You can't go out; you must be here. From the day these children are born your life is planned; you've got to put it round that child'. Third, as the above quotation indicates, the process is protracted long beyond the normal. Many mothers would not leave their 5-year-old children to come home from school to an empty house. Few, however, would still need to be there to receive a 15-year-old, with the prospect of still needing to be there when the 'child' is 25.

Thus while successive governments since the 1950s have advocated community care for dependent people, they have not provided adequate facilities for this to become a meaningful way of handling them. Coupled with community apathy and even hostility, this has meant that care becomes the responsibility of the family (and specifically of the female carer). An apparently progressive and humanitarian policy turns out in practice to make little difference to the lives of dependent people. What it does do is to impose additional burdens – both economic and social – on their informal carers.

The specific problems and their scale can be illustrated by describing the lives which some mothers live while providing 'community care' for their handicapped children. Among the mothers interviewed by Abbott and Sapsford (1987a), Mrs Allison was the mother of a 14-year-old Downs' syndrome daughter with a weak heart. She lived in a remote village with poor public transport, so a car was essential. Her daughter Brenda had to go to a hospital 20 miles away every 3–4 months for a check-up, and her heart would not stand much physical exercise, so transport was needed even to go shopping. However, the family could not afford two cars, so Mrs Allison was more or less house-bound during the week unless she added driving her husband half an hour each way to and from work to her already busy schedule. She was further tied to the house by the need to supervise Brenda and was well aware of the contrast between her situation and that of other mothers:

> You've got to have your wits about you the whole time . . . not that she's mischievous, but you've got to watch what she's doing . . . If you'd got a girl that's nearly fifteen you wouldn't, for example, have to be finding people to look after her if you want to go out . . .

Then there was the work, and expense, of constant washing and drying, with a child who was not 'out of nappies' until the age of 12:

> I used to get up two or three times in the night to take her to the toilet to try and keep her dry . . . Cost me a fortune in plastic pants and what-not, and extra bedding because, I mean . . . a certain amount of bedding does get soiled, although there's plastic sheets . . . [Also] she's a shocking picker . . . a couple of pairs of socks go West in a week, or two or three pairs of pants go West in a week.

She had to do a load of washing every day of the week. Additional expense was incurred by Brenda's poor circulation, which entailed extra heating, thermal underwear, thermal under-blankets and specially thick sheets.

Mrs Friedmann experienced even more heavy demands. Her brain-damaged 13-year-old daughter was blind, immobile and doubly incontinent, and her husband's employment often took him away from home for several days at a time:

> It's a constant care because she can't even sit up. Every single move she makes has to be done for her. She can't even turn over...
>
> You need more than two hands. It takes two of us to wash her hair... I lay her right across the side here... and somebody holds her and her head's just hung over the sink... everything is just like a big operation...
>
> It's very difficult because she's on a very limited diet... everything is liquidized and tipped in... You can't bribe her [to eat] because she can't see... if she doesn't like it she'll reject it...
>
> I do have a lot of contact with her, I pick her up and I hold her and I carry her. But... she's thirteen... and I'm getting older as she's getting older... At twenty years I'm not going to be able to lift her... I'm permanently tired because she is heavy...
>
> ... the hours of crying when she gets frustrated and upset. The mental side when you can't do anything apart from hold her and nurse her and care for her...
>
> If she's got a toothache or a stomach-ache she can't tell you and she screams... You can't help her because you don't know what's wrong with her...
>
> You're constantly on call... if she cries or something [the school] just pick up the phone and say 'We're bringing her home'.
>
> We can't go out together as a family... You can't lay in bed, you can't go out and have a party on a Saturday night... because you know early in the morning Gerry can't get up... They need far more attention... Everything is done with Gerry in mind so she really calls the tune in this house. Where we go, who visits, who stays. Holidays. Everything. There's not one thing that doesn't really centre around Gerry.

Informal care and state policy

The concern in the last 15 years about the public expenditure implications of an ageing population, in the context of a more general commitment to monetarist economic policy and welfare retrenchment, has resulted in a renewed emphasis on informal care. It is not just a simple concern to contain public expenditure, however, but a broader ideological move to redraw the boundaries between personal and state involvement in welfare. The ensuing debate about the impact of post-war collectivism on personal responsibility and its role in the creation of a 'dependency culture' led to a call for a return to individual responsibility. In practice, this meant arguing for familial responsibility for the care of dependants. Not only was family and informal care seen to be cheaper, it was also promoted as being a morally superior form of care. As the Griffiths Report on community care put it, 'families, friends, neighbours and other local people provide the majority of care... this is as it should be' (Griffiths 1988: 5). Baldock and Ungerson (1991: 148) illustrate the use of moral judgements to justify reliance upon informal care. They argue that the proposed dichotomy – in its crudest form – is that the 'formal' system substitutes skill for tenderness, is contractual, hierarchical, subject to rigid divisions of labour laid down through collective bargaining procedures, with bureaucratically managed resources in scarce supply; in contrast, it is suggested, the 'informal' system is spontaneous, loving, flexible, and untrammelled by ideas of rigid divisions of labour (except, though this is rarely spelt out, the sexual division of labour). To conclude, care in the community is then seen as good, care at home better and care by the family as best.

Government policies of community care and decarceration obviously have an impact on the role and nature of informal carers. There has been a policy shift in favour of an explicit recognition of and commitment to the promotion of informal care. Community care policy over the last decade has encouraged statutory agencies to support informal carers – this was explicitly embraced in the National Health and Community Care Act 1990. Government policies have also encouraged a shift in responsibility from the NHS to social services departments and from institutional to domiciliary care. However, this shift has not been accompanied by a growth in community services. Recent Department of Health statistics, for example, show that the projected growth in home and community-based nursing services has not occurred to any significant extent (see Table 8.1). This means that informal carers are expected to take on a greater burden of care.

Despite the rhetoric demonstrating a concern to 'support carers', there has been an unwillingness on the part of the government to provide the kind and level of services which might better support carers. As Twigg and

Table 8.1 Numbers of initial contacts by community nurses, 1989–93 (thousands).

	1989–90	1990–91	1991–92	1992–93
District nursing	2304	2136	2154	2128
Community psychiatric nursing	246	255	268	304
Community mental handicap nursing	22	22	20	22
Total	2572	2413	2442	2455

Source: Department of Health (1995).

Atkin (1995) notes, despite 'repeated exhortations' in the National Health and Community Care Act 1990 and in the Disabled Persons Act 1970, there has been little real policy guidance or practical support for carers. This has placed a great strain on carers. Whatever the benefits of unpaid family care in the home to the dependent person, we must also recognize the costs to the carers. A full appreciation of the impact of caring on carers' lives must take into account the effect on employment opportunities, earnings potential, increased household expenditure, physical illness, disability and emotional stress (Parker 1985). It is interesting to note that widespread public support for increasing the role of the informal sector may not really exist. A survey by West (1984: 441) on public attitudes towards family responsibilities concluded that:

> In the sample as a whole the idea of family care alone receives support from only a minority of respondents . . . The public as a whole are strongly supportive of professional and service involvement in the care of dependent persons.

Gender and informal care

A major impetus behind the increased visibility of informal care has come from feminist academics concerned to point out the gender implications of this form of care, and the viability and desirability of strategies designed to increase still further reliance on this sector. This concern stems from a recognition that women form the majority of carers and that the concentration of women in this type of unpaid work has important implications for their personal autonomy and ability to undertake paid work. As Finch (1984: 43–4) put it:

> . . . feminists have increasingly insisted on making explicit the true meaning of 'community care' as it applies to elderly and handicapped people – i.e. for community read family, and for family read women.

The argument for increasing the range of options available to dependent people is a strong one, and for many dependent people care in their own home or that of their family is no doubt a preferred option. There are, however, many dependent people who do not wish to live with their family, not least because this may undermine their independence and they fear becoming a burden to their families. In addition to this we must also consider the implications of the 'quality of care' and the 'choice' argument from the viewpoint of the carer. It is important to recognize that one person's free choice may mean denial of choice to another. As Twigg and Atkin (1995: 7) note:

> There is an essential duality of focus involved when addressing the issue of care. Caring takes place in a relationship, and one cannot focus on the interests of either the carer or the cared-for person to the exclusion of the other.

Taking on the care of a dependent relative does change the lives of those who take on the caring role and the lives of other members of the family, not just at the time but for the foreseeable future. There are financial, social and emotional implications. The wages that the female carer earned or may have earned in the future will be lost, other members of the family may have to turn down promotion or overtime, outside contact with other relatives or friends may be severely curtailed or completely foregone, and the carer will have less time and energy to devote to the care – including the 'emotional care' – of the rest of the family. Even when support and other services are available, carers may be reluctant to ask for them or may not even know they exist (see, for example, Abbott 1982). In research carried out by Abbott and Sapsford (1987a) in a new town, a mother who had to carry her 13-year-old daughter everywhere had to wait until she fell down the stairs and injured herself before she was offered a stair lift. The same mother found that respite care had to be booked so long in advance that she could rely on it only when social and physical exhaustion meant that she felt she could no longer cope. It was also evident that parents often did not understand or know about the full range of services available to them. **Normalizing** lives for dependent people may in effect de-normalize the lives of carers.

The tendency to present informal care as the only alternative to large, monolithic and segregative Victorian-styled institutions, rather than seeing the two as polar ends of a continuum of possibilities, may have served a useful ideological function in pricking the conscience of families and reaffirming their 'duty' to care. When feminists have suggested that community care need not mean family care, they are not proposing a return to Victorian standards but to the development of new forms of **residential care** which would enable both carers and the cared-for to lead as independent and 'normal' lives as possible:

> ... enabling people to maintain links with relatives or friends to whom they are emotionally close, that is, people who care 'about' them; but ... removing the compulsion to perform the labour of caring.
>
> (Finch 1990: 55)

Hilary Graham (1993b) acknowledges the emphasis in feminist perspectives on the providers of care, often to the neglect of the experiences of those receiving care – a point picked up by Morris (1993), who is fiercely critical of feminists for failing to consider the needs of disabled people. Morris argues that the focus on carers' needs has sidelined the fundamental question of why dependency arises in the first place (and hence why carers are required). In so doing, they have failed to challenge the social and economic factors which disabled people have to confront and unwittingly collude with the creation of their dependency (Morris 1993: 47). For many women in particular, the roles of carer and cared-for cannot easily be separated however, as they typically shift between the two and at times women may perform both roles simultaneously (as many disabled or pregnant women do). From the point of view of the person who is cared-for, community care can be seen both as a policy to perpetuate oppression and/or as a means of promoting independence:

It is the mechanism which enables them to receive personal care outside institutional settings; yet it is also the tool that can leave them dependent for intimate personal care at the mercy of others.
(Graham 1993b: 127)

In addition to feminist concerns about the desirability of increased reliance on informal care from the viewpoint of carers, there are some concerns about the viability of such policies. Demographic changes resulting in increased levels of dependency coupled with changes in family structure, and particularly increased levels of divorce, separation and lone parenting, together result in higher dependency ratios (with fewer women caring for more dependants) and more tenuous kinship links. What obligations will a woman have towards an ex-mother-in-law or a step-daughter, for example?

Increased geographical mobility, in the context of the free movement of people throughout the EU and increased levels of inter-regional mobility as labour follows capital in the search for work, means that, increasingly, many potential carers live substantial distances from their elderly parents. The increase in labour market participation rates for women across Europe in both full- and part-time work and the demise of the male breadwinning family model, as women increasingly constitute an important source of family income, also raises questions about the continued availability of unpaid labour for informal care. Finch and Groves (1983: 506) add to this by commenting:

There is a tendency also to ignore the issue of whether women will continue to accept their cultural designation as carers, or whether they will explicitly reject it, in ideology and in practice, in increasing numbers.

Together these pan-European social trends and their implications for the supply of informal care are likely to encourage the development of state policies aimed at reinforcing and reconstructing traditional family responsibilities. One such initiative concerns the introduction of systems of payment for informal care.

Informal care and the 'carer': Who provides care?

Studies of informal care in the 1970s and 1980s suggested that most of it was provided by women (see, for example, Wilkin 1979; Nissel and Bonnerjea 1982; Walker 1982; Finch and Groves 1983; Abbott and Sapsford 1987a; Lewis and Meredith 1988), and that this was often at a considerable social and psychological cost to the women providing it (Braithwaite 1990). The Foreword to Gillian Dalley's (1988: ix) *Ideologies of Caring* outlines some key concerns about the role of carers in the informal sector:

Where does the responsibility for providing care for dependent people lie? How can the services be offered in ways which do not rely on women to do the unpaid work of caring for members of their own family?

Women as informal carers

A study by the Equal Opportunities Commission (EOC) in 1984 compared the contribution of men and women in the caring of elderly dependent people and found that assignment of caring tasks was gendered and was conditioned not just in terms of the relationship with the dependant but also by the nature of the task involved. Women were much more likely to take responsibility for personal and domestic care duties and the contribution of male family members, while substantially less than that of women, was largely restricted to auxiliary care. These findings are also reported in a study by Gillian Parker (1985: 30), which argued that to talk of community or family care is:

> ... to disguise reality. In fact, ... 'care by the community' almost always means care by family members with little support from others in the 'community'. Further, care by family members almost always means care by female members with little support from other relatives. It appears that 'shared care' is uncommon; once one person has been identified as the main carer other relatives withdraw.

This point is reinforced by Twigg and Atkin (1995: 17), who found that:

> Caring largely devolved on individual carers and shared care was rare ... [where they did act as direct care providers] ... Families helped with more distant and social aspects, such as sitting with the cared-for person, providing transport or shopping, and were rarely involved in the intimate tasks of personal care.

Men as informal carers

However, more recent research has indicated that men are also involved in informal care. Arber and Gilbert (1989b) indicated that the same proportion of men as women care for a disabled spouse and that 40 per cent of elderly parents looked after by an unmarried child at home are cared for by a son. Arber and Gilbert (1989a) suggest two ideal-type caring trajectories: first, a lifelong co-resident trajectory where the care role is gradually taken on, generally as a response to a changing dependency relationship; and, second, a trajectory where care is explicitly taken on, the cared-for either joining the household or being cared for in another household. Men are equally as likely as women to be carers in the first trajectory, but women, and especially married women, are more likely to be the carers in the second. Men are also more likely than women to take on a temporary care role, for example when their wives are ill, reverting to a more traditional masculine role when their wives recover (Cliff 1993). Ungerson (1990) found that men were more likely to take on a caring role out of love, and women more out of duty.

The 1990 General Household Survey (OPCS 1995) found that 6.8 million people provide informal care: 1.6 million to someone in the same household and 5.2 million to someone living in another household (see Table 8.2). Fifteen per cent of people over the age of 16 were providing care for someone who was sick, disabled or elderly. The care they provided

Table 8.2 Carers' relationships to dependants.

Person being cared for	In the same household	In another household	Total
Total carers (millions)	1.6	5.2	6.8
Spouse	41%	—	10%
Child over 16	10%	10%	3%
Child under 16	8%	—	2%
Parent	23%	39%	35%
Parent-in-law	6%	15%	13%
Other relation	10%	20%	18%
Friend/neighbour	2%	25%	19%

Source: OPCS (1995: table 8.22).

included personal care, giving medicine, physical help, providing company and 'keeping an eye out'. Four per cent of men and women are caring for someone living in the same household, and 10 per cent of men and 13 per cent of women care for someone living in another household.

The amount of care provided by these informal carers is considerable; for example, 40 per cent of female and 15 per cent of male co-resident carers provide 35+ hours a week of care, while 34 per cent of women and 22 per cent of men providing care to someone not co-resident devote 10 or more hours a week (Arber and Ginn 1995). Arber and Ginn's analysis of the 1990 General Household Survey data indicates that, although women provide more informal care than men, men do provide considerably more of it than the literature has until now assumed. In terms of co-residential care, men provide care for spouses and children, and non-married men provide care for parents living in the same household. Married women, as well as providing care for husbands and children, are also the main providers of care to parents and parents-in-law. Women provide considerably more care for dependants living in another household, particularly married women. Twice as many women as men provide personal care, but there is evidence of a strong cross-sex taboo in the provision of personal care except for spouses and children. It is also less acceptable for an informal carer to provide personal care for friends, neighbours and non-close relations.

Gender and responsibility for informal care

Research using detailed qualitative techniques rather than the more superficial approach of large-scale survey questionnaires has consistently found that women take on more responsibility for informal care than men, both in providing more care and in taking the responsibility for managing and organizing it (see, for example, Finch and Groves 1983). Abbott and Sapsford (1987a), for example, found that fathers played little or no role in providing care for their children with learning disabilities; indeed, they often played a smaller part in the care of the disabled child than other children in their own families or fathers in families without a disabled child. Nissel and Bonnerjea (1982) found that, in families caring for an elderly parent, wives spent on average two to three hours a day undertaking essential care tasks, whether or not they were in paid employment; husbands, on the other hand, spent on average eight minutes. Twigg *et al.* (1990) suggest that women are mainly responsible for the provision of personal and physical care; men are more likely to take on the role of informal helpers. Where men do take on a major caring role, it tends to be for their elderly, disabled wives.

The question of the apportionment of caring roles within the family may, therefore, be more complex than previous research has suggested, requiring more in-depth analysis of the structuring of family obligations and a 'hierarchy of care' which runs from the spouse as first choice through daughters (second choice) to other close relatives (Qureshi and Walker 1989, cited in Graham 1993b: 127). While spouses might be assumed to take first responsibility for the care of their partner, irrespective of gender, once that relationship breaks down various gendered assumptions may come into play to determine which family member assumes the role of primary carer.

Children as informal carers

While much of the attention has been focused on women as carers, more recently concern has been expressed about children caring for disabled parents. Although considerable concern has been expressed, there is little evidence available on the numbers involved or the extent of care undertaken. However, increased awareness of this issue has been prompted by the implementation of both the Children Act 1989, which defines and clarifies the rights of children, and the National Health and Community Care Act 1990, which requires local authorities to take account of the needs of carers. Parker (1993) found that parents who are disabled do not wish to rely on the support of their children, while Lonsdale (1990) found that disabled mothers had clear ideas about what support it was appropriate for their children to give them. Aldridge and Becker (1993) undertook an ethnographic 'quality of life' study of young carers which sought to reveal the impact of caring on children's educational and psycho-social development and the opportunities available to them. The study found some 300 young carers (defined as carers under the age of 18, providing primary care for a sick or disabled relative in the home) in Nottinghamshire (based on a national estimate of 10,000 such carers). The findings of the study present a disturbing picture of children caring for a parent often suffering from a degenerative disease (such as multiple sclerosis or muscular dystrophy) with caring tasks ranging from light cleaning, washing up and preparation of meals to financial transactions, lifting, toileting and dealing with incontinence. The young carers interviewed expressed a need for additional support in three key areas: (1) improved formal services, (2) better information and (3) more emotional support.

The authors highlighted the need for a balance to be struck between 'liberating' young carers (from their caring role) and 'protecting' them.

Many of them would have welcomed more support, particularly to over-come their sense of isolation, but showed a general distrust of social workers and a fear of 'intervention' in their lives. Many child carers were missing a considerable amount of school and suffering restricted social lives and career opportunities as a result of their caring role. A second follow-up study (Aldridge and Becker 1994) focused on the recipients of care to ascertain how parents felt about their children taking primary responsibility for their physical and emotional well-being. The study found that although many parents felt that their children should not have to provide primary care and had clearly held views about the appropriate-ness of certain tasks, many preferred their children to care for them rather than professionals from outside the family.

Some parents had concealed their dependency on their children carers in order to maintain, as near as possible, a 'normal' family structure. They feared that if the professionals came to realize the degree of their depend-ency, it might result in them questioning their abilities, as parents, to look after their children in a situation of reciprocal dependency, where the child is both the carer and the cared-for. While many parents experienced a strong sense of guilt and fear in relying upon their children to care for them, they saw caring as a private matter and exercised various means of control over their children in order to maintain the care required and prevent withdrawal from caring. These attempts to keep the relationship 'private' also resulted in an unwillingness to involve professionals in their own care, although the parents felt that it was the role of the profes-sionals to provide for their children's needs. While most parents believed that their children cared through love and affection, the findings of the previous survey showed that the children themselves referred more to a lack of choice and their being socialized into the role.

Black carers

The needs of Black carers have also been highlighted in recent research. Atkin and Rollings (1992) have indicated the barriers that exist to Black people getting the services they need. They argue that not only are Black people not offered support services, but those they *are* offered are inap-propriate. They indicate that services need to be made accessible and acceptable to Black people. Service provision is often based on stereotyped and ill-informed views of what the Black community needs. It is often assumed, for example, that elderly Asian people will be cared for by their extended families. Assumptions about the ability of women to take on unpaid care work may apply even less in black communities – where it is more normal for women to have full-time paid employment – than in white communities. The needs of the Black community will grow as its age-structure begins to resemble that of the white majority.

Friends and neighbours

Little attention has been paid to the role of friends and neighbours who provide informal care, as opposed to organized volunteers. Many provide substantial amounts of help with such tasks as shopping, as well as being 'company' for the dependent person, and neighbours are the main source of surveillance of elderly people – they 'look out for them' and alert someone if there appears to be a problem. However, the help given by friends and neighbours is particularly 'fragile' and liable to disruption. Baldwin and Twigg (1992: 124) summarize the key findings of recent work on informal care as follows:

- The care of non-spouse dependants falls mainly on women;
- It is unshared to a significant extent by relatives, statutory or voluntary agencies;
- It creates burdens and material costs which are a source of significant inequalities between men and women;
- Many women nevertheless accept the role of informal carer and, indeed, derive satisfaction from doing so;
- The reasons for this state of affairs are deeply bound up with the construction of female and male identity, and possibly also with culturally defined rules about gender-appropriate behaviours.

Service support for carers

In addition to evidence concerning the differential impact of caring responsibilities on women, particularly in non-spouse relationships, there is growing evidence of indirect discrimination in the allocation of domiciliary services to carers. A 1984 Equal Opportunities Commission report summarizes this evidence and shows how government-funded support services tend to become involved in supporting the work of female carers at a much later stage in the caring process than for male carers. This is particularly the case in relation to the second category, which considers service support to non-spouse carers living with an elderly person. When the non-spouse is female, there is typically no home-help provision, community nursing support is received somewhat later in the process, and intermittent day care tends to be introduced at the point of dependency when male carers would have been offered long-stay residential care.

Twigg and Atkin's (1995) study of service support for carers found that support does not follow simple needs-related criteria (in terms of level of disablement, etc.), but rather socially constructed notions of carers' needs. Here the nature of the kinship relationship, the age and gender of the carer together underpin the attitudes of both service providers and users (including both carers and dependants). In terms of the assumptions of service providers, Twigg and Atkin (1995: 24) found that:

> One of the ways in which gender assumptions were significant was in relation to the visibility of the carer. Actions that were noteworthy in a male carer and resulted in him being recognised as such, were passed over when performed by a female, subsumed under her general domestic role.

Furthermore, service response varied depending on the relationship in question:

Service providers would go to more extreme lengths to support the
continuance of caring where it was between spouses . . . Where the
cared-for person is a parent, the assumptions are different. Privacy is
less strongly defended, and there is a greater tradition of autonomy
and separation.

(Twigg and Atkin 1995: 19)

An equally important factor affecting the receipt of service support
relates to the response of carers themselves to their situation. Twigg and
Atkin found that women are more likely to be 'engulfed' by the caring
relationship, which often takes over their entire lives. These women are
often reluctant to request or accept help, particularly when it is aimed at
them as opposed to the person they look after. Men, on the other hand,
often adopt an 'employment orientation'; they generally find it easier to
maintain boundaries and see their activities as a form of occupation rather
than an extension of family obligation:

Men appear to find it easier to separate themselves from the caring
situation, to set limits on their involvement and to see themselves as
'professional carers' who should legitimately receive support.

(Twigg and Atkin 1995: 24)

Research by Arber and Gilbert (1989b), based on the 1980 General Household Survey (OPCS 1982), also questioned the presumption that elderly
male carers receive much more support than women. They found that
although male carers do receive more help from both the voluntary and
statutory sectors, the differences are much smaller than other research has
suggested. Discrimination was found not to operate against women *per se*
(in that the differences in receipt of services between elderly male and
female carers is not that great), but against households in which non-
elderly married women predominated as carers. The authors conclude:

The major source of variation in the amount of support services received by elderly infirm men and women seems to be not the gender
of the recipients or the gender of the carer but the kind of household
in which they live and, in particular, whether there are others in the
household who can take on the burden of caring.

(Arber and Gilbert 1989b: 141)

Arber and Ginn (1995) conclude that recent policy initiatives will mainly
advantage male carers, mostly because of the cross-sexual taboos on the
provision of care given that there are far more female than male recipients
of care. They conclude that care managers' targeting of support will:

. . . discriminate against both women and co-resident carers. The latter already provide long hours of care equivalent to full-time employment, often with adverse consequences for their health and financial
well-being. If this kind of inequality is to be ended and the positive
benefits of community care – improving choice and independence for
those receiving care – are to be realised, additional resources must be
channelled to local authorities to meet the full cost of transferring
care to the community setting.

(Arber and Ginn 1995: 30)

Paying for Informal Care

Informal care in Britain has been based on two dominant models – familial care, where it is assumed that the carer is financially dependent on a (male) spouse, or the spinster model, where it is assumed that care is being undertaken by a daughter. The costs of caring have to a considerable extent been borne by informal carers themselves, who often have to give up paid employment or modify the type of work they undertake, to take on the caring role.

Invalid care allowance

State income support for carers was non-existent until the 1970s; those who were not entitled to a universal benefit (mainly the elderly) were dependent on means-tested benefits to the extent that they met eligibility criteria. In the 1970s, invalid care allowance was introduced, a means-tested benefit for people under retirement age who gave up paid employment to care for a dependant. Married women were unable to claim this benefit until 1986, when the European Court ruled that this amounted to sex discrimination and the British Government was forced to include them. The benefit is paid only to full-time carers, the person being cared for has to be claiming attendance allowance/disability living allowance, and the rate is equivalent to that of non-householder income support. This means that the carer remains financially dependent either on other members of the household or on the cared-for person.

Paying informal carers

In the last chapter, we considered the development of paid volunteering as a response to the need for increased numbers of volunteers arising from the expansion both in size and responsibility of the voluntary sector. We also noted the impact of such initiatives on the mixed economy of welfare, blurring the boundaries between welfare providers and raising complex questions about the implications of such initiatives for those involved. Resort to the payment of previously unpaid workers for the provision of welfare services is not, however, restricted to voluntary work, and recently there has been an increase in schemes involving the remuneration of informal care. The development of schemes involving payment to informal carers must be considered in the context of demographic change in Western Europe, where the growth in the population of frail elderly people and a falling birth rate have led to an increase in the dependency ratio. This, in turn, has created pressures to develop measures which might increase the overall supply of care-giving labour combined with economic and ideological pressures to restrict public expenditure in the area of social care.

Glendinning and McLaughlin (1993) compared schemes involving payment for carers in Britain (via invalid care allowance) with the Finnish system of home care allowances, in which family and friends are paid 'very substantial' amounts to care for a frail elderly person, focusing in particular on the implications of these schemes for the 'adequacy, autonomy and independence' of both care-givers and those in receipt of care. The system of payment for carers via the social security system (invalid care allowance, the disability living allowance and various other benefits) in Britain as described by Glendinning and McLaughlin (1993: 241) provides for a very low level of benefit (the invalid care allowance in 1993–94 amounted to £33.70 plus additions for dependent children). In addition, entitlement conditions effectively exclude the majority of carers. The invalid care allowance was intended as an earnings replacement benefit and is not therefore available to elderly carers or part-time workers; it is also taken into account in assessments of means-tested benefits. It is only available to carers of severely disabled people (defined as those claiming attendance allowance/disability living allowance), creating an interdependence of benefit. Two-thirds of unsuccessful applications in 1988 were disallowed because the person being cared for was not receiving attendance allowance (Glendinning and McLaughlin 1993: 242). This type of benefit effectively renders many carers financially dependent upon their dependent relative. The low level of the benefit reflects gendered assumptions about the nature of this type of work and represents little more than a token contribution of very restricted availability.

In contrast, the Finnish system of home care allowances forms part of a broad programme of support for home care. It is not a social security benefit but a form of substitute for directly provided statutory services in the form of cash payments. The payment is calculated on the basis of the dependant's needs but paid to the carer by the municipal authorities. Levels of payment vary considerably, with full-time carers receiving £265.25 per month in one authority and £795.76 in another, raising problems of territorial justice; eligibility depends upon the dependant's needs and is not income-related. While apparently generous, the levels of payment are closer to levels of welfare benefits in Finland and fail to compensate carers for their loss of labour market earnings. Indeed, even at these levels, the home care allowances do not appear to increase the supply of carers, the majority of whom are related to, living with, and often the spouse of, the dependent person. They may, however, sustain the care-giving relationship for longer, thus reducing admission to institutional care.

Set in the context of a society in which over 88 per cent of women are economically active in full-time waged work, there is some concern that this form of payment for informal care may constitute a form of exploitation of female labour with payments well below the market rate – 'a means of excluding women from paid labour but not from work' (Glendinning and McLaughlin 1993: 249). The fact that carers themselves received the benefit increased their self-esteem and perceptions of their status. Ungerson (1995: 31) argues that these developments call into question the traditional dichotomy between paid and unpaid work as the activities of informal care are increasingly being commodified, resulting in new social and economic relations which pose particular dilemmas for feminists.

While accepting that any distinction between informal and formal care, based on assumptions that the motivations of informal carers are qualitatively different (reflecting kinship obligation and a 'labour of love' as opposed to a contractual agreement), have always been problematic, the development of forms of remuneration for carers further muddies the waters. It becomes increasingly difficult to argue that formal and informal care are substantially and qualitatively different: 'they both contain elements of labour and love' (Ungerson 1995: 32). In addition to schemes involving direct payment to carers, there is a second, more popular, trend in the provision of cash benefits directly to dependent individuals in the expectation that they will use the money to purchase their own care. (The Community Care Allowance/Disability Living Allowance paid to severely disabled people in Britain is intended to enable the purchase of services.) Austria is currently turning over its entire care system to high cash payments to care-recipients so that they can buy in their own care. Both forms of payment have different implications for the autonomy of carers. While both schemes constitute an explicit recognition 'of the work involved in domestic caring labour and provide the basis for carers' autonomy and a modicum of financial independence . . . the systems are often gendered in conception and are certainly gendered in consequence' (Ungerson 1995: 39).

There is no guarantee that recipients will use the benefits in the way intended (i.e. to buy in care), nor that they will pay appropriate wages. Indeed, Ungerson notes the growing concern in Europe over the development of unregulated 'grey labour' with no guarantees of minimum working conditions, pay levels or workers' rights. Furthermore, the symbolic nature of these payments may be used to encourage carers to remain in the private domain rather than entering paid work. As such, this extra pressure on women to give up paid work may be 'entrapping rather than liberating' (Ungerson 1995: 48). This is especially true of payments channelled through care-recipients, where no minimum wage rates or conditions are specified. Such kinds of payment also tend to reinforce reliance on one single carer, as they typically only identify one person to receive the whole benefit. Schemes involving payment of informal carers thus raise similar issues to those discussed in relation to paid voluntarism:

1 How does the payment of informal carers affect the relationship between the supply of formal and informal labour? Will it affect the level of funding for care workers employed in the public and commercial sectors?
2 What are the implications of payment for the rights, citizenship and quality of life of carers and those receiving care? In particular, how does the public funding of informal care affect the quality of carers' working conditions and the quality of care provided?
3 How do different systems of payment affect the autonomy of carers and the recipients of care?

Conclusions

Informal care – that is, care by relatives and friends, but predominantly close relatives – is the major form of welfare in Britain and always has been. The family is the major institutional location of care and welfare for the majority of the population. The main providers of care are women, as they meet the welfare and care needs of their husbands and children as well as elderly relatives and adult children with care needs. The British classic welfare state was built on the assumption that the nuclear family of husband, wife and dependent children was not only how people lived their lives but how they *should* live them. Women, it was assumed, were and would be financially dependent on their husbands and would meet the care needs not only of their partners and their children but of ageing parents as well (see, for example, Abbott and Wallace 1992). The subsequent development of policies of community care (see Chapter 9) has built on this foundation and assumed that women are willing and available to take on additional caring roles for dependent relatives, friends and neighbours.

We have also seen that women are not the only carers; men and children also take on the burden of caring. However, there is not the same assumed relationship as with women between natural virtues and the caring role, and so not the same moral pressure to care. Women, it is assumed, are natural carers and therefore should be able to take on caring roles and should wish to do so. Women who decline to do so are seen as unnatural, as uncaring. For women there can be no separation, as there can be for men, between 'caring about' and 'caring for'.

In the next chapter, we look at the mixed economy of care by examining the development and operation of policies of community care. These are built on implicit (and, increasingly, explicit) assumptions about the role of informal carers. We have demonstrated above that the burden of care placed on informal carers is often considerably greater than that placed on paid workers. The availability of informal carers and their willingness to continue to play the central role in providing care should not be taken for granted. This is especially the case with women in mid-life who increasingly have jobs as well as providing for the care needs of husbands and children; it is this group, however, who are least likely to be given help by the state welfare services. The needs of black carers are also frequently not met, and there is an increasing awareness of the scandal of child carers.

Summary

• Informal care and the notion of a 'welfare society' has underpinned and determined all other forms of welfare provision throughout British social history.

- 'Informal care' is a concept used to refer to the work done, mainly within the home, in supporting people at various levels of dependency.

- This work is undertaken, primarily by women, on a largely unremunerated basis with important implications for their financial and personal autonomy.
- Recent years have witnessed the growth of fiscal and ideological pressures to further increase the relative contribution of this sector via policies of welfare retrenchment and the promotion of 'community care'. In spite of the rhetoric, however, there is little evidence of a substantial shift in resources to enable carers to shoulder this additional responsibility.

- Gendered assumptions about caring roles permeate policy in this area resulting in discrimination in the allocation of services which substantially increases the burden placed upon women.

- The development of forms of remuneration for informal carers raise complex and contradictory questions; on the one hand they represent an acknowledgement of caring as a form of 'work', but on the other they reinforce caring roles and perpetuate labour market discrimination.

Further reading

Baldwin, S. and Twigg, J. (1992) Women and community care. In M. Maclean and D. Groves (eds), *Women's Issues in Social Policy*. London: Routledge.

Bornat, J., Pereira, C., Pilgrim, D. and Williams, F. (eds) (1993) *Community Care: A Reader*. Basingstoke: Macmillan.

Dalley, G. (1988) *Ideologies of Caring*. London: Macmillan.

Parker, G. (1985) *With Due Care and Attention: A Review of Research on Informal Care*. London: Family Policy Studies Centre.

THE MIXED ECONOMY OF CARE: WELFARE SERVICES FOR DEPENDENT PEOPLE

Introduction

In Chapter 1, we indicated that there is a mixed economy of care in Britain: provision by the state, the commercial sector, the voluntary sector and informal carers. In Chapters 5–8, we used case studies to illustrate the role of each of these sectors. In this chapter, we look not at the separate elements, but at 'the mix'. Recent developments of schemes to promote 'care in the community' best exemplify how the mixed economy of welfare works in practice. We have argued in previous chapters that all dimensions of social policy interact, but this interrelationship is nowhere as explicitly acknowledged as in the development of community care. Indeed, the success or failure of care in the community depends on the careful balance of responsibilities and partnerships both within the statutory sector itself (between different agencies, such as social services, health authorities and housing departments) and between the range of nonstatutory providers. These welfare services together enable dependent people to live in the community. The provision of **domiciliary** services and day care is only one element of community care (Abbott 1992a, 1992b).

This chapter begins by documenting the development of community care strategies in the post-war period. It considers some of the explanations for the increasing attractiveness of this type of policy, including concerns about public expenditure, issues about the 'quality of care', and ideological pressures to shift 'responsibility' further on to individuals and families and away from the state. Finally, the chapter outlines the most recent developments in community care policy and the development of schemes to harness and coordinate the provision of care by the voluntary sector, the commercial sector and the family. This focus on community care illustrates the changing role of the state in contemporary Britain, from one of direct provider (of residential homes and domiciliary services for the elderly, the mentally ill and children) to one of financier, regulator and coordinator of a broad range of inputs.

As a social policy, community care is relatively new in Britain. The term itself was first used in the Report of the Royal Commission on the Law Relating to Mental Illness and Mental Deficiency (Royal Commission 1958). This report recommended a shift of policy from hospital to community care and emphasized the desirability of supported family care. Community care has been supported and promoted by successive governments since the 1960s, not least because it has been seen as a cheaper and more humanitarian alternative to residential care. However, in practice, community care often means either community neglect (especially in the case of mentally ill people transferred from hospital to boarding houses) or care by relatives, especially women. Local authorities have been slow to provide community care services, and individuals with relatives to care for them have been less likely to receive services than those who live alone (see Chapter 8).

There is a long history of a mixed economy of care in the provision of **personal social services**, both domiciliary and day care. However, the greater part of expenditure on personal social services has been accounted for by services provided by the state sector – although, as indicated in Chapter 8, the informal sector has played the major role in actually providing the care. The larger part of state expenditure that has involved purchasing care from the commercial and voluntary sectors has been provided by the Department of Social Security (DSS) to fund or partly fund places in residential and nursing homes. Of residents in commercial and voluntary homes in 1992, nearly 60 per cent were funded in this way (Wistow *et al.* 1994: table 3.5). Local authority expenditure has been modest. In 1991–92, it was 6.4 per cent of total expenditure in England: 3.5 per cent was used to purchase services from the voluntary sector, 1.4 per cent went in general support to the voluntary sector and 1.5 per cent was used to purchase services from the commercial sector. Only a very small part of this expenditure went on non-residential services (Wistow *et al.* 1994: tables 3.1–3.4).

Community care services

Community care is most easily understood as the alternative to institutional care. It consists of a wide range of welfare services which provide care for dependent groups (e.g. elderly people, children, people who are physically disabled, people with **learning difficulties**, or those who are mentally ill) within the community, rather than within institutions such as long-stay hospitals or large residential homes. A community care policy may embrace one or more of the following:

1 Services are provided by the state in the community.
2 Decarceration, i.e. dependent people are no longer cared for in long-stay hospitals.
3 Care is provided by informal carers, especially families.
4 The lives of dependent people are 'normalized' and their contribution to society valued.

Michael Bayley (1973) made a distinction between 'care in the community' and 'community care'. The former concerns geographical location, in that people are cared for not in large hospitals, but instead reside in small local hospitals, or hostels or with their families. The latter suggests that people are cared for by both formal and informal agencies, and relatives, in the community. Government policies have tended to emphasize the responsibility of families to care for their dependent members. Other research suggests that informal support and help from the community is rarely forthcoming. As Martin Bulmer (1987: x) has pointed out:

> 'Community' as a concept invokes images of the family to convey the warmth and intimacy which its bonds are supposed to foster . . . The term 'community care' appeals to sentiment and postulates a range of supportive ties which may not actually exist in practice, thus putting the burden of care upon particular family members.

The election of the Conservative government in 1979 gave a new impetus to community care, partly because it was integral to that government's commitment to the importance of the family, commercial markets and the voluntary sector in providing welfare, and partly because of an increasing concern about the cost of providing for a growing number of elderly people needing care.

Development of community care

Before the welfare state

Jack Tizzard (1964) was unable to trace the origins of the idea of community care as a policy objective. However, Scull (1977) indicated that the policy was considered in the late nineteenth century but could not be implemented he argues, for lack of community services. The 1904–1908 Royal Commission on the Care of the Feeble-Minded, although mostly concerned with institutional care, did advocate guardianship and supervision in 'the community'. The 1929 Wood Committee recommended greater use of all forms of community supervision, and by the late 1930s experts were suggesting that, given favourable conditions, the mentally handicapped could be supervised at home.

Certainly, psychological and sociological research in the 1950s and 1960s strongly suggested that all children developed better, both cognitively and emotionally, if cared for in a family environment (Bowlby 1954; Lyle 1958, 1959a, 1959b; Tizzard 1964) and that hospitals and other large institutions were dehumanizing (Barton 1959; Goffman 1961; Wing and Brown 1970; King *et al.* 1971). Furthermore, the founding of the welfare state meant that facilities existed in the community ready to be drawn upon by people with special needs and their carers. The policies also fitted in with the ideology of welfare and equality of opportunity that was developing in Britain (see, for example, Scull 1977). In the case of the mentally ill, the development of psychotropic drugs which could 'control' the 'unaccept-able' behaviour of many was a key factor. An important selling point at the time seems to have been that policies of community care appeared to be cheap as well as humanitarian alternatives to residential care. As Scull indicated, the general welfare services introduced in the 1940s were avail-able to meet the needs of dependent groups – specific services did not have to be provided.

Community care in the welfare state

Scull (1977) has pointed out that while the rejection of institutional care in asylums and other long-stay institutions was based on research findings that demonstrated the dehumanizing nature of such care, the advocacy of community care was not based on research demonstrating its efficacy. Furthermore, what community care means has never been fully clarified. In general, it seems just to mean care outside large-scale institutions – remote, impersonal asylums or other long-stay institutions. Community care can mean living in a small local hospital, a hostel, a group home, in lodgings, independently or with a family. It can mean that a range of services are provided, such as sheltered workshops, community nursing, home care, social work support, respite care, day care and so on, or that families are left entirely to fend for themselves.

In the last 30 years or so, then, community care for dependent groups has become a policy objective in most western countries. In Britain by the 1950s, residential care, especially in large institutions, was being criticized for children deprived of a normal home life (Bowlby 1954) as well as the mentally handicapped, the mentally ill and older people (National Coun-cil for Civil Liberties 1951; Townsend 1962). Subsequently, a number of academic studies of long-stay residential institutions suggested that they were dehumanizing (e.g. Barton 1959; Goffman 1961; Wing and Brown 1971), and official enquiry reports indicated that residents were ill-treated. King *et al.* (1971) argued that organizational factors were a key to the problems faced in providing adequate, personalized care in institutional set-tings. The Report of the Royal Commission on Mental Health (1954–58) suggested community care as an alternative to hospitalization, and the Mental Health Act 1959 advocated community care for mentally ill and mentally handicapped people. A government report in 1964, 'The Development of Community Care', recommended the development of a family-oriented service and an expansion of non-institutional day care and domiciliary services, staffed by professional workers, in expanding local authority health and welfare departments, while recognizing that some residential care might still be necessary. The Seebohm Committee (1968) argued that the existence of community care remained an illusion. Government policy throughout the 1970s was to implement community care, but the extent to which community services did actually develop has been questioned. A number of welfare benefits were also introduced to assist dependent people with the costs of living in the community. These included benefits which were not means-tested, such as mobility allowance and attendance allowance paid to disabled people themselves, as well as means-tested income maintenance benefits, including invalidity benefit and the invalidity care allowance paid to carers (but withheld from married women until 1986; see Chapter 5).

Normalization

By the late 1970s, besides community care, 'normalization' was being advocated – the idea that dependent people should lead as normal a life as possible in the community (see Department of Health and Social Security 1980; see also P. Jenkin 1980, then Secretary of State for Social Services, quoted in Abbott 1982: 161). Community care has continued to be advocated by governments as a major policy objective. However, the emphasis has switched from the provision of services by health and social services department to informal care with support as necessary:

> Whatever level of public expenditure proves practicable, and however it is distributed, the primary sources of support and care for elderly people are informal and voluntary . . . It is the role of public authorities to sustain and where necessary develop but never displace such support and care . . . Care in the community must increasingly mean care by the community.
>
> (DHSS 1981a: 3)

Furthermore, when services are required, they are to be purchased by the local authority from the commercial and voluntary sectors as well as being provided directly by social services and the health authority. The state agencies are to act as

> . . . enabling authorities . . . securing the delivery of services not simply by acting as direct providers, but by developing their purchasing and contracting role to become enabling authorities.
>
> (DSS 1989: para. 313)

It is argued that services should be targeted at those most in need and directed at maintaining people in the community with, wherever possible, informal carers playing a major role: 'the reality is that most care is provided by family, friends and neighbours' (DSS 1989: para. 2.3).

Community care in the 1990s

Since the end of the 1970s, the British Government has been committed to policies of community care for all dependent groups. The most recent restatement of this commitment was the enactment of the provisions in the White Paper, *Caring for People* (Department of Health 1989c), in the Health and Community Care Act 1990, whose community care provisions were implemented in April 1993. The most significant development of recent years has been concern about the implications of demographic change (and the rise in the proportion of elderly people) for social policy expenditure. By the early 1980s, the government came to realize that if more very dependent people were to live in the community rather than in long-stay residential hospitals, then costs would escalate unless much of this care was undertaken by informal carers. Nearly half of all social security payments in 1993–94 were made to the elderly (CSO 1995: 135) and, between 1980 and 1989, social security expenditure on elderly people in residential care rose from £10 million to £1000 million (Lewis *et al.* 1995: 75). The Family Policy Studies Centre estimated the economic 'value' of informal care to be between £15 billion and £24 billion per year in 1989. Such calculations are difficult to make with accuracy as the defining feature of this sector is its informal and largely hidden nature. The figure is useful, however, if only to illustrate the contribution of the sector in comparison with total government expenditure on social services in 1987–88, which amounted to £3.34 billion (DHSS 1987). Of particular concern has been the resource implications of increasing numbers of long-stay and geriatric beds in residential and nursing homes, especially in the commercial and voluntary sectors. These places have to a considerable extent been funded by the DHSS, what the Audit Commission referred to as a perverse incentive to residential care. The evidence suggests that elderly people prefer to remain in the community, but the support services are not available (Abbott and Lankshear 1992).

The new community care policy was embodied in the 1990 National Health Service and Community Care Act, which required local authorities to make substantial changes in the way they managed and delivered services. The Act envisaged that social services departments would become 'enabling authorities' responsible for the stimulation and coordination of 'independent' providers within a mixed economy of care. Local authorities were also required to separate the purchaser and provider functions within social services departments as a means of reducing direct social service provision and encouraging the buying-in of commercial and voluntary services to support informal care. Through more effective joint planning, social services departments were to oversee the development of a 'seamless service' within a mixed economy of service provision. The intention behind these policies was to reinforce the role of informal care through the provision of additional domiciliary support in the form of home care, meals on wheels and community nursing to prevent caring relationships from breaking down as a result of high levels of dependency.

The move towards community-based care also marked an ideologically motivated shift away from direct public provision in favour of a 'mixed economy of care', and from provider/professional-led services to needs-led services. The introduction of new procedures for assessment, which emphasized 'needs-led' care, may be interpreted as a positive initiative aimed at reducing bureaucracy and the power of welfare professionals and genuinely empowering service users. In practice, however, the rhetoric of user **empowerment** may mean little more than a shift from being clients to consumers within a managed market. Lewis *et al.* (1995: 75) express similar misgivings about the meaning of 'user-centredness' in the community care context:

> Many academic commentators have highlighted the issue of whether it is possible to represent this claim as the empowerment of users, or whether it is merely an attempt to increase their standing as consumers of services.

In summary, then, the key objectives of the 1990 legislation were:

1 To facilitate the development of services in the community, which will enable dependent people to live in their own homes.
2 To ensure that the needs of users are prioritized, that is to change from service-led to needs-led provision.
3 To ensure that needs are assessed by care managers who are responsible for purchasing packages of care.
4 To ensure that the voluntary and independent sectors are major providers of services.
5 To ensure better value for the public monies spent on community care.
6 To ensure that services are targeted at those most in need.

Thus the key role of social services departments is to be the lead authority and to purchase and coordinate care within a social care market, a market that they are responsible for stimulating. This must be done in consultation with health authorities. The intention is that there will be a shift in the balance of welfare provision from the state to the voluntary, commercial and informal sectors with the establishment of market forces that will drive down the cost of service provision. Services will be targeted at those most in need – that is, those most likely to require admission to residential care if services were not provided. Four key concerns remain:

1 The balance between institutional and community services.
2 The balance between supply-led and needs-led services.
3 The balance between the provision of services by the public sector and the commercial/voluntary sectors.
4 The balance between funding and provision by the NHS and local authority social services.

Older people and community care needs

A major concern, then, has been the growth in the number of individuals in the population aged 65 years and over, both in absolute terms and as a percentage of the UK population as a whole. In 1988, the population of the UK was estimated to be 57.1 million (CSO 1991), of whom 18 per cent were aged 65 years or older (Arber and Ginn 1991), compared with 5 per cent in 1901. The proportion of the population aged 65 or over is not expected to alter much over the next 30 years, but there is concern regarding the predicted growth in the numbers of individuals aged 85 years and over – that is, those most likely to require help in performing daily living tasks. The proportion of people in this age group is expected to grow by 62 per cent in the next 20 years. By 2001, there will be over one million people aged 85 and over, and about half of these are likely to need assistance with some aspect of daily living.

People aged 65 and over account for a large percentage of health and welfare spending. Half of all NHS spending goes on this age group; they also account for 50 per cent of district nursing workload, and 75 per cent of those aged 65 and over visit their GPs regularly. The projected increase in the numbers of older people, especially the frail elderly, will put increased pressure on resources which are already stretched. Arber and Ginn (1991) estimate that expenditure on health and personal social services will have to rise by 12 per cent in real terms over the next 40 years, if expenditure per person in each age group is to remain constant.

However, there is complex 'fracturing', creating overlapping constituencies of older people, with clear contrasts of circumstances and needs. The most obvious of these fracture-lines are those between the frail and the fit and healthy, and between those who have adequate economic resources and the poor elderly. Those who have adequate resources are often in a position to purchase their own social care services from the commercial sector; those who do not are dependent on state support.

Old age and dependency

Thus old age, even *very* old age, is not synonymous with dependency and ill health; nor is it synonymous with financial dependency on the state. A minority are extremely dependent (25 per cent of those aged 65+ living in private households are moderately or severely incapacitated; see Table 9.1 and OPCS 1982). However, there is a close relationship between advancing years on the one hand and the increasing incidence of physical

Table 9.1 The degree of disability of elderly people living at home, by age group.

Age (years)	Total sample (n)	Degree of disability			
		None (%)	Slight (%)	Moderate (%)	Severe (%)
65–69	1620	65	22	10	3
70–74	1218	53	26	16	6
70–74	861	35	33	25	7
80+	875	22	24	31	22
Total	4374	49	26	17	8

Source: Evandrou (1991); figures derived from OPCS (1982).

disabilities and mental incapacities on the other. There is also a gender imbalance: the greater life expectancy of women means they form an ever increasing proportion of those surviving into advanced old age. Women are also more likely than men to be dependent on state benefits in old age, being less likely to have a private pension. The need for care in old age, and especially the need for care from formal services, is mediated by a number of factors, including the household circumstances of the elderly person, their socio-economic circumstances, their extended family net-works and the type of disability or ill health they suffer. Changes in these other factors suggest that the growth in the numbers of older people will provide a formidable challenge to health and social care agencies. The erosion of public sector resources for providing services to support older people means that it is difficult to provide services at present, let alone for increased numbers in the future. The decline in the numbers of young people in the 1970s because of low birth rates, means that there will be difficulties recruiting nurses and other care workers, especially to work with older people. Care of the elderly relies heavily on informal carers, but the increasing number of elderly people is not matched by a similar increase in potential carers (see Chapter 8). Challis et al. (1989) suggest that there is a need for the state sector to support informal carers; if not, they will collapse under the strain and become dependent themselves.

An analysis of the OPCS Disability Survey (OPCS 1988) and the 1987 General Household Survey (OPCS 1989a) gives an indication of 'at-risk' groups and the care needs of older people. The Disability Survey provides information on people whose impairment affects their ability to perform the normal activities of daily living. Six million adults in Britain who live in private households are disabled, of whom about 70 per cent are aged 60 and over. Of the more than one million severely disabled adults, 75 per cent are aged 60 and over. An analysis of the 1987 General Household Survey (Evandrou et al. 1986) showed that 42 per cent of those aged 65+ have difficulty cutting their own toenails, 12 per cent need help to walk across the road, or could not do so at all, and 8 per cent are unable to take a bath or shower or wash themselves all over, or need help in doing so. The need for help with personal care increases with age (Table 9.2). If

Table 9.2 The proportions of older people living in private households unable to perform specified tasks, by age group.

	Tasks						
Age (years)	Cutting toenails	Bathing oneself	Shaving (males only)	Washing face/hands	Feeding oneself	Climbing stairs	Getting to toilet
65–69	16	4	1	—	—	4	1
70–74	24	5	1	1	1	5	1
75–79	34	10	1	1	—	10	2
80–84	48	16	3	1	1	17	2
85+	65	31	7	3	2	31	7
90+	78	35	20	12	4	34	15

Source: OPCS (1989: tables 12.14 and 12.31).

these figures are extrapolated for all those aged 65+, there are approximately one million older people who are unable to go outside and walk down the street and about three-quarters of a million who are unable to bath, shower or wash themselves. By the year 2001, these figures will probably have increased by 25 per cent. (More than 80 per cent of this increase will be accounted for by people aged 85 and over.)

Caring for older people

The major source of help for those unable to care for themselves is relatives and other informal carers (see Chapter 8). Government policy also assumes that informal carers will continue to be the main providers of care for older people, and while it is stated that public services should support informal carers, in practice they often receive little, if any, help from statutory services.

Box 9.1 A proposed hierarchy of the care preferences of older people

A In older person's own home – self-care

B In older person's own home – care provided by co-resident:
   1 Spouse
   2 Same-generation relative
   3 Child, or someone other than kin

C In older person's own home – care provided by non-resident
   4 Child
   5 Other relative
   6 Neighbour, friend, volunteer

D In caregiver's home – care provided by co-resident
   7 Unmarried child
   8 Married child

Domiciliary support services such as home helps and community nurses may perform an enabling role for older people in any of these caring contexts.

Source: Arber and Ginn (1991).

Arber and Ginn (1991) suggest that informal care is the form of care preferred by older people themselves, who wish to stay in their own homes for as long as possible (Table 9.3, Box 9.1). However, research suggests that older people increasingly prefer the support of professionals when they have care needs and are not living with a spouse (Phillipson 1990). A 1988 Gallup poll found that 57 per cent of those interviewed believed that responsibility for care should shift towards the state (*Guardian*, 2 November 1988, quoted in Phillipson 1992), while in a survey of older people in South Glamorgan, Salvage *et al.* (1988, 1989) found that

Table 9.3 Proportions of elderly people in Britain receiving help with daily activities, 1985.

Source of help	Steps and stairs (%)	Personal care tasks (%)	Cutting toenails (%)	Shopping (%)	Cleaning windows (%)
Total sample (n)	119	92	988	880	963
Spouse	40	47	15	34	33
Other in household	24	39	5	16	15
Relative	21	8	6	18	11
Friend	3	1	—	8	2
Nurse/health visitor	2	4	2	—	—
Home help	—	1	—	7	19
Chiropodist	—	—	68	—	—
Paid help	—	—	—	1	12
Other	10	—	4	16	8

Source: Victor (1991: 150).

Table 9.4 Sources of personal help and domestic care for severely disabled elderly men and women (percentages).

Source of help	Personal care			Domestic care		
	Men (%)	Women (%)	Total (%)	Men (%)	Women (%)	Total (%)
Spouse	66	28	39	65	20	33
Other in household	12	32	26	14	36	30
Relative not in household	8	20	17	20	17	17
Friend/neighbour	1	5	4	5	5	5
State services	12	14	14	16	14	14
Paid help	1	—	<1	2	2	2

Source: OPCS (1987) and Arber and Ginn (1991: 148).

although a majority of respondents wanted to remain in the community for as long as possible receiving family care – and this was especially true of men – they did not think that carers should be expected to make too extreme a sacrifice. For example, they did not think a daughter should be expected to give up her paid employment. Older people also seem less prepared than in the past to be dependent on their children, especially if it involves a long-term commitment (Lee 1985) or personal care (Ungerson 1987).

There is little evidence, however, that statutory services are being provided to support informal carers, and the needs of elderly carers in particular do not seem to be being met (Wenger 1990). Older people living alone are much more likely to receive statutory services than those living with other people. Although 14 per cent of elderly women and 7 per cent of elderly men are severely disabled and need help with **personal** and **domestic care**, the majority receive help from informal sources, mainly from a spouse if they are men, but women are more likely to receive help from relatives or other informal carers (Table 9.4).

Statutory services

Only a very small percentage of people aged 65 and over receive statutory services. About 7 per cent of those aged 65+ have a home help, rising to 36 per cent of those aged 85+. Three per cent of those aged 65+ have meals delivered to the home, rising to 11 per cent of those aged 85+ (OPCS 1987). Twenty per cent of those aged 65+ are visited by a district nurse during the course of the year, about 6 per cent at least once a month (OPCS 1982, 1989). Of those aged 75 and over, 6 per cent attend a day centre and 1 per cent a day hospital. However, provision of home helps varies widely in different parts of the country, metropolitan counties having a higher ratio than shire counties. The ratio of community nurse to older people is roughly constant across the country, though a higher proportion are receiving services at any one time in shire counties (5.6 per cent) than in metropolitan counties (3.7 per cent).

A number of concerns have been raised about the provision and deployment of domiciliary care services. Sinclair and Williams (1990) summarize these under three headings: inflexibility, resource allocation and caring style. They suggest that the domiciliary services are not sufficiently flexible to meet the care preferences of individual clients; that is, to provide what is wanted, when it is wanted and in a way that fits in with the client's informal care networks. Services are not provided to those most in need and little concern is shown for the needs of informal carers. (However, there is a problem here: most clients and other potential users would prefer an extensive service that provides domestic help, while government community care policies require that services be concentrated on highly dependent people who might otherwise be admitted to residential care.) In terms of caring style, it is suggested that social service workers encourage dependency (Abbott 1992a) and do not obtain medical advice on the causes of problems.

The home help service is seen as particularly central to community care (SSI 1987, 1988; Lawson 1991), but there has been considerable debate as to how it should be used. Increasingly, it has been suggested that the service should be targeted at a small number of very dependent people and provide an intensive and frequent service, including personal care. However, the majority of home help hours are still devoted to domestic work, and the majority of clients receive a small number of hours of home help (Sinclair and Williams 1990). Bebbington and Davies (1983) estimated that 64 per cent of those in need of a home help were not being visited by one, while 22 per cent of those being visited were not in need. Old people living in rural areas and in need were the least likely to receive the service. Neill et al. (1988), in an analysis of applicants for residential care, found that while 70 per cent of those who lived alone received one or more domiciliary services (home help, meals on wheels, district nurse), only 51 per cent of those who lived with another elderly person did so, and only 31 per cent of those who lived with a person or persons of a younger generation. District nursing was the only service which was not significantly more likely to be provided to older people if they lived alone.

Preventing the move into residential care

There is also debate about whether the home help service can substitute
for residential care. Lawson (1991) suggested that the amount of home
help input makes little difference to whether or not an elderly person is
admitted to residential care. Others suggest that the service cannot be
seen as an alternative to residential care, simply because it is never dis-
pensed in sufficient quantity to provide such an alternative (Sinclair and
Williams 1990), while Victor and Vetter (1988) have pointed to the need
not only to increase the amount of time devoted by conventional home
helps but also to provide more personal care. There has been no clear
policy of substituting the home help service for residential care (Bebbington
and Tong 1986), and between the mid-1970s and the mid-1980s the provision of home helps per thousand elderly people actually fell (Audit
Commission 1986; Jamieson 1991a).

Evaluation of schemes aimed at providing a home care service are mixed.
Reports of the development of domiciliary care schemes aimed at providing a flexible home help service that provides more personal care and
care at unusual hours are generally enthusiastic about the outcomes; the
problems seem to lie in the relationship between home helps and district nurses (Hunter *et al.* 1988; Sinclair and Williams 1990; Abbott 1992b).
Davies *et al.* (1990) demonstrated the importance of good field coordination between social services and community nursing. However, evaluations of schemes that have been based on developing a more flexible
home help service suggest that while there is a reduction in the number
of elderly people entering residential care and using district nursing services, the cost to social services is considerably increased (Latto 1984;
Abbott 1992b). Specific projects undertaken in the 1980s to assess the
possibility of maintaining vulnerable elderly people in their own homes,
who would otherwise require hospital or residential care, suggest that
home care assistants, under the supervision of qualified staff and with
multidisciplinary assessment, can meet the needs of these elderly people.
Evaluation of the projects, however, also suggests that it is necessary for
health and social service input to be integrated under one management
structure (see, for example, Challis *et al.* 1989; Baldock 1991). However,
the lack of integration of the community health and social services and
the issue of which service should provide personal care may actually
mitigate against providing community care for vulnerable elderly people
(Abbott 1992a; 1992b).

Indeed, it is not clear that residential care can be substituted by domiciliary services in any straightforward sense, even when home helps provide social and personal care as well as domestic help. Evaluation of
successful 'experiments' indicates that if effective and efficient care is to
be provided to those with a high and complex mix of needs, then it
requires careful coordination and integration at the level of the individual
user. Research suggests that frail elderly people can be maintained in their
own homes at a cost lower than that of residential care, but that care
management is essential. The most successful 'experiments' have used
care workers who perform all care tasks, including those usually undertaken by home helps, nurses and care assistants (see Abbott 1992a).

Dant and Gearing (1990), commenting on successful British projects aimed at maintaining frail elderly people in their own homes, pointed out that, while there have been short-term cost savings (i.e. per month), long-term costs are higher because those who remain in the community live longer (!). This means that community care for very frail elderly people may be more expensive in the long term than residential care. Further, they suggest, expanding community services cannot be limited to those who would otherwise be moved into residential care. It may well be that services will have to be provided for those who would otherwise struggle on in the community without them. In this situation, Dant and Gearing suggest, residential care may be the cheapest option.

Sinclair (1990), however, in a review of the literature on residential care, suggested that better assessment and the provision of better services might prevent admissions to residential care. Research asking social workers whether applicants for, or inmates of, residential care could have been kept out of residential care suggests that at least some of them could have been. Biggs (1988), in a study of residents of private care homes supported by supplementary benefit, suggested that only 7 per cent did not need residential care at the time of admission. A further 10 per cent could have been enabled to live in the community with intensive home care services. However, the social work assessors making these judgements varied considerably in their evaluations, from the view that only 5 per cent could have been maintained in the community with intensive support up to a figure of 61 per cent. Neill et al. (1988) has suggested that, at a conservative estimate, about a third of residents of both private and local authority homes could have been enabled to remain in the community with intensive domiciliary support.

The vast majority of older people, including the very elderly, care for themselves or are cared for by informal carers. Only a minority receive domiciliary services, and home helps/carers and meals on wheels are mainly provided to elderly people living alone. While there is some evidence that residential care can be a positive choice, the vast majority of older people want to remain in the community, with support from their families and statutory services, for as long as possible.

Providing care in the community

It is important to recognize, when considering the interaction of services providing community care, that not all welfare services are provided or funded by the state sector (in other words, by government or local authorities). There are many different providers of health and social care:

1 The commercial sector, e.g. private residential homes, domestic services.
2 The voluntary sector, e.g. home nursing, day centres, domestic help, baths, transport.
3 The state sector, e.g. hospitals, GPs, dentists, district nurses.
4 The informal sector, e.g. parents, wives, mothers, daughters.

Any of the four sectors can provide help. For example:

1 *The state*: an elderly person may be assessed as needing help by the local authority and be provided with a home help and/or meals on wheels (allocated and funded by the state).
2 *The voluntary sector*: an elderly person may have a home help provided by, for example, Age Concern (a charity) and go to an Age Concern day centre for meals, or have meals delivered by a voluntary organization such as the Women's Royal Voluntary Service.
3 *The commercial sector*: an elderly person may have help from a commercial home help agency, or, quite simply, pay someone to come in and cook, shop, etc., and/or purchase meals from a cafe or restaurant.
4 *The informal sector*: help may be provided by relatives, friends or neighbours.

Who *pays* for the care is a more complex question:

1 The state could provide the services, using its own employees, or it could purchase the required services from the voluntary or commercial sectors or even the informal sector. Whatever the case, the elderly person is likely to be 'means-tested' and, on a sliding scale, required to make a contribution to the cost of providing the service, if her or his income exceeds a bare minimum or savings exceed a certain sum (generally the levels set out for supplementary pensions).
   If the elderly person is sufficiently disabled, he or she will be entitled to an attendance allowance, which is not means-tested and which could be used to purchase the additional services that were needed. If a relative provides considerable care for an elderly person in receipt of the allowance, he or she might be eligible for a carer's allowance – a weekly, means-tested benefit for those not in paid employment providing full-time care. (For details of benefits, see the Child Poverty Action Group's *National Welfare Benefits Handbook*, which is updated annually.)
2 The voluntary sector may provide services, paying for them out of donations and/or grants made by the state. Volunteers may give their time free. Recipients of services may or may not pay a charge for the service, and the charge may or may not be means-tested.
3 The commercial sector provides services for a fee; they could be paid for by the state, the elderly people themselves or relatives.
4 Employers may provide services for ex-employees, and the receipt of an employer private pension will enhance the possibility of an elderly person purchasing services from the state and other sectors.
5 Relatives may purchase the help elderly relatives need rather than provide themselves.

As with the question of who provides the care, more than one sector could be paying for it.

The skills mix in community care

The needs of elderly people living in the community can be met by more than one agency, and when more than one service is required a number of providers may be involved. This may include more than one sector providing care and more than one purchaser – that is, a mixed economy of provision requiring a **skills mix**. A person's needs may be met by more than one statutory agency, but it is likely that other sectors will also be involved, almost always including the informal sector. The 1990 legislation requires that when a client has complex needs, a care manager should assess their needs and ensure that they receive an appropriate package of care.

There is clearly a need to coordinate packages of care for those whose needs require a complex mix of skills. It is also necessary to ensure that services are being provided by the most appropriate agencies, even when a user is receiving only a single service. This means that it is essential to define the boundaries between health and social care for elderly and disabled people. The Social Services Inspectorate suggested that, 'it may be helpful for agencies to agree a schedule of care tasks which would normally be undertaken by one or other agency or by either' (SSI 1991). The SSI went on to point out that under the 1990 National Health Service and Community Care Act, the health authority is responsible for bringing **social care needs** to the attention of the local authority, and vice versa. They suggest that there needs to be local agreement as to the responsibility of agencies for those tasks that can be, or are already being, carried out by employees of both agencies. The National Association of Health Authority Trusts (NAHAT, undated) has attempted to make clear those tasks that are the responsibility of health services and those which should fall on the local authority, but they had to define a number of tasks as 'both/either': washing and dressing, escorting clients, some toileting tasks, the administration of medicines, encouraging social and emotional skills, elements of advice and counselling, and teaching clients' carers and relatives. Under the legislation, care managers are responsible for assessing needs and purchasing a package of care; the services required can be purchased from the state, the commercial or the voluntary sector. In some cases, the elderly person or an informal carer may be given the money with which to purchase the necessary services.

The skills mix: A case study

Research carried out in Cornwall immediately prior to the implementation of the community care legislation, Abbott (1992a; 1992b) found a range of providers of community care. And this was in a rural area where the range of services, especially those provided by voluntary organizations and the commercial sector, is likely to be significantly less than in urban areas. In three differing GP practices, broadly similar services were available, provided by 'informal' carers, the voluntary sector, the commercial sector and the statutory agencies. The following is a description of what provision was available (taken from Abbott 1992a).

Informal carers, especially when residing in the same household as the dependent person, were the main providers of community care. However, many disabled and older people did not have anyone living with them to provide day-to-day care. Often the elderly person's main informal carer was his or her spouse, who in turn needed considerable support. Relations, friends and neighbours also often provided support. However, this was not always possible and was always liable to break down. This was especially the case if too much was expected. When there was someone in the same household who could provide care, outside agencies provided support and specialized services. Some of the elderly people purchased services themselves. The main services purchased were chiropody (to have a home visit) and cooked meals (see Box 9.2).

Box 9.2 The main commercial services available in Cornwall in 1992

1 Chiropody – mainly to obtain a home visit
2 Domestic help
3 Night nursing
4 Gardening
5 Window cleaning
6 Caring/day-sitting
7 Meals:
  (a) 'Flying Pies' – a daily meals delivery service, which also caters for special diets.
  (b) Cafes and public houses, which provide pensioners' meals in the winter in one of the study areas.

A number of voluntary groups were identified who provided help for the elderly. The two major volunteer organizations were Age Concern and the Women's Royal Voluntary Service (WRVS). Age Concern's main activity was providing transport – cars for hospital appointments, chiropody, day care, etc. They also ran a club for the over-65s in one area and a luncheon club in another. The WRVS delivered and organized Meals on Wheels on behalf of social services, who were responsible for assessing need and allocating the service.

There was also a day centre run by a church group but with only short-term funding. It opened on Tuesdays and Thursdays, providing a centre that anyone in the community could attend. Morning coffee, lunch and afternoon tea were available; lunch had to be booked in advance. On Thursdays the group had an Age Concern bus and were able to provide transport to the centre. A volunteer bureau in one of the towns kept a list of volunteers willing to provide help such as shopping, befriending and transport. Volunteer drivers were paid 23 pence per mile (in 1992), and the charge was passed on to users. The bureau also provided a 'Carers' Break' scheme, which provided care and supervision to dependent people in their own homes to give carers a break. The service was able to organize care during the daytime and overnight and to cover for holidays. Users were charged for the service at cost (there was no administrative charge). Finally, the Echo Centre, a day-care facility for disabled people in one town, was partly funded by social services and partly by a charity. It opened 5 days a week. Physically disabled people could attend on as many days as they liked; Tuesdays to Thursdays were reserved for people aged 16–65. In addition, Macmillan nurses provided a counselling service for the terminally ill and Curie nurses a night-sitting service.

The services provided by the county council, the FHSA, the health trust and the health authority for the client groups included in the project can be categorized broadly into 10 groups (see Box 9.3).

Box 9.3   Services provided by the NHS and the local authority

1 Domestic help, i.e. housework
2 Social care, including meals on wheels, shopping, collecting pensions, etc.
3 Personal care, e.g. washing, dressing, help with mobility
4 Nursing care, both adult and psychiatric
5 Day care
6 Chiropody
7 Provision of aids and adaptations
8 Respite care
9 Sheltered housing
10 GP services

Box 9.4   The providers of health and social services in Cornwall in 1992

1 Home helps
2 District nursing teams
3 Practice nurses
4 Health visitors
5 Community psychiatric nurses
6 Geriatric liaison nurses
7 Parkinsons liaison nurses
8 Chiropodists
9 Occupational therapists
10 Wardens of sheltered housing
11 Day-care nurses and auxiliaries
12 The district council's Alarm System Control Centre

The *main* providers of community care to the client group involved in the research, however, were statutory services – home helps, district nursing teams and GPs. The first two of these groups showed the greatest overlap of service provision, in the area of personal care. All the professional groups, however, provided essential elements of community care (see Boxes 9.4 and 9.5).

Box 9.5 Summary of community care services and providers in the Cornish research

Service	FHSA	Social services	Health authority	Community care trust	Housing authority	Voluntary sector	Commercial sector
Domestic help		x[a]				x	x
Meals		x[e]	x[c]				x
Laundry service			x[d]				x
Housing					x		x
Sheltered housing					x		x
Personal care		x		x		x	x
Bathing		x	x[c]				
Chiropody				x			x
Dentist	x						x
Optician	x						x
Occupational therapy		x	x[c]				
Physiotherapy			x[c]				
Adult nursing	x[b]		x[c]	x			
Community psychiatric nursing			x				
Geriatric liaison nursing			x				
General practitioner	x						
Health visiting				x			
Befriending/ visiting						x	
Day-sitting						x	
Night-sitting						x	
Day care		x	x				
Respite		x	x				
Transport		x		x		x	

[a] Only as part of a package of care for new referrals.
[b] By the practice nurse.
[c] Only as part of day hospital provision.
[d] Only in clients' homes in two areas.
[e] But delivered by WRVS voluntary sector.
Source: Abbott (1992a: table 4).

It is apparent, then, that a range of services is available for elderly people, provided by a number of providers. Each of the main sectors is involved in provision and the services may be provided free at the point of delivery by the local authority and/or health services, or the state may purchase the services on behalf of the elderly person from the commercial and/or the voluntary sector. Alternatively, the elderly may be required to pay in full or part for the services or purchase them themselves. Some state services, for example district nursing, GPs and chiropody, are provided free at the point of delivery for all older people assessed as needing them, whereas home help services and meals on wheels can involve a means test, with those with an income above a declared minimum having to make a contribution to the cost of service provision.

The mixed economy of care

The range of problems with which welfare providers need to deal in order to maintain elderly people in their own homes is immense and goes beyond the services discussed in the case study. There are three major areas of concern:

1 *Financial difficulties*: many elderly people have very low incomes (see Chapter 5).
2 *Health and personal problems*: not all elderly people are ill, but as a group they are more likely to suffer from chronic conditions such as arthritis or degenerative conditions such as dementia. Many of the health problems typically associated with older people not only need constant medical attention but also reduce the patient's mobility; for example, many older people are unable to manage stairs easily, if at all. They may also have physical difficulties with shopping, cooking their own meals, keeping the house clean and even washing themselves.
3 *Social problems*: many older people in Britain are isolated either because they have no family or friends or because they do not live near them. Even when family and friends live nearby, older people are sometimes reluctant to leave their homes for fear of crime or because they find public transport inadequate or because of a physical difficulty. The increasing tendency of married women to enter paid employment (see, for example, Abbott and Tyler 1995) means that daughters now have less time than in the past to visit elderly parents.

The four sectors together tend to deal with these problems as follows. Financial difficulties are often alleviated by provisions such as housing benefit, rate rebates, pensions (provided by the state, by employers or through commercial insurance schemes) and heating allowances, and/or through financial help from family or friends. Health and personal needs are met by a range of services, including packages of care purchased by care managers (social service workers who assess needs), access to or visits from a GP, home visits by a district nurse or psychiatric nurse, meals on wheels to provide a cooked meal, occupational therapists to assess the

need for aids such as chair-lifts or bath-hoists, home helps to perform
social and personal care tasks (ranging from shopping and collecting
pensions to bathing and dressing), the local housing department to ar-
range a transfer to 'sheltered' accommodation, or friends and/or family
members to helping with cooking, cleaning and personal care. Finally,
many *social problems* can be overcome by providing access to free transport, cheap-rate telephone calls, cheap off-peak cinema and theatre tickets
or drop-in clubs and coffee bars; people who visit in another capacity
(home helps, district nurses, etc.) also have an important role to play
here. This is by no means an exhaustive list, but it shows the range
of services required to meet the aims of community care for older people
(see Table 9.5).

Table 9.5 Welfare sectors and community care provision for older people.

| Service | Sector | | | |
	State	Commercial	Voluntary	Informal
Financial	Retirement pensions, community care allowance	Private pensions, annuities, occupational pensions, interest on savings		Financial support from relatives
Housing	Council housing (sheltered housing)	Owner-occupied housing, rented housing	Housing associations	Accommodation provided
Personal care	District nursing, nursing, home helps, day care	Commercial nursing and home help agencies, private day care	Voluntary sector nursing (e.g. Macmillan), day care (e.g. Age Concern), night-sitting (e.g. Marie Curie)	Relatives
Social care	Home helps, alarms	Domestic agencies, alarms, restaurants, cafes, public houses, meal delivery services	Voluntary sector, home helps, visiting services, meals on wheels	Friends/relatives neighbours, surveillance by neighbours/ friends
Domestic	Home helps	Domestic agencies, gardening agencies, window cleaners	Voluntary agency services	Friends/ relatives/ neighbours
Medical/ nursing/ health	District nursing, chiropody, dentist, GP, NHS physiotherapy, etc.	Nursing agencies, chiropody, dentist, pharmacist, physiotherapy, etc.	Voluntary nursing (e.g. Macmillan)	
Transport	Ambulance service	Taxis	Car service (e.g. Age Concern)	Friends/ relatives/ neighbours

Conclusions

In this chapter, using the example of community care and with special reference to older people, we have illustrated the way in which the mixed economy of care works in practice. Until the introduction of the new community care policy in April 1993, the statutory sector was the main provider of formal services, except in the area of residential care, where the commercial and voluntary sectors were significant providers. The 1993 legislation required the local authorities to stimulate a social market, purchasing services from the commercial and voluntary sectors. Provision was to be needs-led – that is, care managers were to assess the needs of elderly people and their informal carers and purchase services to meet those needs. However, while at the time of writing a full evaluation of the policy has not been conducted, indications are that it is unlikely to bring about the radical changes hoped for by the government. Cash limits on local authorities mean that not all assessed needs can be met and that only the most vulnerable can be provided with services. Informal carers continue to receive little support. It has been suggested that one possible scenario is that a smaller number of very vulnerable people will remain on enhanced services, with other, less vulnerable people receiving none.

It is not yet clear to what extent a social care market has been or will be stimulated outside of residential care. Whatever voluntary/commercial sector provision develops is likely to be patchy, most evident in middle-class suburban areas and least evident in rural areas. Furthermore, the extent to which a social care market with the flexibility to meet individual needs will develop is also debatable. Local authorities are likely to want to negotiate contracts and get the best value for money, and this may mean contracting with a monopoly supplier, resulting in a service-led rather than needs-led approach (Lewis *et al.* 1995). Even with care management it may be difficult to provide a seamless web of care, particularly in the area of personal care, where there is the question of whether this should be provided/payed for by health or social services (Abbott 1994).

Community care is likely to continue to be provided in the main by the informal sector, with those who have the ability to buy care for themselves or have relatives prepared to do so purchasing services from the commercial and voluntary sectors. Poor older people, especially those living alone, and including a disproportionate number of women and people from ethnic minority groups, will continue to be dependent on the state for support, even if the state purchases services for them from the commercial and voluntary sectors.

Summary

- This chapter has focused on the relationship between the different providers within the mixed economy of welfare using, as an example, recent developments in community care policy.

- The development of community care has drawn considerable support from the critique of residential caring institutions. It is, however, important to distinguish between policies supporting 'care in the community' (more locally-based community services) and those supporting 'care by the community' (usually meaning informal or family care).

- The 1990 National Health Service and Community Care Act required local authorities to make substantial changes in the way they managed and delivered services shifting emphasis away from direct service provision to one of co-ordinator/financier/regulator of the mixed economy.

Further reading

Arber, S. and Ginn, J. (1991) *Gender and Later Life: A Sociological Analysis of Resources and Constraints*. London: Sage.

Wistow, G., Knapp, M., Hardy, B. and Allen, C. (1994) *Social Care in a Mixed Economy*. Buckingham: Open University Press.

WELFARE PLURALISM IN THE 1990s:
THE CHANGING ROLE OF THE STATE

Introduction

The previous chapters have shown how the study of social policy amounts to much more than a simple study of state provision. The field of social policy analysis has recently been described by Rose (1993: 221):

> ... any study of goods and services of primary importance to the majority of individuals must consider non-state as well as state sources of welfare. In the abstract we can define total welfare in the family (TWF) as the sum of goods and services produced by the household (H), the market (M) and the state (S) ... This perspective includes, regardless of source, the goods and services essential to the majority of households, such as income, food, housing, personal social services, education, health and transportation.

Rose's definition is useful in that it begins by defining the type of resources (goods and services) we are interested in – namely, those which are of primary importance to the majority (a relative definition) – and also because it demonstrates the importance of a mixed economy of provision.

We could add to this definition the specific contribution of the voluntary sector and focus on individual as opposed to family welfare, as the latter confuses family and household and assumes (a) that we all live in families and (b) an equal distribution of resources within the family. This is clearly not the case, as both the provision and receipt of 'family/household' resources is uneven and gendered. Total personal welfare (TPW) thus depends on our access to support from the informal, voluntary, statutory and commercial sectors:

$$TPW = I + V + S + C$$

We have seen how, although the terminology is relatively new, the existence of welfare pluralism is not. What has happened in recent years is an increasing pressure for a fundamental shift in the balance of responsibilities within the welfare mix, with more emphasis on individual and community responsibility. The growth in non-statutory provision was not going to occur overnight, as a simple response to welfare retrenchment; important questions have arisen concerning the capacity and coverage of these forms of provision, leading to new forms of state intervention to support, direct and control their contribution. This has resulted in the growth of increasingly complex relationships between the respective sectors with important implications for the changing, if not declining, role of the state.

This final chapter considers the feasibility and desirability of attempts to substitute state provision with that provided by the commercial, voluntary and informal sectors and the implications for the role of the state in the late 1990s. It begins by outlining some of the key arguments put forward by proponents of New Right ideology which have underpinned the shift in government policy since 1979. Of prime concern here is the relationship between freedom, equality and state welfare.

Liberalism and the welfare state

When we talk about Liberalism here, we are not referring to the doctrines of the Liberal Democrat Party in Britain but to a school of political thought defined by Hayek as 'concerned mainly with limiting the coercive powers of all government in the interest of liberty and a free society' (cited in Hindess 1987: 120). Central to this tradition is the notion that the market is the best (and only effective) means of allocating social goods and that state intervention (in resources allocation) distorts the operation of the free market and undermines individual liberty. In other words, state intervention is coercive and should be carefully circumscribed. Faced with the alternative of a command-style economy (where the state intervenes substantially in matters of resource allocation and planning) and a society based on 'voluntary cooperation' within a free market, Liberals contend that it is only the latter that safeguards the principle of consumer choice. As Friedman and Friedman (1980: 41) put it:

... choice plays an important role. Our decisions about how to use our resources, whether to work hard or to take it easy, to enter one occupation or another, to engage in one venture or another, to save or to spend – these may determine whether we dissipate our resources or improve and add to them.

When the state becomes involved in directing personal decisions about spending, saving and insuring, it is behaving in a coercive manner, undermining our freedom of choice.

Liberals have been critical of the development of collective welfare provision on a number of grounds. The most important of these has been the desire to contain the costs of and responsibilities for welfare in order to delimit the parameters of legitimate state intervention. This concern to 'roll back the state' reflects more than a simple desire to reduce public expenditure in the face of recession and the potential escalation of costs as a result of demographic change and the development of new and expensive forms of medical treatment. It reflects a broader commitment, which lies at the heart of liberal thinking, to principles of freedom and choice, and a belief that universal state welfare is inherently damaging.

Supply, demand and the price mechanism

Social policy, as we have seen, is centrally concerned with matters of resource allocation, at finding ways of matching the provision of social goods with social needs. For Liberals, the only way to ensure that an individual's welfare needs are met is via the free market: only the price mechanism can coordinate efficiently and effectively the demand for and supply of social goods. The argument here is that the unfettered market will respond sensitively to consumer demand by providing goods and services at an appropriate price. Consumers are the best judges of their own needs (not professionals) and consumer demand backed by resources (spending power) translated via the price mechanism becomes the incentive for provision:

> ... the economic market is superior to the political ballot box in its ability to cater sensitively for minorities ... Small groups of customers with unusual needs or preferences can invariably find a supplier to meet their distinctive requirements at a price.
>
> (Harris and Seldon 1979: 68)

State provision, on the other hand, cannot respond in the same way to consumer preferences. It is viewed as bureaucratic, paternalistic and susceptible to pressure both from pressure groups and from welfare professionals whose behaviour may reflect self-interest as much as client needs. Within this debate lies a critique of social science research on the grounds that the state can never achieve the knowledge base required to plan and distribute goods and services effectively. George and Wilding (1994: 21) put the argument like this:

> Supporters and advocates of rationalist social planning believe that the relevant facts can be known, that from this knowledge plans to

secure desired ends can be developed, that the plans can be successfully implemented and the desired aims achieved. The New Right are highly dubious of all this. They speak with contempt of the fallacies of constructivist rationalism and the failure to accept the limitations of human reason.

They go on to cite a leading proponent of New Right ideology who writes of 'the epistemological impossibilities of successful central planning' (Gray 1992, cited in George and Wilding 1994: 22). Central planning on the scale required to provide acceptable universal welfare services which meet individual needs is thus seen as impracticable; only the 'hidden hand' of the price mechanism is able to achieve this. The alternative is for welfare professionals/planners to make decisions about human needs and appropriate forms of provision; such decisions may, however, be tainted with paternalism.

Not only is state provision likely to be at odds with consumer preference, it also distorts the operation of the free market – and the price mechanism – to the extent that important goods and services may not be supplied at all. It could be argued, for example, that the development of universal health care restricted the opportunities for the commercial sector to flourish and develop new and innovative forms of treatment. It does this in two main ways: first, by reducing the purchasing power of consumers through heavy taxation and, second, by creating state monopolies which undermine free competition.

Taxation as coercion

The high levels of taxation required to finance collective social policies necessitate serious incursions by the state into people's private lives, which, according to leading protagonists, amount to unacceptable levels of state interference severely restricting the ability of unsatisfied consumers to meet their needs through the commercial market. In this sense, taxation itself becomes a form of coercion for, as Friedman and Friedman (1980: 89) suggest, 'an essential part of economic freedom is freedom to choose how to use our income: how much to spend on ourselves and on what items; how much to save and in what form; how much to give away and to whom'.

We could perhaps illustrate this point by reference to education policy. The enormous cost of funding state education is met from public funds via taxation. As such we are all obliged to contribute, whether we have children or not and whether we wish to use those services or not. We may, for example, wish to send our children to a private school – perhaps of a particular religious denomination – which may cost no more than a place in a state school. This 'preference', however, may be undermined by a lack of resources as our income is eroded through taxation. On the other hand, we may have children who lack the 'ability' to gain access into higher education – and yet we, as parents, have to contribute towards the university education of children whose earnings potential in future years will exceed that of our own children (LeGrand 1982). Not only does this situation frustrate our own desires for the education of our children, it also restricts the growth of the commercial sector and of alternative forms of provision because it tampers with the price mechanism. If a sufficient number of parents were 'free' to allocate their educational resources in a certain direction, then, arguably, the commercial sector would respond by providing the sort of schooling they desired – and the more parents demanded that particular type of schooling the more competition would ensue, resulting in downward pressure on pricing and a more efficient service. Any dissatisfied consumers could then withdraw their support and the service would either have to improve or collapse as new players came into the market. Thus freedom of choice is realized. The responsiveness of the commercial sector ensures that service provision is highly sensitive to consumer demands, a feature absent in state-funded services. This argument is neatly summarized by Green: 'No system will ever be responsive to customers if producers receive payment whether or not their work is satisfactory' (cited in George and Wilding 1994: 28).

   Recent government proposals for changes in the funding of higher education have suggested the replacement of existing mandatory grants and loans with a privatized loans scheme, and the introduction of vouchers or 'educational entitlements' to pay fees as a means of both reducing costs and increasing consumer choice.

Consumer choice and the market

We saw in the quote from Hayek (p. 212), that Liberals do not feel that the state should be involved in coercing individuals into predetermined expenditure regimes; they should be free to decide how and when to allocate their resources. This not only preserves freedom of choice but also reinforces individual responsibility. LeGrand (1995) rehearsed some of the arguments about individual responsibility and freedom of choice in a recent study of the role of the state in the redistribution of income across the life-cycle (intrapersonal distribution as opposed to interpersonal distribution between social groups). He began by asking the question:

> why do many countries have some kind of compulsory state social insurance system whose intention is, at least in part, to redistribute income across the life cycle? . . . a case can be made that state intervention in the redistribution of life cycle income is neither necessary nor desirable – this despite the fact that, in the absence of state intervention, individuals' incomes fluctuate widely throughout their lifetimes . . . if people do not like the income fluctuations [life] events induce, they are in a position to do something about it . . . they can save, borrow; they can insure.
>
> (LeGrand 1995: 22)

LeGrand distinguishes here between the case for interpersonal and intrapersonal redistribution on the grounds that if problems of low income are dealt with by the state, the arguments for life-cycle redistribution are less clear (everyone has the opportunity to make provisions).

The imperfect market

If markets operated perfectly and provided a reliable means of evening out and insuring against life-cycle inequalities, there would arguably be no need for state intervention. In reality, however, markets are imperfect. LeGrand notes, in particular, the problems of insurance and labour market failure and the problems caused by externalities (which arise when the production/consumption decisions of some individuals have repercussions on the lives of others). He cites the example of environmental pollution resulting in external costs to individuals which they may not have predicted, and vaccination programmes which may result in external benefit (in that even if you are not vaccinated yourself, you gain benefit from high levels of societal immunization). Finally, he notes the problem of 'myopia', where people behave in a short-sighted fashion and fail to provide adequate cover for sickness and old age. This is not a problem of market failure as such, but highlights a fundamental weakness of free market economics based on the concept of individual rationality. In practice, it seems neither markets nor consumers can be relied upon to behave in a rational manner.

Hindess (1987) similarly questions the Liberal assumption that free markets and the price mechanism constitute an effective means of distributing scarce social resources and notes, for example, the alternative Marxist view of the price system, particularly as the means for the determination of wage levels as 'the crucial mechanism of the exploitation of the working class by the capitalist class. Here the appearance of voluntary exchange masks an underlying exploitative relationship' (p. 124). According to Hindess, both Marxism and Liberalism share the tendency to 'essentialize' the market; in the former the market becomes a vehicle for exploitation and the maldistribution of resources, whereas in the latter it becomes the 'hidden hand' ensuring the satisfaction of consumer choice. LeGrand (1995: 31) is more cautious: 'Ultimately the question as to which is the "best" system for engaging in intrapersonal redistribution is an empirical one: which system fails the least?'

Charitable capitalism?

The preceding section has looked at the impact of statutory provision on individual consumer choice (in terms of how they choose to meet their personal welfare needs) and the tension which exists between state provision and the commercial 'for-profit' sector. Clearly there are implications here for the development of the voluntary sector too. In the example of educational choice given above, parents may have preferred a school in the voluntary sector. Indeed, many denominational schools are voluntary organizations and many private schools have charitable status. The ability to exercise that choice and back it with resources would encourage voluntary sector schools. There is another issue at stake here, however. If you read the quote from Friedman and Friedman (1980: 89) above once again, you will notice that they refer not only to our personal spending but also to our giving. This final point broadens the argument from one simply concerned with the rights of an individual to choose the best means of meeting their personal welfare needs to the relationship between the market, the state and voluntarism. Just as the burden of taxation is seen to restrict individual spending decisions, so it controls the means and direction of voluntary effort. While the main thrust of New Right thinking is in the direction of individual responsibility, they have also argued that the welfare state has damaged individuals' sense of social responsibility; that state incursion into social responsibility results in people taking the view that they have discharged their social responsibilities once they have paid their taxes:

> If our benign and cooperative relations with our fellow citizens become instead functions of the state, then we are indeed reduced to merely atomistic individuals pursuing our own self-interest.
> (Willetts 1992, cited in George and Wilding 1994: 33)

Voluntarism and philanthropy

The idea of a close relationship between **individualism** and voluntarism was central to Margaret Thatcher's belief in philanthropic capitalism under which the greater accumulation of wealth produced in an unfettered market would 'trickle down' to poorer sections of society. While the market ensures that most needs are met, altruism – or philanthropy – provides the best means of mopping up residual problems. Altruism is preferred by Liberals because it does not involve any element of 'compulsion'; individuals are free to choose whether and how to assist others. From this perspective, altruism is incompatible with universal state provision. Ware (1990: 187) summarizes the argument as follows:

> ... state provision of welfare diminishes the 'altruistic spirit', because would-be philanthropists can see no point in such activity if they are merely duplicating the supply of goods and services to those in need.

We saw in Chapter 2 some of the problems of philanthropic welfare in the nineteenth century, and particularly its association with paternalism and social engineering. In Chapter 7, we saw that the relationship between free market capitalism and philanthropy is more complex and how the expectation of greater philanthropy as society becomes more affluent has not been met in practice. Turning the argument on its head, Titmuss (1973) has presented a view that collective welfare provision actually promoted altruism and a sense of social responsibility in a society dominated by market values. In a similar vein, Ware (1990: 186) has argued that:

> ... in general, the extension of market mechanisms in a society makes it less possible for that society to rely on altruism in meeting needs ... the pursuit of self-interest in the market clashes with the ethos of helping others: the greater the permeation of market relations into social interactions, the more likely it is that self-interested attitudes

will displace altruistic beliefs generally . . . the extension of the market does tend to corrode altruism.

On a more pragmatic point, it is increasingly uncertain that the voluntary sector will have the capacity to expand to fill the gaps in provision left by a receding state sector without further and substantial injections of public money (and associated centralizing tendencies). Furthermore, in those areas that have seen large-scale transfers of public money from directly provided services to voluntary organizations (such as housing associations; see Chapter 6), this raises questions about the accountability of public money and the regulation of the sector as well as concerns about the impact of such forms of financial dependency on the very ethos of voluntarism itself.

The free market and the authoritarian state

So far we have considered New Right arguments against the extension of state intervention in social welfare and against the very idea of central planning. This form of 'economic liberalism' which sees the market as the only effective means of allocating resources is heavily critical of state incursion into areas of personal responsibility on the grounds that it undermines the market but also because of the extension of state paternalism and control over people's private lives. Whilst economic liberalism forms a dominant school of thought within the New Right, it exists alongside a somewhat different tradition referred to as 'social authoritarianism'. This uneasy co-existence has resulted in some often contradictory policies. The social authoritarian perspective holds that, whilst the role of the state in social policy should be strictly contained within a residual welfare system, state intervention in some aspects of social life is both necessary and desirable in order to support the moral fabric of society and to restore traditional values of individual responsibility, the family and the work ethic.

Education: local autonomy and central control

The tension between 'economic liberals' (who wish to see wholesale state retrenchment) and 'social authoritarians' (who see the state as an important defender of public morality), and the contradictions that ensue, can be seen in the process of education reform over the past decade. The key focus of concern here has been with the position of local education authorities (LEAs), which the government has presented as coercive, unrepresentative and inefficient public bureaucracies responsible for restricting parental/consumer choice. The main policy response has been to 'free' individual schools from LEA control by enabling them to 'opt-out' and take on 'grant-maintained status'. Grant-maintained schools then obtain their funds directly from central government, including an allowance to cover services which the school would have received from the

LEA. The autonomy of individual schools has also been increased through the introduction of the local management of schools (LMS), which requires that LEAs devolve over 85 per cent of their budgets to the school governing bodies, giving governors greater powers over key financial and management issues. In addition, parents and children have been given increased rights to select the school of their choice. Alongside these changes to state schools, the government has also increased its support for private schools through the expansion of the assisted places scheme, which enables selected private schools to offer places to a certain number of children at reduced fees depending on parental income (announced at the Conservative Party Conference in 1995). To that extent, the policy shifts fall neatly into the broader Liberal objectives of increasing consumer choice, reducing the power of state monopolies and the decentralization of decision-making. The same piece of legislation (the 1988 Education Reform Act), however, also introduced various measures which represented a marked centralization in educational policy. The introduction of the National Curriculum, with strict guidelines dictating the range of subjects to be delivered and the proportion of school time to be allocated to each, together with clear prescriptions for assessment, represented a marked concentration of power and control away from democratically elected local authorities into the hands of central government. Of particular interest here is the emphasis placed within the National Curriculum on Christianity as the dominant form of both religious education and worship within schools (the National Curriculum does not apply to private schools).

Together with the shift to state funding for opted-out schools, these changes amount to a transfer of power away from education authorities and individual schools, providing a good example of how, in its regulatory role, the state has become increasingly interventionist and coercive.

Housing policy

Another area which has witnessed contradictory pressures of both retrenchment and centralization, with important implications for public expenditure and local autonomy, is that of housing policy. If we look at privatization in the area of housing – and the promotion of owner-occupation in Britain – it is clear that policy changes in favour of increased owner-occupation have resulted in some major shifts in public expenditure. Malpass and Murie (1994) note that, although housing cutbacks accounted for over 75 per cent of all public spending reductions in 1980, with capital spending falling to less than a tenth of its 1976–77 real level,

> To see the pattern of housing expenditure solely in terms of cuts is misleading. On top of expenditure cuts there has been a transfer in the balance of effective public expenditure away from the public sector and direct investment and towards the support of owner occupation.
> (Malpass and Murie 1994: 107)

What may at first appear as a net reduction in public expenditure may, when subjected to more rigorous analysis, amount to simply a transfer of subsidy. The public expenditure implications of shifts in housing policy have been obscured by problems with statistics. The government's view of what constitutes public spending as set out in the annual White Paper on public expenditure excludes two important areas of spending on housing. Housing benefit appears in overall figures on public spending but not as housing expenditure, while mortgage interest tax relief is not defined as public spending at all. These two components of housing expenditure have dominated the pattern of housing finance in the 1990s, as the general subsidy to local authority housing (through the Housing Revenue Account) has been virtually eliminated (Willis and Cameron 1993: 51). The cost of housing benefit for council and private tenants in 1992–93 was some £7.5 billion and the cost to the Exchequer of mortgage tax relief amounted to three times the cost of other housing expenditure in 1990–91 (Malpass and Murie 1994: 108).

If we add to these subsidies the costs of the government's 'Right to Buy' policy, discounts on council house sales and the increasing costs of income support to help with mortgage costs for those people who have lost their jobs or are unable to keep up their mortgage payments, a picture emerges not of public expenditure cuts as a result of privatization, but rather of a massive transfer of housing resources. This situation has been described by Malpass and Murie (1994: 109) as:

> . . . a transfer, from the public sector to the support of owner occupation, from investment to subsidy, and from the subsidisation of the production of public housing to the subsidisation of individual consumption reflect[ing] other priorities which have tended to override public expenditure considerations.

The role of the state in relation to housing policy has not, therefore, declined but shifted and public expenditure has increased. These policy shifts reflect a broader ideological commitment to owner-occupation as a preferred form of tenure; one which promotes independence, individual responsibility and profit. In the process, we have witnessed a marked centralization of responsibility and control as local housing departments have seen their autonomy cut (with the imposition of the statuatory Right to Buy, a moratorium on new building for general needs and changes in the financing of council housing).

It could be argued that this increase in state control, which has significantly undermined the power of democratically elected local authorities regarding their housing stock, was simply a necessary temporary measure to expedite the sale of municipal housing and that, once completed, the state could then withdraw. We saw in Chapter 6, however, that the gradual replacement of housing authority functions by housing associations (particularly in relation to new building), funded directly through the Housing Corporation by central government, represents another example of centralization.

Clearly, the New Right do not totally reject any role for the state in welfare. While it views collective universal provision as wasteful and inefficient, as responsible for the creation of a 'dependency culture' and erosive of individual and social responsibility, it accepts that the state remains an important source of support for those without recourse to private, family or voluntary support. In this respect, the debate shifts from one concerned with levels of state intervention to one of forms of state intervention. The general view here is that where the state does get involved, its role should be limited to the provision of residual, safety-net services.

Universal versus selective benefits

Selective benefits have been favoured by the Right (and more recently by 'New Labour') on the grounds of efficiency and effectiveness. The extension of more complex entitlement criteria, including means-testing, enable the state to target available social resources more closely on those who are in genuine need and deserve state support and avoid squandering public money on those who either have sufficient personal resources or have brought improvidence upon themselves. This debate has crystallized in recent months in the debate over child benefit, one of the few remaining universal social security benefits. The general view has been that the benefit is too low to deal effectively with the problem of child poverty, that it would be prohibitively expensive to increase the level of payments and that finite resources would be better spent targeting those children in real need. On the other hand, the benefit has been defended on the grounds that it represents society's responsibility towards its children (that this is a social as much as a personal responsibility) and that working mothers help to pay for it through their national insurance contributions. In addition, feminists have pointed out that, even in families with adequate aggregate income levels, which would be denied entitlement in a means-tested system, it is false to assume that income is distributed equally (by male breadwinners); it therefore forms an important source of direct support to mothers who can be relied upon to pass it directly on to their children (Lister 1990b). The assumption that selective benefits are more efficient has also been questioned in the face of evidence of low take-up (of family credit, for example) and the high costs involved in administering and policing means-tested benefits. The most recent figures available on the take-up of income-related benefits suggests that only 66 per cent of those eligible to claim are actually doing so (DSS 1994). Furthermore, Table 10.1 demonstrates the administrative costs of welfare benefits:

Table 10.1 Administrative costs of various benefits.

Benefit	Cost as % of benefit expenditure	Average weekly cost per beneficiary (£)
Retirement pension	1.2	0.6
Child benefit	2.1	0.4
Income support	10.2	5.4
Council tax benefit	10.3	0.7
Unemployment benefit	17.5	9.1
Social Fund	61.1	2.4

Source: DSS (1995b).

Whereas only about 1 per cent of the cost of retirement pensions is taken up by administration and about 2 per cent of the child benefit budget, administrative costs account for 17 per cent of the unemployment benefit budget and a staggering 61 per cent of the Social Fund.

A further, ideologically motivated, preference for selective benefits comes from the social authoritarian wing, which advocates a clear role for the state in the promotion and sanctioning of certain forms of social behaviour – in order to preserve a preferred moral order. An important aspect of this is the removal of benefits seen as undermining traditional forms of personal and social responsibility (such as lone-parent's benefits, for example, which may encourage parenthood), in order to pressurize potential recipients into seeking recourse to support from the family or into entering the labour market. To complement this, various incentives or 'carrots' may be offered in the form of carefully circumscribed, selective forms of entitlement, which reinforce rather than undermine traditional sources of responsibility. We saw in Chapter 4 how entitlement to many forms of social security in Britain are conditional upon the recipient's behaviour; unemployment benefit, for example, is dependent upon the recipient satisfying the 'availability for work' criteria – 'To be available you must be willing and able to accept any suitable job offer at once' (CPAG 1995: 13). While some rules can be justified on the grounds of equity and accountability for use of public money (why should someone receive sickness benefit when they are not sick or a student grant when they are not studying?), other conditions have been advocated by the New Right as a means of sanctioning certain forms of social behaviour. Gilbert (1981, cited in George and Wilding 1994: 39) summarizes this approach as one which 'stresses the centrality of marriage and family ties to the work effort of men and therefore to any attempt to take poor families out of the poverty trap. Social policy must therefore be deliberatedly directed to strengthening the male role in families'.

If we return to the previous example of unemployment benefit and the availability for work criteria, we can see how gendered presumptions come into play, reinforcing familial roles and female dependency. The CPAG handbook offers potential claimants with children or adult dependants the following advice:

> ... the new client advisor will want to know what plans you have for their care if you get a job. Because you have to be available for work at short notice, you must be able to show that you have a plan worked out or the adjudication officer is likely to refuse your claim for benefit.
>
> (CPAG 1995: 17)

Such conditions may come into play even in cases such as this, where the applicant is claiming a contributory benefit.

Other forms of incentive have evolved which seek not only to reinforce traditional gender roles but also to safeguard the continued supply of informal care. Chapter 8 examined the development of schemes of payments to informal carers, in the face of demographic change and increasing dependency ratios and concern about the potential costs to the state.

Such schemes reflect a recognition that, despite New Right rhetoric, it may not be feasible to rely on an unsupported informal sector to supply the additional labour required to meet these growing demands. To some extent, the state must accept responsibility for part of this 'problem', as monetarist economic policy emphasizing the movement of labour as opposed to capital (of workers as opposed to jobs) has encouraged the breakdown of extended families and communities, resulting in an uneven distribution of dependency and caring labour.

It is arguable that such forms of payment also reflect a concern about the needs and autonomy of carers. The Disabled Persons Act 1986 introduced for the first time an explicit recognition of the relationship between carers' needs and those of the person cared for. Section 8 of this Act requires a local authority, when assessing the needs of disabled people, to have regard for the carer's ability to continue to provide care on a regular basis. While falling short of a recognition that carers themselves have important needs, this nevertheless represented a substantial departure from previous legislation and policies and was really an attempt to ensure that services were provided at a point before the caring relationship broke down, resulting in admission to residential care (Ackers 1989). The inclusion of this 'right' did not, however, bring about an expansion in services designed specifically for carers. Indeed, in many cases, where services were introduced, they subsequently became the victim of local government expenditure cuts. This was certainly the case of an innovative scheme introduced in Avon to promote the care in the community of elderly persons with dementia through comprehensive day care provision and carer support services (Ackers 1986). This successful project was closed down as it fell in the grey area of uncertain financial responsibility between health and social services.

In the absence of schemes of this nature, and of a genuine attempt to recognize the burden which long-term caring places on carers, it may become increasingly difficult to rely upon informal carers to fill the gap left by the withdrawal of state services. The reduction in institutional care provided by the state will thus be replaced not by care in the community but, instead, by private residential care, funded and regulated by the state. The 1984 Residential Homes Act gave social services and health authorities new powers to supervise and regulate the commercial and voluntary sectors. It has been argued, however, that these powers are inadequate and the sheer number of applications, in a resource-constrained environment, has resulted in less than rigorous and patchy implementation: 'The number of instances of abuse of patients that have been coming to light seems to indicate that some homes are run by totally unsuitable people' (Ware 1990: 157).

Since the introduction of changes in benefit regulations in 1983, which allowed elderly people in private residential care to claim their fees back from the Department of Social Security, the number of private residential care homes has increased from 1871 in 1975 to 9235 in 1992. During the same period, the number of private nursing homes increased from 1000 to 4000 (Laing and Buisson 1993). Under the community care reforms in 1993, responsibility for assessing the type of care required and paying the fees was shifted from the Department of Health to local authorities and,

in the National Health Service and Community Care Act 1990, local authorities were required to purchase residential services from the commercial and voluntary sectors in preference to state provision. In the context
of a rapidly increasing market as a result of demographic change, these
policy changes have led Davis (1993) to the conclusion that 'the majority
of private homes would not have opened to admit the large numbers of
people needing care unless public funds had been available'. Not even the
commercial sector, it seems, can be relied upon to fill the gaps in social
provision, particularly in the case of high levels of dependency and for
low-income groups. State intervention, in the form of public funding, is
required in order to promote the profitability of certain key areas of provision and this brings with it calls for a high level of accountability and
surveillance, which may itself stifle some of the apparent advantages of
commercial provision (such as its capacity for innovation and flair and
the disciplining function of risk). When private monopolies have guaranteed funding from the state they may, in practice, operate in a very similar
way to state monopolies, which were at least subject to some form of
democratic control (via elected local authorities, etc.).

Conclusions

This chapter has outlined some of the objectives underlying New Right
attempts to shift the balance of responsibilities within the mixed economy
of welfare. It has also evaluated the effect of some of the changes in the
context of these objectives. While the role of the state has undoubtedly
changed in recent years, there is little evidence to suggest a reduction in
state intervention in social policy. Indeed, the effect of social policy legislation and economic policy in the last decade has been to transfer public
expenditure from direct provision by the state into the subsidization of
the commercial and voluntary sectors with some real increases in public
expenditure. In addition, the erosion of local authority responsibilities in
the areas of housing and education (coupled to changes in local government finance) represents a marked centralization of power and resources
at the expense of local autonomy. To that extent, the central state – or
the government – has become more interventionist. In other respects,
we have seen how changes in the basis of social entitlement, particularly
in relation to social security benefits, have led to a greater incursion in
people's private lives in an attempt to 'engineer' social relations.

In terms of the efficiency argument – and the critique of excessively
bureaucratic public monopolies – some of the changes introduced within
the NHS and education have resulted not in a slimming down of bureaucracy but in the introduction of a new tier of financial management
modelled on the private sector. Recent proposals to introduce new forms
of training for headteachers responsible for managing large and complex
budgets, together with training for school governors, for example, reflect
the growth of a new army of financial managers in almost every sector of
the welfare state as budgets are devolved. Serious concerns about the
escalating costs of administration within the NHS were raised at the 1995

Conservative Party conference and led to a new commitment to cut the costs of administration by 25 per cent.

Shifting the responsibility for welfare provision away from the state has clearly not resulted in any major savings to the Exchequer which could then translate into a reduction in taxation. Indeed, there is evidence to suggest that New Right policies have resulted in an overall increase in levels of taxation, particularly in indirect taxation, through taxes on spending and through increases in national insurance contributions. In that sense, the desire to increase personal freedom through a restoration of purchasing power to consumers has not been realized. However, if the 'hidden hand' has failed to stimulate the private and voluntary sectors, the introduction of new forms of fiscal and financial subsidy have undoubtedly brought about a growth in non-statutory provision. On the face of it, the increased diversity of provision has resulted in the widening of 'choices' available to some consumers. Those with the personal resources to purchase private education and health care may now receive increased subsidies from the state. In practice, this may have brought private provision within the reach of a wider populace. The impact of unemployment, downward pressure on wages and increased levels of taxation, together with reduced benefits and higher levels of contribution within the state sector (for prescriptions, student finance, council house rents, etc.), have meant that, for the majority, the talk of choice is empty rhetoric; they are not free to choose.

In Chapter 1, we referred to Marshall's prediction that the growth of the welfare state would bring about a new form of social citizenship, protecting citizens from labour market dependency and modifying pre-existing patterns of social distribution based on class. The changes in the British welfare system over the past two decades have, however, operated in a 'commodifying' capacity, leading to a progressive strengthening of the relationship between economic position and access to key social resources. The greater emphasis on individual responsibility – and labour market achievement – has been particularly damaging to women's personal autonomy as the male breadwinning family model has been reinforced. The greater emphasis on informal care as the primary source of provision for the care of children, elderly and disabled persons has further undermined women's already fragile relationship with the labour market and reinforced dependency within marriage. It remains to be seen whether the growth of casual and flexible labour markets (promoting greater 'opportunities' for women to combine paid work with unpaid labour in the home), together with the introduction of schemes involving cash payments to informal carers, will increase women's autonomy or result, instead, in new forms of exploitation and inequality.

Summary

- This final chapter has examined the changing role of the state in relation to social welfare.

- Policies of welfare retrenchment over the past 15 years have been fuelled by monetarist concerns to reduce public expenditure, 'free up' the private sector and reduce state incursion in people's private lives.

- Central to the liberal critique is the view that state welfare has undermined both individual freedom and voluntary effort. This has led to policies of welfare retrenchment and a diversion of resources to support private and voluntary effort.

- Available evidence suggests that these policies have not met with their objectives; that there has been no major impact on public expenditure (and in some cases it has actually increased); that the expectation of greater philanthropy has not been met and that the freedom of many people has been substantially restricted as a result.

Further reading

Friedman, M. and Friedman, R. (1980) *Free to Choose*. Harmondsworth: Penguin.

George, V. and Wilding, P. (1994) *Welfare and Ideology*. Hemel Hempstead: Harvester Wheatsheaf.

Hayek, F.A. (1960) *The Constitution of Liberty*. London: Routledge and Kegan Paul.

Hindess, B. (1987) *Freedom, Equality and the Market*. London: Tavistock.

GLOSSARY

Absolute poverty: *see* Poverty, absolute.

'Actively seeking work': in order to qualify for unemployment benefit, it is necessary to demonstrate that steps are actively being taken to find employment.

Altruism: concern for others, putting others before oneself.

Artefact explanation: a spurious correlation – an apparent relationship due to the effect on both elements of some third factor.

Attendance allowance: benefit paid to people with care needs who require assistance night and/or day. Replaced by disability living allowance for those under retirement age.

Basic income: an income paid to all irrespective of work performed or needs experienced.

Behavioural explanation: the assumption that poverty, poor educational achievement, poor health, etc., can be explained by the behaviour of the people themselves; for example, that poor health is the outcome of a freely chosen but inappropriate lifestyle.

Benefits, earnings-related: benefits which vary according to the level of previous earnings.

Benefits, flat-rate: benefits paid at a single rate for all, as opposed to 'earnings-related' benefits.

Benefits, insured: welfare benefits paid on the basis of an insurance contribution record (e.g. unemployment pay).

Benefits, means-tested: welfare benefits paid on the basis of a financial test of means; paid only to those with a low income and/or low levels of saving (e.g. income support).

Benefits, non-contributory: welfare benefits paid without requiring a record of insurance contributions or a test of means (e.g. child benefit, non-contributory invalidity benefit).

Benefits, selective: *see* Benefits, means tested.

Benefits, universal: welfare benefits paid as of right, without a financial means test (e.g. insured and non-contributory benefits).

Bureaucracy: hierarchical management of an organization with strict vertical lines of superordination and subordination.

Charity Organizations Society: a major philanthropic society of the nineteenth century opposed to the morally enervating effects of 'charity as gift', whose aim was the promulgation of surveillance over charitable donation to ensure that they were properly used by their recipients.

Commercial sector: providers of welfare services as a commercial proposition, for profit.

Community: a concept used to refer to (1) people living in a geographical location, (2) groups of people with a sense of identity and commonality, (3) a group of people linked together through social relationships, or (4) a group of people linked by a common culture.

Community care: the provision of services to enable dependent people (1) to live outside of large residential institutions, (2) to live in their own homes or (3) to live in as 'normal' an environment as possible. Variously taken to mean the location of care or the source of care – care *in* and *by* the community.

Community care grant: a grant paid out of the Social Fund to allow the purchase of basic household items to enable someone to live in the community.

Competitive tendering: putting up service contracts for 'auction' to commercial and other concerns, with the intention of accepting the cheapest offer which promises to provide the service efficiently and effectively.

Conservatism: a set of political beliefs emphasizing social order and tradition; associated with the Conservative Party in Britain.

Correlation: systematic co-variation, such that the value of one variable is to some extent predictable from the other. Examples include the relationship of height and weight or social class and income.

Cycle of deprivation: *see* Poverty cycle.

Dependency: a state of reliance on the support of welfare services – can be financial, physical and/or psychological.

Dependent population: people who are not economically active. Generally used to refer to those below the age of paid employment (children) and people over the age of retirement.

Deprivation, material: being unable to afford the basic goods and services taken for granted in a given country.

Deprivation, social: being unable to participate in normal day-to-day social activities. This may be the result of material deprivation, but it could be because of, for example, old age or disability.

Deterrence: making a behaviour or course of action unattractive to someone; for example, measures used to deter people from applying for state benefits.

Disability living allowance: non-contributory, non-means-tested benefit paid to people under the age of retirement who need constant care by day and/or night and/or have severe mobility problems. With the exception of the terminally ill, there is a qualifying period of 6 months.

Discrimination: to exclude someone from goods, services, employment, housing, etc., because of some characteristic (e.g. gender, colour, race) or to offer them inferior terms. Generally used when a person or group is disadvantaged by the exclusion.

Disincentive to work: the argument that high levels of social security benefits to the unemployed will make them less likely to seek paid employment.

'Dole': colloquial term for unemployment benefit.

Domestic care needs: needs for help with domestic cleaning.

Domiciliary care: personal, social and domestic care provided in a person's home. Provision of domiciliary care is seen as a means of enabling people to remain in their own homes, people who might otherwise have had to move into residential care.

Earnings-related benefits: *see* Benefits, earnings-related.

Effectiveness: doing what was intended in the least costly way, meeting objectives. The Conservative government have argued that effective policies are those that are targeted at those most in need.

Efficiency: carrying something out in the least costly way while still achieving the intended outcome; minimization of waste.

Eligibility: entitlement to. Generally used to mean that a person meets the criteria for receiving a welfare benefit and/or service.

Empowerment: giving people the power to make decisions for themselves. This can involve giving them money so that they can purchase services for themselves and/or knowledge so that they can make informed choices.

Endemic: latent, always present in the population (generally used in relation to diseases).

Epidemic: a major outbreak of a contagious condition (generally used in relation to diseases).

Equality: equal treatment – everyone being treated, in some sense, in the same way.

Equity: fair treatment – the treatment of like cases in the same way.

Ethnic minority: a group having a different culture from the majority of the population. In Britain, the term is most frequently used to refer to people of Afro-Caribbean or southern Asian descent. Often used to refer to all non-white groups in Britain.

Eugenics: the argument that the race can be improved either by encouraging the 'fit' to breed (positive eugenics) or by preventing the 'unfit' from breeding (negative eugenics).

Expressed needs: the welfare needs that people themselves say they have.

Fabian Movement: a political movement and philosophy associated with one wing of the Labour Party, which believes in social reformation through gradual change; supporters of a classic welfare state with universal benefits and equity.

Family: a group of people related by kinship ties. In modern Britain, generally used to refer to the 'nuclear family' of mother, father and dependent children, as opposed to the 'extended family', comprising a wider group of relatives.

Felt needs: needs that people feel they have.

Fiscal policy: state economic policy, especially with reference to taxation.

Fiscal welfare: redistribution through the tax system (e.g. tax relief on mortgage interest).

Flat-rate benefit: *see* Benefits, flat-rate.

Friendly Society: a mutual aid organization developed for the protection of its members; usually concerned with sickness, unemployment and old age.

Fundholder: *see* GP fundholders.

Gender roles: roles taken on by men and women that are associated with one gender. Assumed to be the result either of natural (biological) differences or of social expectations (socialization).

General practitioner: *see* GP.

GP (general practitioner): a medical doctor who provides a comprehensive medical service for a list of patients in the community.

GP fundholders: GPs who have devolved budgets to provide and purchase medical care on behalf of their patients.

Gross domestic product (GDP): the total income of a country.

Gross national product (GNP): the value of a country's total production.

Health inequalities: *see* Inequalities, health.

Health selection: the argument that an individual's social class is determined at least in part by his or her health; that is, those who are healthiest are the 'fittest' and are upwardly socially mobile.

Healthy Cities Project: policy advocated by the World Health Organization for joint strategies by health authorities and local government to improve the health of residents by both target-setting and policy initiatives.

Horizontal redistribution: redistribution between people in different social circumstances, without necessarily having regard to resources. Often used to refer to redistribution across the life course.

Household: a group of people who share accommodation and other resources.

Housing benefit: means-tested benefit for those on low income to assist with the cost of rented housing.

Housing tenure: the basis on which people occupy housing – owner occupation, rental (private), rental (council), rental (housing association).

Ideology: a set of interrelated values and beliefs.

Income support: means-tested benefit for unemployed/non-employed people, who may also be in receipt of other income maintenance benefits such as unemployment pay or disability living allowance.

Individualism: (1) the argument that each person, individually, is able to take action independently of other people in society (i.e. individuals can take control of their own lives and make decisions for themselves); (2) the view that poverty, educational failure, etc., can be explained by the inadequacies (biological or acquired) of individuals themselves.

Individualistic policies: policies which focus on each individual separately.

Inequalities, health: the differential health experiences of groups in society. Most frequently used to refer to inequalities in health between socially and economically privileged and deprived or less privileged groups.

Inequalities, material: the differential access to goods and services (e.g. housing, health services, income, diet, etc.) experienced by socially and economically privileged and deprived or less privileged groups.

Informal carer: one who cares for another, being neither employed to do so nor a member of a voluntary organization. Generally the spouse or parent, or child, of the dependent person, but may include other relatives, friends and neighbours.

Informal sector: the provision of welfare by family and friends without payment and generally assumed to be based on feelings of affection but may be based on feelings of duty/loyalty.

Insurance benefits: *see* Benefits, insured.

Laissez-faire: literally 'leave alone'; used to refer to economic policies that argue that the state should not intervene in the economic market.

Learning difficulty (or learning disability): slow intellectual development.

Lesser eligibility: the deterrence principle enacted in the 1832 Poor Law, that those given relief (benefits) should be treated less favourably than the poorest person not on relief.

Liberalism: the argument that individuals must be left free to make choices and that the state should make minimal intervention in society, providing only a legal framework and defence.

Life chances: the differential opportunities for economic, educational and social success. Often argued to be based on social class of birth; those with middle-class parents being said to have superior life chances to those with working-class parents.

Life-course: the series of changes that take place as people go through the course of their lives; biological and social changes including, for example, childhood, adolescence, adulthood, marriage, parenting, bereavement and old age.

Life expectancy: the number of years that a person can expect to live, on average. Usually given for life expectancy at birth but can be calculated from any given age.

Lone-parent family: the head of the family in which there is only one parent, through death, divorce or separation. In Britain, 90 per cent of single parents are women. *See also* Single parent.

Low pay: an income less than that paid on average in a country. There is considerable disagreement as to what counts as low pay, however.

Managed market: term used to refer to the internal markets set up by the National Health Service and Community Care Act 1990 to encourage competition between providers of health care in Britain. (Also referred to as Quasi-markets.) Also used to refer to the social market that the same legislation required to be stimulated in the provision of community care. However, the former can be distinguished from the latter in that the vast majority of providers of services in the health sector are NHS Trusts, while for the latter social services departments have been explicitly required to stimulate the voluntary and commercial sectors as providers.

Manual workers: people who work with their hands. Often referred to as the 'working class'.

Marketization: the process of making the delivery of state welfare services more like services delivered by the commercial sector. Can be achieved either by 'privatization' or by introducing managed markets.

Material inequalities: *see* Inequalities, material.

Means test: a test of financial means (income and/or savings) to determine eligibility for benefits and/or services.

Means-tested benefits: *see* Benefits, means-tested.

Medicine, alternative: also referred to as complementary medicine, and includes traditional medicine. Health care treatment that falls outside conventional scientific medicine (e.g. homeopathy, acupuncture, traditional Chinese medicine, osteopathy, chiropraxis, aromatherapy).

Medicine, conventional: scientific medicine as generally practised by qualified medical doctors in Britain and including the work of professions allied to medicine, and nursing care.

Middle class: *see* Social class

Mixed economy of welfare: the provision of welfare services and benefits by more than one sector – state, commercial, voluntary, informal.

Mobility allowance: an allowance formerly paid to people who could not walk or had great difficulty in walking. Claimants had to be eligible for the allowance before their 65th birthday. Now incorporated within disability living allowance for those aged under 65.

Morbidity: ill health.

Mortality: death.

Mutual aid: the principle of joining together with others to provide help or support for each other in times of adversity.

National efficiency: term used at the time of the Boer War to refer to the ability of people, particularly the working class, to undertake military service or to work in factories, etc.

Needs: problems experienced by people that welfare is aimed at overcoming.

New Right: the term used to refer to the ideologies espoused by the political right since the late 1970s, particularly in Britain and the United States. Generally combines a commitment to Conservative values in terms of morality and the family with Liberal (free-market) economic principles. Also referred to as Thatcherism or Reaganism.

NHS Trusts: an agency within the health service providing services for purchase (e.g. hospitals, community services, ambulance services).

Non-contributory benefits: *see* Benefits, non-contributory.

Non-employed: those who do not have and are not seeking paid employment (e.g. students, people over the age of retirement, women with full-time domestic responsibilities).

Non-take-up: failure to claim benefits, most commonly associated with means-tested benefits.

Normalization: enabling people to live as normally as possible; empowering people to participate in society.

Nuclear family: *see* Family.

Occupational schemes: *see* Pension, occupational.

Occupational welfare: *see* Welfare, occupational.

Paternalism: the principle of doing things for people's benefit, without seeking their consent.

Patriarchy: literally, 'rule of the father'. Now generally used to refer to a society in which men have power over women.

Pauperism: term used under the New Poor Law to refer to the state of being dependent on relief (benefits).

Pension, occupational: retirement pension provided by an employer, to which the employee may or may not have contributed during his or her working life. Benefits are based on years of service.

Pension, private: a pension – usually on retirement but could be, for example, on permanent disability – arranged by an individual with an insurance company.

An employer may contribute to a private pension. Benefits are based on contributions paid.

Pension, state: retirement pension paid by the state on the basis of a contribution record. Those who have not opted out may be entitled to an additional earnings-related element.

Pension, supplementary: a means-tested pension paid to retirement pensioners on low income.

Performance indicators: targets used to assess work performance; usually associated with employment in which employees are on performance-related pay. May also be used for measures of the effectiveness of a department or service.

Performance-related pay: an element of earned income dependent on achieving agreed targets; often related to the uprating of pay.

Personal care needs: needs for help with personal care tasks such as toileting, washing and dressing.

Personal social services: the range of services, including social work, residential and domiciliary care, which are the statutory responsibility of local authority social services departments.

Philanthropy: term used to refer to charitable work where there is the expectation that the recipients of charity will reform/change their behaviour.

Policy vacuums: gaps in policy and provision.

Poor Law infirmary: hospital for the poor, in the nineteenth and early twentieth centuries.

Poverty: severe deprivation, usually associated with inadequate resources, especially financial. How it shall be measured is disputed.

Poverty, absolute: the inability to provide for basic food and shelter; starvation.

Poverty, feminization of: the argument that poverty is a major problem for women because of the growth of women dependent on means-tested benefits, either as heads of single-parent households or as elderly women.

Poverty, relative: being poor in relation to average standards of living in a society; not being able to participate in the day-to-day activities that are taken for granted by others.

Poverty, subsistence: having just sufficient resources to live at the bare minimum.

Poverty cycle: the movement in and out of poverty (however defined) experienced across the life course by low income groups.

Poverty trap: a situation that arises when people's income increases and they move off welfare benefits, such that their net income does not increase or increases only marginally.

Premature death: death occurring before the average life expectancy has been achieved.

Private sector: *see* Commercial sector.

Privatization: transfer to the commercial or perhaps voluntary sector of previously state-owned services.

Progressive taxation: a fiscal policy that means that, as income rises, the amount of tax paid/deducted rises.

Provident Society: *see* Friendly Society.

Public sector: services managed and financed by the state.

Quasi-market: *see* Managed market.

Redistribution: transfer of resource from some people to others, or from one life-stage to another.

Registrar General's Classification: an occupational class measure that divides occupations into five category bands, roughly by income and status.

Relative poverty: *see* Poverty, relative.

Reluctant collectivists: a term used to refer to Conservative politicians in the 1940s to 1970s who reluctantly supported the welfare state in Britain.

Remuneration package: the sum total received from an employer, including salary plus additional rewards such as use of car, health insurance, sick pay, pension plan, workplace nursery, etc.

Residential care: care in which help and support is provided in a residential setting; usually seen as 'more normal' than care in long-stay hospitals.

Residual welfare state: a welfare state that makes only minimum provision at a minimum level for those on low incomes. Eligibility for benefits is generally means tested.

Residuum: term used in the nineteenth century to refer to the unemployed dependent on relief from the workhouse. The term 'underclass' has been used to refer to the same population in the 1980s and 1990s.

Retirement: leaving paid employment. In Britain, the retirement age is often seen as synonymous with entitlement to a state pension – currently at age 60 for women and 65 for men. However, early retirement is not uncommon, and in some occupations it has become the norm for men and women to retire at 60.

Safety net: residual welfare services and/or benefits for those on low incomes or without income altogether, who would not otherwise be able to provide for themselves.

Sanitary reform: usually used to refer to the public health reforms in the nineteenth century concerned primarily with the provision of sewers and clean water.

Selective benefits: *see* Benefits, means-tested.

Selectivity: a policy of focusing resources on people in need; usually involves financial means testing.

Single parent: a parent (normally a mother) who has never married and is bringing up children on her own.

Skills mix: the combination of services from different agencies and/or different grades or kinds of staff, differently trained and qualified, to best satisfy the needs of a given client or group of clients.

Social care needs: needs for help with tasks such as cooking, shopping, transport and collecting pension.

Social class: the division of the population into economic groups. Social classes are generally said to share social and economic interests. Marxists see the major division as that between those who own the means of production – the owners/capitalists – and those who have to sell their labour – the workers. They argue that capitalist societies such as Britain are ruled so that, in the main, the interests of the capitalist class is secured. Most social scientists, however, argue that there are a number of social classes in Britain which have their own interests and try to protect them. The official categorization of social class is that devised by the Registrar General. The population is divided into six main groups or classes:

1   professional and higher managerial
2   semi-professional, lower management
3.1 routine non-manual
3.2 skilled manual
4   semi-skilled manual
5   unskilled manual.

Children and married women are generally classified by the occupation of the (male) Head of Household. This practice has been the subject of considerable debate (see Abbott and Sapsford 1987b; Abbott and Wallace 1996).

Social control: control exercised by some people over others, either for the benefit of society generally or for the benefit of a specific social group. People are controlled when they are made or induced to act in ways in which they would not otherwise choose, in order to receive benefits/ services, or when their options are restricted.

Social deprivation: *see* Deprivation, social.

Social Fund: a cash-limited fund established by the Social Security Act 1986. There are two elements: community care grants and loans.

Social policy: policies designed to meet people's welfare needs. The study of social services and the welfare state.

Social problem: a problem which is seen to relate to society as a whole or specific groups within it. Can be seen as a problem for society and/or a problem that has social as opposed to individual causes. For example, crime is seen as a social problem because it creates problems for society generally; it may be seen as having social and/or individual causes.

Social security: income maintenance benefits. In Britain, the term refers to insured and means-tested benefits.

Social stigma: *see* Stigma.

State: the formal political institutions of a society, including both central and local government.

State retirement pension: *see* Pension, state.

Statutory services: services provided or at least purchased by the public sector and prescribed by law or regulation.

Stigma: literally 'visible blemish'; a sense of shame, a 'spoiled identity', a loss of status.

Stigmatized: socially rejected because of actual or assumed physical and/or moral characteristics.

Structural dependency: dependency caused by economic position and relationship to society, rather than by people's individual characteristics or behaviour.

Subsistence poverty: *see* Poverty, subsistence.

Supplementary pension: *see* Pension, supplementary.

Surveillance: literally 'oversight'; the monitoring of behaviour/performance of a group or individual.

Targeting: directing services and/or benefits to those most in need; usually involves using financial means tests and/or strict criteria of eligibility.

Tenure: in housing policy, the right by which people occupy their house (e.g. renting from a housing association, owner-occupation).

Underclass: a group below the class system, dependent on state benefits. Used both by those who see the group as excluded by structural factors from participating and by those who see the underclass as morally undesirable.

Unemployed: those who do not have paid employment and are actively seeking it.

Unemployment trap: the situation where people are better off on benefit than in paid employment.

Universal benefits: *see* Benefits, universal.

Universality: the distribution of benefits or services to everyone – or at least everyone in a broad category.

Vertical redistribution: redistribution between people on different levels of wealth or income; usually redistribution from the wealthier to the poorer members of society.

Voluntary provision: provision made by the voluntary sector, that is, non-governmental organizations.

Voluntary sector: independent provision which is not for profit, usually on the basis of charity or mutual aid.

Welfare dependency: dependency on welfare, i.e. state, benefits. The New Right has argued that the provision of welfare benefits means that those on them become dependent – that is, they develop a psychological state such that they do not seek to help themselves by, for example, finding employment, but are content to remain on benefit. The welfare state is said to stifle initiative and incentives to hard work and independence and to encourage the attitude that 'the state will provide'.

Welfare, employment: *see* Welfare, occupational.

Welfare, occupational: welfare provided through the workplace.

Welfare needs: *see* Needs.

Welfare pluralism: the provision of welfare by more than one sector, and the argument that it should be so provided.

Welfare rights: the rights of people (citizens) to welfare.

Welfare state: a state that organizes/provides welfare services – that is, services to deal with a wide range of social problems. The classic Welfare State is one where the state is seen as the provider of a comprehensive range of welfare services.

REFERENCES

Abbott, P.A. (1982) Towards a social theory of mental handicap. PhD thesis, Thames Polytechnic.

Abbott, P.A. (ed.) (1988) *Material Deprivation and Health Status in the Plymouth Health District*. Plymouth: University of Plymouth, Department of Applied Social Science.

Abbott, P.A. (1992a) *Stage I Report on the Skills Mix Project*. Research Report to Cornwall Social Services. Plymouth: University of Plymouth, Department of Applied Social Science.

Abbott, P.A. (1992b) *Rationalising the Skills Mix in Community Care for Disabled and Older People*. A Report of Research in Cornwall. Plymouth: University of Plymouth, Community Research Centre.

Abbott, P.A. (1994) Conflict over the grey areas: District nurses and health visitors providing community care. *Journal of Gender Studies*, 3: 299–306.

Abbott, P.A. and Ackers, L. (in press) Women and employment. In T. Spybey (ed.), *Britain in Europe*. London: Routledge.

Abbott, P.A. and Giarchi, G. (in press) Health. In T. Spybey (ed.), *Britain in Europe*. London: Routledge.

Abbott, P.A. and Lankshear, G. (1992) *Caring for Older People: Estimating Needs for Services in Devon*. Research Report to Devon Social Services. Plymouth: University of Plymouth, Community Research Centre.

Abbott, P.A. and Payne, G. (1990) Travelling for surgery: The case of heart disease. Paper presented to the *Annual Conference of the British Sociological Association*, Manchester, April.

Abbott, P.A. and Sapsford, R.J. (1987a) *Community Care for Mentally Handicapped Children: The Origins and Consequences of a Social Policy*. Milton Keynes: Open University Press.

Abbott, P.A. and Sapsford, R.J. (1987b) *Women and Social Class*. London: Tavistock.

Abbott, P.A. and Sapsford, R.J. (1988) The body politic: Health, family and society. Unit 11 of Open University course D211, *Social Problems and Social Welfare*. Milton Keynes: The Open University.

Abbott, P.A. and Sapsford, R.J. (1990) Health visiting: policing the family? In P.A. Abbott and C. Wallace (eds), *The Sociology of the Caring Professions*. Basingstoke: Falmer Press.

Abbott, P.A. and Sapsford, R.J. (1994) Health and material deprivation in Plymouth: An interim replication. *Sociology of Health and Illness*, 16: 252–9.

Abbott, P.A. and Tyler, M. (1995) Ethnic variation in the female labour force. *British Journal of Sociology*, 46: 339–53.

Abbott, P.A. and Wallace, C. (eds) (1990a) *The Sociology of the Caring Professions*. Basingstoke: Falmer Press.

Abbott, P.A. and Wallace, C. (1990b) Introduction. In P.A. Abbott and C. Wallace (eds), *The Sociology of the Caring Professions*. Basingstoke: Falmer Press.

Abbott, P.A. and Wallace, C. (1990c) Social work and nursing: a history. In P.A. Abbott and C. Wallace (eds), *The Sociology of the Caring Professions*. Basingstoke: Falmer Press.

Abbott, P.A. and Wallace, C. (1992) *The Family and the New Right*. London: Pluto.

Abbott, P.A. and Wallace, C. (1996) *An Introduction to Sociology: Feminist Perspectives*. London: Routledge.

Abel-Smith, B. and Titmuss, K. (eds) (1987) *Selected Writings of Richard M. Titmuss: The Philosophy of Welfare*. London: Allen and Unwin.

Abel-Smith, B. and Townsend, P. (1965) *The Poor and the Poorest*. London: Bell.

Abrams, P. (1977) Community care: Some research problems and priorities. *Policy and Politics*, 6: 125–51.

Acheson Report (1988) *Public Health in England: The Report of the Committee of Inquiry into the Future Development of the Public Health*. Cm 289. London: HMSO.

Ackers, H.L. (1986) *Evaluation of the Trefgarne Initiative for Carers of Elderly Persons with Psychiatric Disorders*. Report to the Social Services Committee, County of Avon. Plymouth: University of Plymouth, Community Research Centre.

Ackers, H.L. (1989) The social construction of disability and its research implications. Paper presented to the *Annual Conference of the British Sociological Association*, Plymouth, April.

Ackers, H.L. (1994) Citizenship, Dependency and Gender in Comparative Social Policy Analysis. Paper presented to a conference on *Employment, Work and Society*, Canterbury, September.

Aldridge, J. and Becker, S. (1993) *Children Who Care*. Loughborough: Loughborough University in association with Nottingham Association of Voluntary Services.

Aldridge, J. and Becker, S. (1994) *My Child, My Carer – The Parent's Perspective*. Loughborough: Loughborough University in association with Nottingham Health Authority and Nottingham Association of Voluntary Services.

Ambrose, P. and Colenutt, B. (1975) *The Property Machine*. Harmondsworth: Penguin.

Appleby, J., Smith, P., Ranade, W., Little, V. and Robinson, R. (1994) Monitoring managed competition. In J. LeGrande and R. Robinson (eds), *Privatisation and the Welfare State*. London: Allen and Unwin.

Arber, S. (1990) Opening the 'black box': inequalities in women's health. In P. Abbott and G. Payne (eds), *New Directions in the Sociology of Health*. Basingstoke: Falmer.

Arber, S. and Gilbert, N. (1989a) Transitions in caring: Gender, life course and care of the elderly. In B. Bytheway, T. Keil, P. Allat and A. Bryman (eds), *Becoming and Being Old*. London: Sage.

Arber, S. and Gilbert, N. (1989b) Men: The forgotten carers. *Sociology*, 23: 111–18.

Arber, S. and Ginn, J. (1991) *Gender and Later Life: A Sociological Analysis of Resources and Constraints*. London: Sage.

Arber, S. and Ginn, J. (1995) Gender differences in informal caring. *Health and Social Care in the Community*, 3: 19–31.

Arber, S., Gilbert, N. and Evandron, M. (1988) Gender, household composition and receipt of domiciliary services by disabled people. *Journal of Social Policy*, 17: 153–75.

Arblaster, L. and Hawtin, M. (1993) *Health, Housing and Social Policy*. London: Socialist Health Association.

Armstrong, D. (1984) *The Political Anatomy of the Body: Medical Knowledge in Britain in the Twentieh Century*. Cambridge: Cambridge University Press.

Arnold, P., Bochel, H., Brodhurst, S. and Page, D. (1993) *Community Care: The Housing Dimension*. York: Joseph Rowntree Foundation.

Arnott, M. (1987) Second-class citizens. In A. Walker and C. Walker (eds), *The Growing Divide*. London: Child Poverty Action Group.

Ascher, K. (1987) *The Politics of Privatisation: Contracting out Public Services*. London: Macmillan.

Ashton, H. (1991) Psychotropic drug prescribing for women. *British Journal of Psychiatry*, 158 (suppl. 10): 30–35.

Ashton, J. and Seymour, H. (1988) *The New Public Health*. Buckingham: Open University Press.

Atkin, K. and Rollings, J. (1992) Informal care in Asian and Afro/Caribbean communities: A literature review. *British Journal of Social Work*, 22: 405–418.

Atkinson, A.B.L. (1989) *Poverty and Social Security*. London: Harvester Wheatsheaf.

Audit Commission (1986) *Making a Reality of Community Care*. London: HMSO.

Audit Commission (1992) *Developing Local Authority Housing Strategies*. London: HMSO.

Baine, S., Benington, J. and J. Russell (1993) *Changing Europe: Challenges Facing the Voluntary and Community Sectors in the 1990s*. London: NCVO.

Balcombe, J., Strange, N. and Tate, G. (1993) *Wish You Were Here: How UK and Japanese-owned Organisations Manage Attendance*. London: The Industrial Society.

Baldock, J. (1991) England and Wales. In R.J. Kraus, J. Baldock, M. Knapsen, M. Thorslund and C. Tunnissen (eds), *Care for the Elderly: Significant Innovations in Three European Countries*. Boulder, CA: Campus/Westview Press.

Baldock, J. (1992) The personal social services: The politics of care. In V. George and S. Miller (eds), *Social Policy 2000: Squaring the Welfare Circle*. London: Routledge.

Baldock, J. and Ungerson, C. (1991) 'What d'ya want if you don' want money?' – A feminist critique of 'paid volunteering'. In M. Maclean and D. Groves (eds), *Women's Issues in Social Policy*. London: Routledge.

Baldwin, S. and Falkingham, J. (eds) (1994) *Social Security and Social Change*. London: Harvester Wheatsheaf.

Baldwin, S. and Twigg, J. (1992) Women and community care. In M. Maclean and D. Groves (eds), *Women's Issues in Social Policy*. London: Routledge.

Banks, O. (1981) *Faces of Feminism*. Oxford: Martin Robertson.

Baratz, M.S. and Grigsby, W. (1971) Thoughts on poverty and its elimination. *Journal of Social Policy*, 1: 119–34.

Barker, D., Halman, L. and Vloet, A. (1992) *The European Values Study, 1981–1991: Summary Report*. Gordon Cook Foundation.

Barnett, S. and Saxon-Harold, S. (1992) Interim report: Charitable giving. In R. Jowell, L. Brooks, L. Dowds and D. Ahrendt (eds), *British Social Attitudes: The 9th Report*. Aldershot: Dartmouth Publishing.

Barry, A., Carr-Hill, R. and Glanville, J. (1991) *Homelessness and Health: What do We Know? What Should be Done?* Centre for Health Economics, Discussion Paper No. 84. York: University of York.

Bartlett, W. and LeGrande, J. (1994) The performance of trusts. In J. LeGrande and R. Robinson (eds), *Privatisation and the Welfare State*. London: Allen and Unwin.

Bartley, M. (1994) Unemployment and ill health: Understanding the relationship. *Journal of Epidemiology and Community Health*, 48: 333–7.

Barton, R. (1959) *Institutional Neurosis*. London: Wright.

Bayley, M. (1973) *Mental Handicap and Community Care*. London: Routledge and Kegan Paul.

Beattie, A. (1984) Health education and the science tender: Invitation to a debate. *Education and Health*, January, pp. 9–16.

Beattie, A. (1991) Knowledge and control in health promotion: A test case for social policy and social theory. In J. Gabe, M. Calan and M. Bury (eds), *The Sociology of the NHS*. London: Routledge.

Bebbington, A. and Davies, B. (1983) Equity and affluence in the allocation of the personal social services. *Journal of Social Policy*, 12: 246–52.

Bebbington, A. and Tong, M.S. (1986) Trends and changes in old people's homes: Provision over twenty years. In M. Judge and I. Sinclair (eds), *Residential Care for Elderly People*. London: HMSO.

Benzeval, M. and Webb, S. (1995) 'Family poverty and poor health'. In M. Benzeval, K. Judge and M. Whitehead (eds), *Tackling Inequalities in Health*. London: King's Fund.

Benzeval, M., Judge, K. and Solomon, M. (1992) *The Health Status of London: A Comparative Perspective*. Initiative Working Paper No. 1. London: King's Fund.

Benzeval, M., Blane, D., Judge, K., Marmot, M., Power, C., Whitehead, M. and Wilkinson, R. (1994) *Society and Health*, Issue 1. London: King's Fund Institute and Centre for Health and Society.

Benzeval, M., Judge, K. and Whitehead, M. (1995a) The role of the NHS. In M. Benzeval, K. Judge and M. Whitehead (eds), *Tackling Inequalities in Health*. London: King's Fund.

Benzeval, M., Judge, K. and Whitehead, M. (1995b) Unfinished business. In M. Benzeval, K. Judge and M. Whitehead (eds), *Tackling Inequalities in Health*. London: King's Fund.

Benzeval, M., Judge, K. and Whitehead, M. (eds) (1995c) *Tackling Inequalities in Health*. London: King's Fund.

Beresford, P. and Craft, S. (1984) Welfare pluralism: The new face of Fabianism. *Critical Social Policy*, 9: 23–8.

Best, R. (1995) The housing dimension. In M. Benzeval, K. Judge and M. Whitehead (eds), *Tackling Inequalities in Health*. London: King's Fund.

Beveridge, W. (1948) *Voluntary Action*. London: Allen and Unwin.

Bines, W. (1994) *The Health of Single Homeless People*. Housing Research Findings No. 128. York: Joseph Rowntree Foundation.

Blackburn, C. (1991) *Poverty and Health: Working with Families*. Buckingham: Open University Press.

Blaxter, M. (1990) *Health and Lifestyle*. London: Routledge.

Bornat, J., Pereira, C., Pilgrim, D. and Williams, F. (eds) (1993) *Community Care: A Reader*. Basingstoke: Macmillan.

Bottomley, 'V. (1992) Building on a solid state. *Community Care*, 2 April, pp. 19–20.

Bowlby, J. (1954) *Maternal Deprivation*. Harmondsworth: Penguin.

Bradshaw, J. (1991) Social security. In D. Marsh and R. Rhodes (eds), *Implementing Thatcherite Policies: Audit of an Era*. Buckingham: Open University Press.

Bradshaw, J., Mitchell, D. and Morgan, J. (1987) Evaluating adequacy: The potential of budget standards. *Journal of Social Policy*, 16: 165–81.

Bradshaw, J., Hicks, L. and Parker, A. (1992) *Summary Budget Standards for Six Households*. Department of Social Policy, Family Budget Unit, Working Paper N. 12. York: University of York.

Braithwaite, B. (1990) *Bound to Care*. Sydney: Allen and Unwin.

Brenton, M. (1985) *The Voluntary Sector in British Social Services*. London: Longman.

Briggs, R. (1988) Boom in private rest homes in Southampton: Impact on the elderly in residential care. *British Medical Journal of Clinical Research and Education*, 296 (6621): 541–3.

British Medical Association (1987) *Deprivation and Ill Health*. London: BMA.

Brown, C. (1984) *Black and White in Britain: The Third PSI Survey*. Aldershot: Gower.

Brown, J.C. (1990) The focus on the single mother. In C. Murray (ed.), *The Emerging British Underclass*. London: Institute of Economic Affairs.

Buckle, J. (1984) *Mental Handicap Costs More*. London: Disablement Income Group Charitable Trust.

Bulmer, M. (1987) *The Social Basis of Community Care*. London: Allen and Unwin.

Cahill, M. (1994) *The New Social Policy*. Oxford: Blackwell.

Campling, J. (1988) Social policy digest. *Journal of Social Policy*, 17: 85–109.

Carstairs, V. (1981) Small area analysis and health service research. *Community Medicine*, 3: 131–9.

Cartwright, A. and Anderson, R. (1983) *General Practice Revisited: A Second Study of Patients and Their Doctors*. London: Tavistock.

Cass, B. (1983) Redistribution to children and to mothers. In C. Baldock and B. Cass (eds), *Women, Social Welfare and the State*. Sydney: Allen and Unwin.

Castle, B. (1981) *The Castle Diaries 1974–1976*. London: Weidenfeld and Nicolson.

Central Office of Information (1948) *The National Health Service*. London: COI.

Central Statistical Office (1991) *Social Trends 91*, 1991 Edition. London: HMSO.

Central Statistical Office (1992) *Social Trends 92*, 1992 Edition. London: HMSO.

Central Statistical Office (1995) *Social Trends 95*, 1995 Edition. London: HMSO.

Challis, D., Darton, R., Johnson, L., Stone, M., Traske, K. and Wall, B. (1989) *The Darlington Community Care Project: Supporting Frail Elderly People at Home.* Canterbury: University of Kent, PSSRU.

Chandler, J. (forthcoming) *Sociology for Nurses and the Caring Professions.* Buckingham: Open University Press.

Child Poverty Action Group (annual) *National Welfare Benefits Handbook.* London: CPAG.

Child Poverty Action Group (1995) *Rights Guide to Non-Means-Tested Benefits.* London: CPAG.

Church of England Working Party (1985) *Faith in the City.* London: Church House.

Clarke, J. (1988) Social work: The personal and the political. Unit 13 of Open University course D211, *Social Problems and Social Welfare.* Milton Keynes: The Open University.

Clarke, J., Cochrane, A. and McLaughlin, E. (eds) (1994) *Managing Social Policy.* London: Sage.

Cliff, D. (1993) Health issues in male early retirement. In S. Platt, H. Thomas, S. Scott and G. Williams (eds), *Locating Health: Sociological and Historical Explorations.* Aldershot: Avebury.

Cohen, R. (1991) If you have everything second-hand, you feel second-hand: Bringing up children on income support. *FSU Quarterly*, 46: 25–41.

Cole, I. and Furbey, R. (1994) *The Eclipse of Council Housing.* London: Routledge.

Commission on Social Justice (1993) *The Justice Gap.* London: Institute for Public Policy Research.

Committee of Vice Chancellors and Principals (1995) *Universities and the Health of the Nation.* London: CVCP.

Community Development Project (1977) *The Costs of Industrial Change.* London: HMSO.

Conservative Party (1987) *Conservative Party Manifesto 1987.* London: Conservative Central Office.

Cook, J. and Watt, S. (1992) Racism, women and poverty. In C. Glendinning and J. Millar (eds), *Women and Poverty in Britain in the 1990s.* Hemel Hempstead: Harvester Wheatsheaf.

Cornwell, J. (1984) *Hard-Earned Lives: Accounts of Health and Illness from East London.* London: Tavistock.

Cox, D. (1991) Health service management: A sociological view – Griffiths and the non-negotiated order of the hospital. In J. Gabe, M. Calan and M. Bury (eds), *Sociology of the Health Service.* London: Routledge.

Craig, P. (1991) Costs and benefits: A review of research on take-up of income-related benefits. *Journal of Social Policy*, 20: 537–65.

Dale, J. and Foster, P. (1986) *Feminists and State Welfare.* London: Routledge and Kegan Paul.

Dalley, G. (1988) *Ideologies of Caring.* London: Macmillan.

Dant, T. and Gearing, B. (1990) Keyworkers for elderly people in the community: Case managers and care co-ordinators. *Journal of Social Policy*, 19: 331–60.

Davies, B. and Challis, D. (1990) *Matching Resources to Needs in Community-Based Care.* Aldershot: Gower.

Davies, E., Dilmot, A., Flanders, S., Giles, C., Johnson, P., Ridge, M., Stork, G., Webb, S. and Whitehouse, E. (1992) *Alternative Proposals on Tax and Social Security.* Commentary No. 29. London: Institute for Fiscal Studies.

Davies, J. and Kelly, M. (eds) (1992) *Healthy Cities: Research and Practice.* London: Routledge.

Davies, S. (1987) Towards the remoralisation of society. In M. Loney, R. Bocock, J. Clarke, A. Cochrane, P. Graham and M. Wilson (eds), *The State or the Market.* London: Sage.

Davis, A. (1993) Community care. In P. Spurgeon (ed.), *The New Face of the NHS.* London: Longman.

Davis Smith, J., Rochester, C. and Hedley, R. (1995) *An Introduction to the Voluntary Sector*. London: Routledge.

Day, P., Henderson, D. and Klein, R. (1993) *Home Rules, Regulation and Accountability in Social Housing*. York: Joseph Rowntree Foundation.

Deacon, A. and Bradshaw, J. (1986) Social security. In P. Wilding (ed.), *In Defence of the Welfare State*. Manchester: Manchester University Press.

Dean, H. (1994) The last of persistent poverty. In V. George and S. Miller (eds), *Social Policy Towards 2000: Squaring the Welfare Circle*. London: Routledge.

Department of Health (1989a) *Working for Patients*. Cm 555. London: HMSO.

Department of Health (1989b) *Income Generation: A Guide to Local Initiatives*. London: HMSO.

Department of Health (1989c) *Caring for People*. London: HMSO.

Department of Health (1990) *Key Indicators of Local Authority Social Services 1988/9*. London: HMSO.

Department of Employment (1991) *New Earnings Survey*. London: HMSO.

Department of Health (1992) *The Health of the Nation: A Strategy for Health in England*. Cm 1986. London: HMSO.

Department of Health (1993) *Managing the New NHS*. London: Department of Health.

Department of Health (1995) *Health and Personal Social Services Statistics for England, 1994*. London: HMSO.

Department of Health/OPCS (1993) *Health Services Indicators Data Set*. London: HMSO.

Department of Health and Social Security (1976) *Prevention and Health: Everybody's Business*. London: HMSO.

Department of Health and Social Security (1964) *The Development of Community Care*. London: HMSO.

Department of Health and Social Security (1980) *Committee of Enquiry into Mental Handicap Nursing and Training* (The Jay Report). London: HMSO.

Department of Health and Social Security (1981a) *Growing Older*. Cmnd 8173. London: HMSO.

Department of Health and Social Security (1981b) *Contractual Arrangements with Independent Hospitals and Nursing Homes*. London: HMSO.

Department of Health and Social Security (1981c) *Report of a Study on Community Care*. London: HMSO.

Department of Health and Social Security (1983) *Report of the Social Security Advisory Committee*. London: HMSO.

Department of Health and Social Security (1985) *Reform of Social Security*, Vol. 1. London: HMSO.

Department of Health and Social Security (1987) *Health and Personal Social Services in HM Treasury, Government Expenditure Plans 1986–7 to 1988–9*. London: HMSO.

Department of Social Security (1989) *Children Come First*, Vols 1 and 2. London: HMSO.

Department of Social Security (1991a) *Social Security Statistics 1990*. London: HMSO.

Department of Social Security (1991b) *Report on Government Expenditure Plans 1991/2 to 1993/4*. Cm 1514. London: HMSO.

Department of Social Security (1992) *Households Below Average Income*. London: HMSO.

Department of Social Security (1994) *The Take-Up of Income-Related Benefits 1991*. Analytical Services Department, DSS. London: HMSO.

Department of Social Security (1995a) *Reform of Social Security: Programme for Action*. Cm 9691. London: HMSO.

Department of Social Security (1995b) *Report on Government Expenditure Plans 1995/6 and 1996/7*. London: HMSO.

Derby City Hospital NHS Trust (1995) NHS league tables – how the Trust stands. *General News*, 5 July, p. 3.

Derbyshire Welfare Rights Service (1993) *Poverty in Derbyshire – Income Support*. Matlock: Derbyshire County Council.

Dominelli, L. (1983) *Anti-Racist Social Work*. London: Macmillan.

Donzelot, J. (1980) *The Policing of Families*. London: Hutchinson.

Douglas, J.W.B. (1964) *The Home and the School*. London: McGibbon and Kee.

Doyal, L. (1995) *What Makes Women Sick: Gender and Political Economy*. London: Macmillan.

Enthovan, A.V. (1985) *Reflections on the Management of the National Health Service*. Occasional Paper No. 5. London: Nuffield Private Hospital Trust.

Equal Opportunities Commission (1984) *Carers and Services: A Comparison of Men and Women Caring for Dependent Elderly People*. Manchester: EOC.

Esau, P. and Berthoud, R. (1991) *Independent Benefits for Men and Women*. London: Policy Studies Institute.

Esping-Anderson, G. (1990) *The Three Worlds of Welfare Capitalism*. Cambridge: Polity Press.

Eurostat (1990) *Poverty in Figures*. Luxembourg: European Community Statistical Office.

Evandrou, M. (1990) *Challenging the Invisibility of Carers: Mapping Informal Care Policy*. Working Paper WSP/49. London: LSE Suntay/Toyota Centre for Economic and Related Disciplines.

Evandrou, M. (1991) Care for the elderly in Britain: State services, informal care and welfare benefits. In J. Pacolet and C. Wilderom (eds), *The Economics of Care of the Elderly*. Aldershot: Avebury.

Evandrou, M., Arber, S., Dale, A. and Gilbert, N. (1986) Who cares for the elderly? Family care problems and receipt of statutory services. In C. Phillipson, M. Bernard and P. Strang (eds), *Dependency and Interdependency in Old Age: Theoretical Perspectives and Policy Alternatives*. Beckenham: Croom Helm.

Family Policy Studies Centre (1989) *Family Policy Bulletin 6*. London: FPSC.

Fearn, R. (1987) Rural health care: A British success or a tale of unmet need? *Social Science and Medicine*, 40: 309–314.

Fennell, G., Phillipson, C. and Evers, H. (1988) *The Sociology of Old Age*. Milton Keynes: Open University Press.

Field, F. and Owen, M. (1993) *Private Pensions for All: Squaring the Circle*. London: Fabian Society.

Fielding, N., Reeve, C. and Simey, M.C. (1991) *Active Citizens, New Voices and Values*. London: Bedford Square Press.

Finch, J. (1984) Community care: developing non-sexist alternatives. *Critical Social Policy*, 9: 6–18.

Finch, J. (1990) The politics of community care in Britain. In C. Ungerson (ed.), *Gender and Caring: Work and Welfare in Britain and Scandinavia*. Hemel Hempstead: Harvester Wheatsheaf.

Finch, J. and Groves, D. (1983) *A Labour Of Love: Women, Work and Caring*. London: Routledge and Kegan Paul.

Fogelman, K., Fox, H. and Power, C. (1987) *Class and Tenure Mobility: Do They Explain the Social Inequalities in Health Among Young Adults in Britain?* National Child Development Study Working Paper No. 21. London: City University Social Statistics Research Unit.

Forrest, R. and Murie, A. (1988) *Selling the Welfare State*. London: Routledge.

Foucault, M. (1963) *The Birth of the Clinic*. London: Tavistock.

Fowler, N. (1984) Speech by the then Secretary for Social Services to the Joint Social Services Annual Conference, 27 September.

Fox, A.J. and Goldblatt, P. (1982) *Longitudinal Study: Socio-demographic Mortality Differentials*. OPCS Series LS No. 1. London: HMSO.

Fox, A.J. *et al.* (1984) Approaches to studying the effects of socio-economic circumstances on geographical differences in mortality in England and Wales. *British Medical Journal*, 40: 309–314.

Fox, J. and Benzeval, M. (1995) Perspectives on social variations in health. In

M. Benzeval, K. Judge and M. Whitehead (eds), *Tackling Inequalities in Health*. London: King's Fund.

Friedman, M. and Friedman, R. (1980) *Free to Choose*. Harmondsworth: Penguin.

Fry, V., Smith, S. and White, S. (1990) *Pensioners and the Public Purse*. Report Series No. 36. London: Institute for Fiscal Studies.

Gabe, J. and Williams, P. (1993) Women, crowding and mental health. In R. Borridge and D. Ormandy (eds), *Unhealthy Housing: Research, Remedies and Reform*. London: E. and F. Spong.

George, V. and Wilding, P. (1972) *Motherless Families*. London: Routledge and Kegan Paul.

George, V. and Wilding, P. (1994) *Welfare and Ideology*. Hemel Hempstead: Harvester Wheatsheaf.

Giarchi, G. (1990) Distance decay and information deprivation: Health implications for people in rural isolation. In P.A. Abbott and G. Payne (eds), *New Directions in the Sociology of Health*. Basingstoke: Falmer Press.

Ginsberg, N. (1992) *Divisions of Welfare*. London: Sage.

Gladstone, D. (ed.) (1995a) *British Social Welfare: Past, Present and Future*. London: UCL Press.

Gladstone, D. (1995b) Introduction: Change, continuity and welfare. In D. Gladstone (ed.), *British Social Welfare: Past, Present and Future*. London: UCL Press.

Gladstone, F. (1979) *Voluntary Action in a Changing World*. London: Bedford Square Press.

Glendinning, C. (1983) *Unshared Care: Parents and their Disabled Children*. London: Routledge and Kegan Paul.

Glendinning, C. (1992a) Employment and 'community care': Policies for the 1990s. *Work, Employment and Society*, 6: 103–111.

Glendinning, C. (1992b) Community care? The financial consequences for women. In C. Glendinning and J. Millar (eds), *Women and Poverty in Britain in the 1990s*. Hemel Hempstead: Harvester Wheatsheaf.

Glendinning, C. (1992c) Residualisation *vs* rights: Social policy and disabled people. In N. Manning and R. Page (eds), *Social Policy Review 4*. Canterbury: Social Policy Association.

Glendinning, C. and McLaughlin, E. (1993) Paying for informal care: Lessons from Finland. *Journal of European Social Policy*, 3: 239–53.

Glendinning, C. and Millar, J. (eds) (1992) *Women and Poverty in Britain in the 1990s*. Hemel Hempstead: Harvester Wheatsheaf.

Glennester, H. (1992) *Paying for Welfare in the 1990's*. Hemel Hempstead: Harvester Wheatsheaf.

Glennester, H., Mataganis, M., Owens, P. and Hancock, S. (1994) GP funding: Wild card or winning hand? In J. LeGrande and R. Robinson (eds), *Privatisation and the Welfare State*. London: Allen and Unwin.

Goffman, E. (1961) *Asylums*. New York: Doubleday.

Goldblatt, P.C. (1989) Mortality by social class, 1971–85. *Population Trends*, 56: 6–15.

Goldblatt, P.C. (1990) Mortality and alternative social classification. In P.C. Goldblatt (ed.), *Longitudinal Study: Mortality and Social Organisation 1971–1981*. OPCS Series L No. 6. London: HMSO.

Graham, H. (1984) *Women, Health and the Family*. Brighton: Wheatsheaf.

Graham, H. (1992) Budgeting for health. In C. Glendinning and J. Millar (eds), *Women and Poverty in Britain in the 1990s*. Hemel Hempstead: Harvester Wheatsheaf.

Graham, H. (1993a) *Hardship and Health in Women's Lives*. London: Harvester Wheatsheaf.

Graham, H. (1993b) Feminist perspectives on caring. In J. Bornat, C. Pereira, D. Pilgrim and F. Williams (eds), *Community Care: A Reader*. London: Macmillan.

Green, D.G. (1993) *Reinventing Civil Society: The Rediscovery of Welfare Without Politics*. London: Institute of Economic Affairs Health and Welfare Unit.

Griffith, B., Illiffe, S. and Rayner, G. (1987) *Banking on Sickness: Commercial Medicine in Britain and the USA*. London: Lawrence and Wishart.

Griffiths, R. (1983) *NHS Management Inquiry Report*. London: HMSO.

Griffiths, R. (1988) *Community Care: Agenda for Action*. London: HMSO.

Groves, D. (1991) Women and financial provision in old age. In M. Maclean and D. Groves (eds), *Women's Issues in Social Policy*. London: Routledge.

Hadley, R. and Hatch, S. (1981) *Social Welfare and the Future of the State: Centralised Social Services and Participating Alternatives*. London: Allen and Unwin.

Halsey, A.H. (1987) Social trends since World War II. In *Social Trends 17*. London: HMSO.

Halsey, A.H., Heath, A. and Ridge, I.M. (1981) *Origins and Destinations: Family, Class and Education in Modern Britain*. Oxford: Oxford University Press.

Ham, C. (1994) Reforming health services: Learning from the UK experience. *Social Policy and Administration*, 17: 87–101.

Ham, C. *et al.* (1989) *Managed Competition: A New Approach to Health Care in Britain*. Briefing Paper No. 9. London: King's Fund Institute.

Hancock, R. and Weir, P. (1994) *The Financial Well-Being of Elderly People*. Social Policy Research Findings No. 57. York: Joseph Rowntree Foundation.

Hantrais, L. (1995) *Social Policy in Europe*. London: Routledge.

Harris, R. and Seldon, A. (1979) *Over-Ruled on Welfare*. London: Institute of Economic Affairs.

Harrison, M. (1994) The Black Voluntary Housing Movement: Pioneering pluralistic social policy in a difficult climate. *Critical Social Policy*, 30: 21–35.

Hatch, S. and Mocraft, I. (1983) *Components of Welfare*. London: Bedford Square Press.

Hawkins, K. (1987) *Unemployment*. Harmondsworth: Penguin.

Hayek, F.A. (1960) *The Constitution of Liberty*. London: Routledge and Kegan Paul.

Haynes, R. (1991) Inequalities in health and health services use. *Social Science and Medicine*, 33: 361–8.

Health Education Authority (1989) *Diet, Nutrition and 'Healthy Eating' in Low-Income Groups*. London: HEA.

Health Education Council (1992) *Allied Dunbar National Fitness Survey: A Report on Activity Patterns and Fitness Levels*. London: Sports Council/HEC.

Hedley, R. and Davis Smith, J. (1992) *Volunteering and Society: Principles and Practice*. London: Bedford Square Press.

Heginbotham, C. (1990) *Return to Community: The Voluntary Ethic and Community Care*. London: Bedford Square Press.

Higgins, J. (1988) *The Business of Medicine*. London: Macmillan.

Hill, M. (1993) *The Welfare State in Britain: A Political History Since 1945*. Cheltenham: Edward Elgar.

Hills, J. (1990) *Income and Wealth*, Vol. 2. York: Joseph Rowntree Foundation.

Hills, J. (1993) *The Future of Welfare: A Guide to the Debate*. York: Joseph Rowntree Foundation.

Hills, J. (1994) *Inquiry into Income and Wealth, Vol. 12: A Survey of the Evidence*. London: Joseph Rowntree Foundation, Income and Wealth Inquiry Group.

Hindess, B. (1987) *Freedom, Equality and the Market*. London: Tavistock.

House of Commons (1993) *Hansard*, Col. 1010, 27 July 1993 and *Hansard*, 18 October 1993. London: HMSO.

House of Commons Social Services Committee (1986) *Fourth Report, Session 1985–86: Public Expenditure and Social Services*. London: HMSO.

House of Commons Social Services Committee (1988) *Sixth Report, Session 1987–88: Public Expenditure and Social Services*. London: HMSO.

Housing Corporation (1993) *Registered Housing Associations in England: Key Facts*. London: Housing Corporation.

Hunt, J.M., Martin, C.J., Platt, S., Lewis, C. and Morris, G. (1988) *Damp Housing, Mould Growth and Health Status*. Edinburgh: Research Unit in Health and Behavioural Change.

Hunter, D.J. (1980) *Coping with Uncertainty: Policy and Politics in the National Health Service*. Chichester: Research Studies Press/Wiley.

Hunter, D. (1994) From tribalism to opportunism: The management challenge to medical dominance. In J. Gabe, D. Kelleher and G. Williams (eds), *Challenging Medicine*. London: Routledge.

Hunter, D., McKeganey, N. and McPherson, I. (1988) *Care of the Elderly: Policy and Practice*. Aberdeen: Aberdeen University Press.

Illsley, R. (1986) Occupational class, selection and the production of inequalities in health. *Quarterly Journal of Social Affairs*, 2: 151–65.

Institute of Economic Affairs (1995) *Dismantling The Welfare State: Tough Love or the Good Samaritan*, Conference materials, March 1995. London: IEA Health and Welfare Unit.

Institute of Health Management (1994) *The Health Service Year Book*. London: IHM.

James, N. (1992) Care = organisation + physical labour + emotional labour. *Sociology of Health and Illness*, 14: 488–509.

Jamieson, A. (1991) Trends in home-care policies. In A. Jamieson (ed.), *Home Care for Older People in Europe*. Oxford: Oxford University Press.

Johnson, I.S., Coyne, A.M., Milner, P.C., Coupland, A.I., Reid, O.T., Heesterman, R.A., Harrison, J., Thorns, G. and Todd, J.N. (1987) *Health Care and Disease: A Profile of Sheffield*. Sheffield: Sheffield Health Authority.

Johnson, N. (1990) Problems for the mixed economy of welfare. In A. Ware and R.E. Goodin (eds), *Needs and Welfare*. London: Sage.

Joint NHS Privatisation Unit (1990) *The Privatisation Experience*. London: JNPU.

Jones, A. (1992) An investigation into the factors affecting the diet of low-income groups. BSc dissertation, University of Northumbria.

Jones, C. (1993) *New Perspectives on the Welfare State*. London: Routledge.

Jones, D., Lester, C. and West, R. (1994) Monitoring change in health services for older people. In J. LeGrande and R. Robinson (eds), *Privatisation and the Welfare State*. London: Allen and Unwin.

Jones, H. (1994) *Health and Society in Twentieth Century Britain*. Harlow: Longman.

Jones, K. (1991) *The Making of Social Policy in Britain 1930–1990*. London: Athlone Press.

Jones, K. and Fowles, A. (1983) People in institutions: Rhetoric and reality. In K. Jones and T. Stevenson (eds), *Yearbook of Social Policy*. London: Routledge and Kegan Paul.

Jones, P.G. and Cameron, D. (1984) Social class: An embarrassment to epidemiology? *Community Medicine*, 6: 37–46.

Joseph, K. (1972) The next ten years. *New Society*, 5 October.

Joseph Rowntree Memorial Trust (1992) *Social Policy Research Findings, No. 31*. York: Joseph Rowntree Memorial Trust.

Jowell, R., Brook, L., Dowds, L. and Ahrendt, D. (eds) (1994) *British Social Attitudes: The 9th Report*. Aldershot: Gower.

Jowell, R., Curtice, J., Brook, L., Ahrendt, D. and Park, A. (eds) (1995) *British Social Attitudes: the 11th Report*. Aldershot: Dartmouth.

Judge, J. and Benzeval, M. (1993) Health inequalities: New concerns about the children of single mothers. *British Medical Journal*, 306: 677–80.

Kendall, J. and Knapp, M. (1995) A loose and baggy monster: Boundaries, definitions and typologies. In J. Davis Smith, C. Rochester and R. Hedley (eds), *An Introduction to the Voluntary Sector*. London: Routledge.

King, R.D., Raynes, N.V. and Tizzard, J. (1971) *Patterns of Residential Care*. London: Routledge and Kegan Paul.

Knight, I. (1984) *The Height and Weight of Adults in Great Britain*. London: HMSO.

Laing and Buisson (1993) *Laing's Review of Private Healthcare 1993*. London: Laing and Buisson.

Lalonde, M. (1974) *A Perspective on the Health of Canadians*. Ottawa: Canadian Government.

Land, H. (1978) Who cares for the family? *Journal of Social Policy*, 7.

Land, H. (1991) Time to care. In M. Maclean and D. Groves (eds), *Women's Issues in Social Policy*. London: Routledge.

Langan, M. and Clarke, J. (1994) Managing in the mixed economy of care. In J. Clarke, A. Cochrane and E. McLaughlin (eds), *Managing Social Policy*. London: Sage.

Langsdale, S. (1990) *Women and Disability*. London: Macmillan.

Latto, S. (1984) *Coventry Home Help Project*. Coventry: Coventry Social Services Department.

Lawson, R. (1991) *Inter-organisational Partnership in the Provision of Home Care for Elderly People*. Discussion Paper No. 626. Canterbury: University of Kent, PSSRU.

Leadbetter, P. (1990) *Partners in Health: The NHS and the Independent Sector*. Birmingham: National Association of Health Authority Trusts.

Leat, D. (1987) *Voluntary Organisations and Accountability: Theory and Practice*. Coventry: University of Warwick.

Leat, D. (1988) Using Social Security payments to encourage non-kin caring. In S. Baldwin, G. Parker and R. Walker (eds), *Social Security and Community Care*. Aldershot: Avebury.

Leat, D. and Gay, P. (1987) *Paying for Care: A Study of Policy and Practice in Paid Care Schemes*. London: Policy Studies Institute.

Lee, G. (1985) Kinship and social support: The case of the United States. *Aging and Society*, 5: 19–38.

LeGrand, J. (1982) *The Strategy of Equality*. London: Allen and Unwin.

LeGrand, J. (1994) Evaluating the NHS reforms. In J. LeGrand and R. Robinson (eds), *Privatisation and the Welfare State*. London: Allen and Unwin.

LeGrand J. (1995) The market, the state and the distribution of life cycle income. In J. Falkingham and J. Hills (eds), *The Dynamic of Welfare: The Welfare State and the Life Cycle*. London: Prentice-Hall/Harvester Wheatsheaf.

LeGrand, J. and Robinson, R. (eds) (1994a) *Privatisation and the Welfare State*. London: Allen and Unwin.

LeGrand, J. and Robinson, R. (1994b) *Evaluating the NHS Reforms*. London: King's Fund Institute.

Lewis, J. (1992) Gender and the development of welfare regimes. *European Journal of Social Policy*, 2: 159–74.

Lewis, J. (1993) Developing the mixed economy of care: Emerging issues for voluntary organisations. *Journal of Social Policy*, 22: 173–93.

Lewis, J. and Meredith, B. (1988) *Daughters who Care*. London: Routledge.

Lewis, J. and Piachaud, D. (1992) Women and poverty in the twentieth century. In C. Glendinning and J. Millar (eds), *Women and Poverty in Britain in the 1990s*. Hemel Hempstead: Harvester Wheatsheaf.

Lewis, J., Bernstock, P. and Bovell, V. (1995) The community care changes: Unresolved tensions in policy and issues in implementation. *Journal of Social Policy*, 24: 73–94.

Lipsey, D. (1994) Do we really want more public spending? In R. Jowell *et al.*, *British Social Attitudes: The 11th Report*. Aldershot: Dartmouth Publishing.

Lister, R. (1989) Social benefit – priorities for redistribution. In Sheffield Group (eds), *The Social Economy and the Welfare State*. London: Lawrence and Wishart.

Lister, R. (1990a) *The Exclusive Society, Citizenship and the Poor*. London: Child Poverty Action Group.

Lister, R. (1990b) Women, economic dependency and citizenship. *Journal of Social Policy*, 19: 445–69.

Lonsdale, S. (1990) *Women and Disability*. London: Macmillan.

Lowe, R. (1993) *The Welfare State in Britain since 1945*. London: Macmillan.

Lynch, P. and Oelman, B.J. (1981) Mortality from coronary heart disease in the British Army compared with the civil population. *British Medical Journal*, 283: 45–7.

Lyle, J. (1958) The effects of an institutional environment upon the verbal development of imbecile children I: verbal intelligence. *Journal of Mental Deficiency*, 3: 122–8.

Lyle, J. (1959a) The effects of an institutional environment upon the verbal development of imbecile children II: speech and language. *Journal of Mental Deficiency*, 4: 1–13.

Lyle, J. (1959b) The effects of an institutional environment upon the verbal development of imbecile children III: The Brooklands Residential Family Unit. *Journal of Mental Deficiency*, 4: 14–22.

Lynn, P. and Davis Smith, J. (1992) *The 1991 National Survey of Voluntary Activity in the UK*. Berkhamstead: The Volunteer Centre UK.

MacGregor, G. (1990) Privatisation on parade. *Health Service Journal*, 3 May, pp. 670–71.

MacIntyre, S. (1986) The patterning of health by social position in contemporary Britain: Directions for sociological research. *Social Science and Medicine*, 23: 393–415.

Mack, J. and Lansley, S. (1985) *Poor Britain*. London: Allen and Unwin.

Mahon, A., Wilkin, D. and Whitehouse, C. (1994) Choice of hospital for elective surgery referral: GPs' and patients' views. In J. LeGrande and R. Robinson (eds), *Privatisation and the Welfare State*. London: Allen and Unwin.

Malpass, P. and Murie, A. (1994) *Housing Policy and Practice*, 4th edn. London: Macmillan.

Marmot, M., Shipley, M. and Rose, G. (1984) Inequalities in death: Specific explanations of a general pattern. *Lancet*, 5 May, pp. 1003–1006.

Marmot, M., Davey-Smith, G., Stansfield, S., Patel, C., North, G.F., Head, J., White, L., Brunner, E. and Feeney, A. (1991) Health inequalities among British civil servants: The Whitehall II Study. *Lancet*, 337: 1367–93.

Marsh, A. and Macky, S. (1993) *Work and Benefits*. London: Policy Studies Institute.

Marsh, G.N. and Channing, D.M. (1986) Deprivation and health in one general practice. *British Medical Journal*, 292: 1173–6.

Marshall, T.H. (1963) *Sociology at the Crossroad and Other Essays*. London: Heinemann.

Martin, J. and White, A. (1988) *The Financial Circumstances of Disabled Adults Living in Private Households*. London: HMSO.

Maslow, A.H. (1970) *Motivation and Personality*, 2nd edn. New York: Harper and Row.

Mason, E.S. (1990) The Asian Mother and Baby Campaign: The Leicestershire experience. *Journal of the Royal Society of Health*, 110: 1–9.

May, M. and Brunsden, E. (1994) Workplace care in the mixed economy of welfare. In R. Page and J. Baldock (eds), *Social Policy Review 6*. Canterbury: Social Policy Association.

Mays, N. and Bevan, G. (1987) *Resource Allocation in the Health Service*. Occasional Papers in Social Administration No. 81. London: Bedford Square Press.

McKeown, T. (1976) *The Role of Medicine: Dream, Mirage or Nemesis?* London: Nuffield Hospitals Trust.

Means, R. (1995) Older people and the personal social services. In D. Gladstone (ed.), *British Social Welfare: Past, Present and Future*. London: UCL Press.

Milliband, R. (1969) *The State in Capitalist Society*. London: Weidenfeld and Nicolson.

Ministry of Health (1944) *A National Health Service*. Cmd 6502. London: HMSO.

Morris, J. (1993) *Independent Lives: Community Care and Disabled People*. Basingstoke: Macmillan.

Morris, J., Cook, D. and Shaper, G. (1994) Loss of employment and mortality. *British Medical Journal*, 308: 1135–9.

Morris, L. (1994) *Dangerous Classes: The Underclass and Social Citizenship*. London: Routledge.

Moser, K.A., Fox, A.J. and Jones, D.R. (1986) Unemployment and mortality in the OPCS Longitudinal Study. In R.G. Wilkinson (ed.), *Class and Health*. London: Tavistock.

Murie, A. (1993) Restructuring housing markets and housing access. In R. Page and J. Baldock (eds), *Social Policy Review 5*. Canterbury: Social Policy Association.

Murie, A. and Forrest, R. (1980) *Housing Market Processes and the Inner City*. Report to the SSRC Inner Cities Working Party.

Murray, C. (1984) *Losing Ground: American Social Policy 1950–1980*. New York: Basic Books.

Murray, C. (1990) *The Emerging British Underclass*. London: IEA Health and Welfare Unit.

Myrdal, G. (1988) *Beyond the Welfare State*. London: Duckworth.

National Advisory Council for Nutritional Education (1983) *A Discussion Paper for Nutrition Guidelines for Health Education in Britain*. London: Health Education Council.

National Association of Citizens' Advice Bureaux (1991) *Barriers to Benefit: Black Claimants and Social Security*. London: NACAB.

National Association of Health Authorities (1988) *Income Generation Schemes in the NHS: A Directory*. Birmingham: NAHA.

National Association of Health Authority Trusts (undated) *Care in the Community: Definitions of Health and Social Care – Developing an Approach (a West Midlands Study)*. Birmingham: NAHAT.

National Council for Civil Liberties (1951) *Fifty Thousand Outside the Law*. London: NCCL.

National Council for Voluntary Organisations (1993a) *Facts and Figures on the Voluntary Sector*. London: NCVO.

National Council for Voluntary Organisations (1993b) *Equal Opportunities in Voluntary Organisations*. Reading List No. 2. London: NCVO.

Neill, J., Sinclair, I., Gorbach, P. and Williams, J. (1988) *A Need for Care?* Aldershot: Avebury.

Newman, G. (1906) *Infant Mortality: A Social Problem*. London: Methuen.

Nicholl, J.P., Beeby, N.R. and Williams, B.T. (1980) Role of the private sector in elective surgery in England and Wales. *British Medical Journal*, 298: 243–7.

Nicholl, J.P., Beeby, N.R. and Williams, B.T. (1989) Role of the private sector in elective surgery in England and Wales 1986. *British Medical Journal*, 198: 243–6.

Nissel, M. and Bonnerjea, L. (1982) *Family Care of the Handicapped Elderly: Who Pays?* London: Policy Studies Institute.

Obaze, D. (1993) Black people and volunteering. In R. Hedley and J. Davis Smith (eds), *Volunteering and Society: Principles and Practice*. London: Bedford Square Press.

Office of Population, Censuses and Surveys (1982) *General Household Survey 1980*. London: HMSO.

Office of Population, Censuses and Surveys (1986) *Mortality Statistics for 1984*. London: HMSO.

Office of Population, Censuses and Surveys (1987) *General Household Survey 1985*. London: HMSO.

Office of Population, Censuses and Surveys (1988) *OPCS Surveys of Disability in Great Britain: The Prevalence of Disability Among Adults*. London: HMSO.

Office of Population, Censuses and Surveys (1989) *General Household Survey 1987*. London: HMSO.

Office of Population, Censuses and Surveys (1991) *Census 1991: Local Base Statistics*. London: HMSO.

Office of Population, Censuses and Surveys (1994) *General Household Survey 1992*. London: HMSO.

Office of Population, Censuses and Surveys (1995) *General Household Survey 1994.* London: HMSO.

Oldman, C. (1991) *Paying for Care: Personal Sources of Funding Care.* York: Joseph Rowntree Foundation.

Oliver, M. (1990) *The Politics of Disablement.* London: Macmillan.

Oliver, M. and Barnes, C. (1991) Discrimination, disability and welfare: From needs to rights. In L. Bynoe, M. Oliver and C. Barnes (eds), *Equal Rights for Disabled People.* London: Institute for Public Policy Research.

Ong, B.N. (1993) *The Practice of Health Service Research.* London. Chapman and Hall.

Oppenheim, C. (1990) *Poverty: The Facts.* London: Child Poverty Action Group.

Organization for Economic Cooperation and Development (1988) *Ageing Populations: The Social Policy Implications.* Paris: OECD.

Owen, D. (1965) *English Philanthropy 1660–1960.* Cambridge, MA: Beltnap Press.

Owen, D. (1981) *Face the Future.* London: Jonathan Cape.

Papadakis, E. and Taylor-Gooby, P. (1987) *The Private Provision of Public Welfare.* Brighton: Harvester.

Parker, G. (1985) *With Due Care and Attention: A Review of Research on Informal Care.* London: Family Policy Studies Centre.

Parker, G. (1990) Spouse carers: Whose quality of life? In S. Baldwin, C. Godfrey and C. Propper (eds), *Quality of Life: Perspectives and Policies.* London: Routledge.

Parker, G. (1993) *With this Body: Caring and Disability in Marriage.* Buckingham: Open University Press.

Parmar, B. (1981) Young Asian women: A critique of the pathological approach. *Multicultural Education,* 9: 19–29.

Parsons, L. and Day, S. (1992) Improving obstetric outcomes in ethnic minorities. *Journal of Public Health Medicine,* 14: 183–92.

Pascall, G. (1986) *Social Policy: a Feminist Analysis.* London: Tavistock.

Pearson, M. (1986) The politics of ethnic minority health studies. In T. Rothwell and D. Phillips (eds), *Health, Race and Ethnicity.* London: Croom Helm.

Pettigrew, A., Ferlie, E. and Mackie, L. (1992) *Shaping Strategic Change.* London: Sage.

Phillipson, C. (1982) *Capitalism and the Construction of Old Age.* London: Macmillan.

Phillipson, C. (1990) *Delivering Community Care Services for Older People: Problems and Prospects.* Stoke-on-Trent: Keele University, Centre for Social Gerontology.

Phillipson, C. (1992) Family care of the elderly in Great Britain. In J. Kosberg (ed.), *Family Care of the Elderly.* London: Sage.

Phillipson, C. and Biggs, S. (1992) *Understanding Elder Abuse: A Training Manual for Helping Professionals.* Harlow: Longman.

Philpott, J. (1994) Unemployment, inequality and inefficiency: The incidence and cost of unemployment. In A. Glynn and D. Milliband (eds), *Paying for Ill Health.* London: Rivers Drain Press.

Piachaud, D. (1979) *The Cost of a Child.* London: Child Poverty Action Group.

Piachaud, D. (1985) *Round About Fifty Hours a Week: The Time Costs of Children.* Poverty Pamphlet No. 64. London: Child Poverty Action Group.

Pinker, R. (1993) Social policy in the post-Titmuss era. In R. Page and J. Baldock (eds), *Social Policy Review,* 5. Kent: Social Policy Association.

Pollock, A.M. and Whitty, I.M. (1990) Crisis in our hospital kitchens: Ancillary staffing during an outbreak of food poisoning in a long stay hospital. *British Medical Journal,* 300: 383–5.

Popay, J. and Bartley, M. (1993) Conditions of formal and domestic labour: Towards an interpreted framework for the analysis of gender and social class inequalities in health. In S. Platt, H. Thomas, S. Scott and G. Williams (eds), *Locating Health: Sociological and Historical Explorations.* Aldershot: Avebury.

Popay, J. and Jones, G. (1990) Patterns of wealth and illness among lone parents. *Journal of Social Policy,* 19: 499–534.

Portillo, M. (1993) Ethics and public finance. Lecture delivered to a *Conference on the Church at Work*, London, September.

Qureshi, H. and Walker, A. (1989) *The Caring Relationship: Elderly People and their Families*. Basingstoke: Macmillan.

Range, W. (1994) *A Future for the NHS?* Harlow: Longman.

Rathbone, E. (1924/1986) *The Disinherited Family*. London: Falling Wall Press.

Reddin, M. (1979) *Universality and Selectivity: Strategies in Social Policy*. London: National Economic and Social Council.

Ridley, N. (1988) Speech to the *Institute of Housing Conference*. June.

Ritchie, J. (1990) *Thirty Families: Their Living Standards in Unemployment*. London: HMSO.

Rose, R. (1993) Bringing freedom back in rethinking priorities of the welfare state. In C. Jones (ed.), *New Perspectives on the Welfare State*. London: Routledge.

Rose, G. and Marmot, M. (1981) Social class and coronary heart disease. *British Heart Journal*, 45: 141–56.

Rowntree, B.S. (1901) *Poverty: A Study in Town Life*. London: Macmillan.

Rowntree, B.S. (1941) *Poverty and Progress*. Harlow: Longman.

Rowntree, B.S. and Lavers, G. (1951) *Poverty and the Welfare State*. Harlow: Longman.

Royal Commission (1958) *Report of the Royal Commission on the Law Relating to Mental Illness and Mental Deficiency*. London: HMSO.

Royal National Institute for the Blind (1991) *Blind and Partially Sighted Adults in the UK*. London: RNIB.

Royston, G. *et al.* (1992) Modelling the use of health services by populations of small areas to inform the allocation of central resources to larger regions. *Socio-Economic Planning Sciences*, 26: 169–90.

Saks, M. (1994) The alternatives to medicine. In J. Gabe, M.D. Kelleher and G. Williams (eds), *Challenging Medicine*. London: Routledge.

Salvage, A. (1988) *Warmth in Winter: Evaluation of an Information Pack for Elderly People*. Cardiff: University of Wales College of Medicine, Research Team for the Elderly.

Salvage, A., Vetter, N. and Jones, D.A. (1988) Attitudes to hospital care among a community sample aged 75 years and over. *Age and Aging*, 17: 270–74.

Salvage, A., Vetter, N. and Jones, D.A. (1989) Opinions concerning residential care. *Age and Aging*, 18: 380–86.

Saraceno, C. (1987) Division of family labour and gender identity. In A. Showstack Sassoon (ed.), *Women and the State*. London: Hutchinson.

Savage, W. (1986) *A Savage Enquiry*. London: Virago.

Saxon-Harrold, S.K.E. and Kendall, J. (eds) (1994) *Researching the Voluntary Sector*, 2nd edn. London: Charities Aid Foundation.

Scull, A. (1977) *Decarceration: Community Treatment and the Deviant*. London: Prentice-Hall.

Seebohm Committee (1968) *Report of the Committee on Local Authority and Allied Personal Social Services*. Cmnd 3703. London: HMSO.

Sheldon, J. (1948) *The Social Medicine of Old Age*. Oxford: Oxford University Press.

Sigerist, H. (1943) *Civilization and Disease*. Chicago: Chicago University Press.

Sinclair, I. (1990) Residential care. In I. Sinclair, R. Parker, D. Leat and J. Williams (eds), *The Kaleidoscope of Care: A Review of Research on Welfare Provision for Elderly People*. London: HMSO.

Sinclair, I. and Williams, J. (1990) Domiciliary services. In I. Sinclair, M. Parker, D. Leat and J. Williams (eds), *The Kaleidoscope of Care: A Review of Research on Welfare Provision for Elderly People*. London: HMSO.

Sinfield, A. (1981) *What Unemployment Means*. Oxford: Martin Robertson.

Skellington, R. and Morris, P. (1992) *Race in Britain Today*. London: Sage.

Smaje, C. (1995) *Health, 'Race' and 'Ethnicity': Making Sense of the Evidence*. London: King's Fund Institute.

Smith, R. (1987) *Unemployment and Health: A Disaster and a Challenge*. Oxford: Oxford University Press.

Social Services Inspectorate (1987) *From Home Help to Home Care*. London: HMSO.

Social Services Inspectorate (1988) *Managing Policy Change in Home Help Services*. London: HMSO.

Social Services Inspectorate (1991) *Care Management and Assessment: Managers' Guide*. London: HMSO.

Spicker, P. (1988) *Principles of Social Welfare*. London: Routledge.

Spicker, P. (1993) *Poverty and Social Security*. London: Routledge.

Spicker, P. (1995) *Social Policy: Themes and Approaches*. Hemel Hempstead: Harvester/Wheatsheaf.

St Leger, F. and Gillespie, N. (1991) *Informal Welfare in Belfast: Caring Communities?* Aldershot: Avebury.

Stern, R., Stilwell, B. and Heuston, J. (1989) *From the Margins to the Mainstream: Collaboration in Planning Services with Single Homeless People*. London: West Lambeth Health Authority.

Strathclyde Regional Council (1993) *The Social Strategy for the Nineties*. Glasgow: Strathclyde Regional Council.

Taylor, M. (1991) *New Times, New Challenges; Voluntary Organisations facing 1990*. London: NCVO.

Taylor, M., Hogget, P. and Langan, J. (1994) Independent organisations in community care. In S.K.E. Saxon-Harold and J. Kendall (eds), *Researching the Voluntary Sector*, 2nd edn. London: Charities Aid Foundation.

Taylor-Gooby, P. (1994) What citizens want from the state. In R. Jowell, L. Brook and L. Dowds (eds), International Social Attitudes: *The 10th BSA Report*. Aldershot: Dartmouth.

Taylor-Gooby, P. (1995) Welfare outside the state. In R. Jowell, J. Curtice, L. Brook, D. Ahrendt and A. Park (eds), *British Social Attitudes: the 11th Report*. Aldershot: Dartmouth.

Taylor-Gooby, P. and Dale, J. (1981) *Social Theory and Social Welfare*. London: Arnold.

Taylor-Gooby, P. and Lawson, R. (eds) (1993) *Markets and Managers*. Buckingham: Open University Press.

Thane, P. (1982) *The Foundations of the Welfare State*. Harlow: Longman.

Thatcher, M. (1981) Speech to *Women's Royal Voluntary Service National Conference*, January.

Thompson, P. (1992) Public sector management in a period of radical change: 1979–1992. *Public Money and Management*, 32: 33–42.

Thunhurst, C. (1985) The analysis of small area statistics and planning for health. *Statistician*, 34: 93–106.

Timmins, N. (1988) NHS regional trust internal market plans. *The Independent*, 14 March.

Tinker, A. (1992) *Elderly People in Modern Society*, 3rd edn. Harlow: Longman.

Titmuss, R. (1955) The social division of welfare. In *Essays on the Welfare State*. London: Allen and Unwin (2nd edition 1962).

Titmuss, R. (1963) *Income Distribution and Social Change*. London: Allen and Unwin.

Titmuss, R. (1968) *Commitment to Welfare*. London: Allen and Unwin.

Titmuss, R. (1973) *The Gift Relationship*. Harmondsworth: Penguin.

Titmuss, R. (1987) *The Philosophy of Welfare: Selected Writings of Richard M. Titmuss*. London: Allen and Unwin.

Tizzard, J. (1964) *Community Care for the Mentally Handicapped*. Oxford: Oxford University Press.

Townsend, J. (1995) The burden of smoking. In M. Benzeval, K. Judge and M. Whitehead (eds), *Tackling Inequalities in Health*. London: King's Fund.

Townsend, P. (1962) *The Last Refuge*. London: Routledge and Kegan Paul.

Townsend, P. (1976) Area deprivation policies. *New Statesman*, 6 August, pp. 168–71.

Townsend, P. (1979) *Poverty in the UK*. Harmondsworth: Penguin.

Townsend, P. (1986) Social inequality and health care. Lecture to a *Joint Meeting of the Economic and Sociology Sections of the British Association for the Advancement of Science*, Bristol.

Townsend, P. (1993) *The International Analysis of Poverty*. Hemel Hempstead: Harvester Wheatsheaf.

Townsend, P., Corrigan, P. and Kowarzik, V. (1987) *Poverty and the London Labour Market: An Interim Report*. London: Low Pay Unit.

Townsend, P. and Davidson, N. (1982) *The Black Report*. Harmondsworth: Penguin.

Townsend, P., Phillimore, P. and Beattie, A. (1988) *Health and Deprivation Inequality and the North*. Beckenham: Croom Helm.

Townsend, P., Simpson, D. and Tibbs, N. (1985) Inequalities in health in the City of Bristol: A preliminary review of statistical evidence. *International Journal of Health Science*, 15: 637–63.

Townsend, P., Whitehead, M. and Davidson, N. (eds) (1992) *Inequalities in Health: The Black Report and the Health Divide* (new edition). Harmondsworth: Penguin.

Transport and General Workers' Union (1994) *In Place of Fear: The Future of the Welfare State*. London: TGWU.

Tudor Hart, J. (1971) The Inverse Care Law. *Lancet*, 27 February, pp. 1405–1412.

Twigg, J. (1989) Models of carers: How social care agencies conceptualise their relationship with informal carers. *Journal of Social Policy*, 18: 53–66.

Twigg, J. and Atkin, K. (1995) Carers and services: Factors mediating service provision. *Journal of Social Policy*, 24: 5–30.

Twigg, J., Atkin, F. and Perry, C. (1990) *Carers and Services: A Review of Research*. London: HMSO.

Ungerson, C. (1987) *Policy is Personal: Sex, Gender and Informal Care*. London: Tavistock.

Ungerson, C. (1990) The language of care: crossing the boundaries. In C. Ungerson (ed.), *Gender and Caring*. Hemel Hempstead: Harvester/Wheatsheaf.

Ungerson, C. (1995) Gender, cash and informal care: European perspectives and dilemmas. *Journal of Social Policy*, 24: 31–52.

Victor, C. (1989) Income inequality in later life. In M. Jefferys (ed.), *Growing Old in the Twentieth Century*. London: Routledge.

Victor, C. (1991) *Health and Health Care in Later Life*. Buckingham: Open University Press.

Victor, C. and Vetter, N.T. (1988) Rearranging the deckchairs on the Titanic: failure of an augmental home help scheme after discharge to reduce the length of stay in hospital. *Archives of Gerontology and Geriatrics*, 7: 83–91.

Vogler, C. (1989) *Labour Market Change and Patterns of Financial Allocation within Households*. Working Paper No. 12. Oxford: ESRC/SCE(I).

Wadsworth, M.E.J. (1986) Serious illness in childhood and its association with later-life achievement. In R.G. Wilkinson (ed.), *Class and Health*. London: Tavistock.

Waine, B. (1992) The voluntary sector – the Thatcher years. In N. Manning and R. Page (eds), *Social Policy Review 4*. Canterbury: Social Policy Association.

Walker, A. (1982) The meaning and social domain of community care. In A. Walker (ed.), *Community Care: The Family, the State and Social Policy*. Oxford: Blackwell/Martin Robertson.

Walker, A. (1990) Blaming the victim. In C. Murray (ed.), *The Emerging British Underclass*. London: Institute of Economic Affairs.

Walker, A. and Walker, C. (eds) (1987) *The Growing Divide*. London: Child Poverty Action Group.

Walker, A. and Walker, C. (1990) The structuring of inequality: Poverty and income distribution in Britain 1979–1989. In I. Taylor (ed.), *The Social Effects of Free Market Policies*. Hemel Hempstead: Harvester Wheatsheaf.

Walker, C. (1993) *Managing Poverty*. London: Routledge.

Walker, R. (1995) *Families, Poverty and Work*. Briefings, 6, Spring 1 and 3. Loughborough: Centre for Research in Social Policy.

Ware, A. (1990) Meeting needs through voluntary action: Does market society corrode altruism? In A. Ware and R.E. Goodin, *Needs and Welfare*. London: Sage.

Ware, A. and Goodin, R.E. (1990) *Needs and Welfare*. London: Sage.

Webster, C. (1993) *Caring for Health: History and Diversity*. Buckingham: Open University Press.

Weir, S. and Lansley, S. (1983) Towards a popular view of poverty? *New Society*, 25 August.

Weller, M. and Tobiensky, R.I. (1989) Psychosis and destitution at Christmas. *Lancet*, 20/30 December, pp. 1509–1511.

Wenger, C. (1990) Elderly carers: The need for appropriate intervention. *Aging and Society*, 10: 197–220.

Wenger, C. (1992) *Help in Old Age: Facing Up to Change*. Liverpool: Liverpool University Press.

West, P., Illsley, R. and Felman, H. (1984) The family, the welfare state and community care: Political rhetoric and public attitudes. *Journal of Social Policy*, 13: 417–46.

Westergaard, J. (1992) About and beyond the 'underclass': Some notes on influences of social climate on British sociology today. *Sociology*, 26: 575–87.

White, A., Nicolas, G., Foster, K., Browne, F. and Cary, S. (1993) *Health Survey for England 1991*. London: HMSO.

Whitehead, C. (1993) Private finance for housing associations. In D. Maclennan and K. Gibb (eds), *Housing Finance and Subsidies in Britain*. Aldershot: Avebury.

Whitehead, M. (1987) *The Health Divide: Inequalities in Health in the 1980s*. London: Health Education Council.

Whitehead, M. (1994) Is it fair? Evaluating the equity implications of the NHS reforms. In R. Robinson and J. LeGrand (eds), *Evaluation the NHS Reforms*. London: King's Fund Institute.

Whitehead, M. (1995) Tackling inequalities: A review of policy initiatives. In M. Benzeval, K. Judge and M. Whitehead (eds), *Tackling Inequalities in Health*. London: King's Fund.

Wicks, D. (1995) Social policy and the active society. In D. Gladstone (ed.), *British Social Welfare: Past, Present and Future*. London: UCL Press.

Wilding, P. (1992) The public sector in the 1980s. In N. Manning and R. Page (eds), *Social Policy Review 4*. Canterbury: Social Policy Association.

Wilkin, D. (1979) *Caring for the Mentally Handicapped Child*. Beckenham: Croom Helm.

Wilkinson, R.G. (1986) Socio-economic differences in mortality: Interpreting data on their size and trends. In R.G. Wilkinson (ed.), *Class and Health*. London: Tavistock.

Wilkinson, R.G. (1992) Income distribution and life expectancy. *British Medical Journal*, 304: 165–8.

Williams, R. (1989) *Social Policy: A Critical Introduction*. Cambridge: Polity Press.

Willis, E. (1993) Volunteers as advocates: Some perspectives for the 1990s. In R. Hedley and J. Davis Smith (eds), *Volunteering and Society: Principles and Practice*. London: Bedford Square Press.

Willis, K.G. and Cameron, S.J. (1993) Costs and benefits of housing subsidies in the Newcastle area: A comparison of alternative subsidy definitions across tenure sectors and income distributions. In D. Maclennan and K. Gibb (eds), *Housing Finance and Subsidies in Britain*. Aldershot: Avebury.

Willmott, P. and Thomas, D. (1984) *Community in Social Policy*. London: Policy Studies Institute.

Wilson, E. (1977) *Women and the Welfare State*. London: Tavistock.

Wilson, E. (1989) Family food systems, preventive health and dietary change: A policy to increase the health divide. *Journal of Social Policy*, 18: 173–83.

Wing, J.R. and Brown, G.W. (1971) *Institutionalism and Schizophrenia*. Cambridge: Cambridge University Press.

Wistow, G. and Henwood, J. (1991) Caring for people: Elegant design or flawed model? In N. Manning (ed.), *Social Policy Review 1990–91*. Harlow: Longman.

Wistow, G., Knapp, M., Hardy, B. and Allen, C. (1994) *Social Care in a Mixed Economy*. Buckingham: Open University Press.

Witz, A. (1992) *Professions and Patriarchy*. London: Routledge.

World Health Organization (1985) *Targets for Health for All*. Copenhagen: WHO.

World Health Organization European Region (1984) *Report of the Working Group on Concepts and Principles of Health Promotion*. Copenhagen: WHO.

Young, B. (1980) Health and housing infestation. *Roof*, July/August, pp. 111–12.

INDEX

RESEARCH METHODS FOR NURSES AND THE CARING PROFESSIONS
Roger Sapsford and Pamela Abbott

This book is about the appreciation, evaluation and conduct of social research. Aimed at nurses, social workers, community workers and others in the caring professions, the book concentrates on relatively small-scale studies which can be carried out by one or two people, rather than large and well-resourced teams. The authors have provided many short, practical exercises within the text and particular emphasis is given to evaluative research including the assessment of the reader's own professional practice. Their clear, accessible style will make this the ideal introductory text for those undertaking research or the evaluation of research for the first time.

This book may be read in conjunction with *Research into Practice: A Reader for Nurses and the Caring Professions* (Open University Press) edited by the same authors.

Contents
Section 1: Introduction – Finding out and making sense – Section 2: Assessing research – Reading research reports – Reading open interviewing research – Reading observation research – Reading about controlled trials – Reading survey research – Reading secondary-source research – Section 3: Doing research – Using secondary sources – Survey research: design and sampling – Experimental practice – Open interviewing – Analysing text – Participant observation and self-evaluation – Evaluation of single cases – Section 4: In conclusion – Writing up – In conclusion – References – Index.

192pp   0 335 09620 4 (Paperback)   0 335 09621 2 (Hardback)

RESEARCH INTO PRACTICE
A READER FOR NURSES AND THE CARING PROFESSIONS

Pamela Abbott and Roger Sapsford (eds)

This book is a collection of examples of research, all concerned in some way with nursing or the study of health and community care. It illustrates the kind of research that can be done by a small team or a single researcher, without large-scale research grants. The editors have selected papers which show a great diversity of approaches: differing emphasis on description or explanation, different degrees of structure in design and different appeals to the authority of science or the authenticity of empathic exploration. They show the limitations typical of small-scale projects carried out with limited resources and the experience of applied research as it occurs in practice, as opposed to how it tends to look when discussed in textbooks. The papers have been organized into three sections representing three distinct types of social science research – 'observing and participating', 'talking to people and asking questions' and 'controlled trials and comparisons'. Each section is provided with an editorial introduction.

Contents

Contributors
Pamela Abbott, Joyce Bernie, George Choon, Robert Dingwall, Susan Fox, Verona Gordon, Nicky James, Mavis Kirkham, Jean Orr, Geoff Payne, Roger Sapsford, Suzanne Skevington.

176pp   0 335 09742 1 (Paperback)